D1174405

CASTE AND THE ECONOMIC FRONTIER

To

MY FATHER

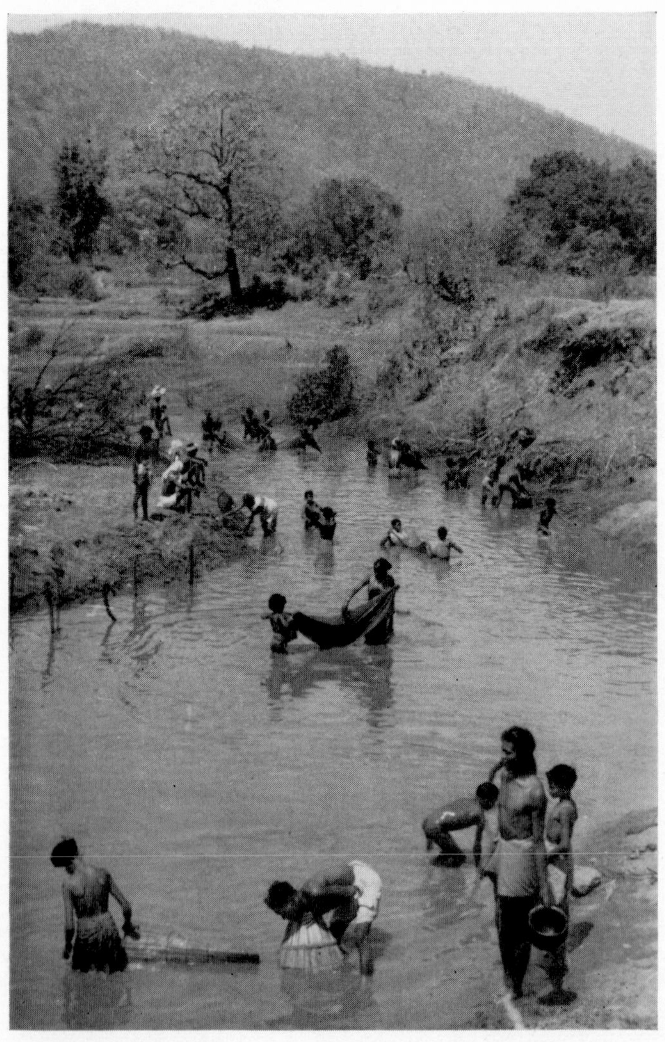

FISHING IN A POND

At the beginning of the hot season, when the harvest is gathered, the people of the village go fishing in ponds and in the Salki River.

All clean castes take part.

The catch is small and provides no more than a relish for one or two meals. Fishing is not a means of making a living, but rather a sport.

CASTE AND THE ECONOMIC FRONTIER

A village in highland Orissa

by

F. G. BAILEY

Lecturer in Asian Anthropology in the School of Oriental and African Studies, University of London

MANCHESTER UNIVERSITY PRESS

Published by the University of Manchester at
The University Press
316–324, Oxford Road, Manchester, 13
1957

U.S.A.
The Humanities Press Inc.
303, Fourth Avenue, New York, 10.

FOREWORD

DURING the last twenty years social anthropologists have extended their field of study to include village communities in different parts of the world and this has already begun to yield dividends: on the one hand, a new dimension has been added to anthropology; and on the other hand, rural studies have been stimulated by a new approach which embodies a distinct body of techniques and concepts. Anthropologists who chose to make field-studies of village communities in countries such as Japan, China, India, Lebanon, Western Europe and elsewhere have had to take into account the fact that these villages formed part of a much wider society and culture, and that the whole has influenced the part, and *vice versa.* The villagers, even when most of them are illiterate, participate in the literary tradition of the larger society. In India to the north of the Vindhyas there are castes of genealogists and bards whose duty it is to record the genealogies, and important events in the life of the families to which they minister. In brief, the field-anthropologist has found that in studying the microcosm he is also studying the macrocosm, and that some knowledge of the latter is essential in order to understand the former. That his work sheds new light on the macrocosm is not only a valuable by-product of his research, but it also opens up new avenues for social anthropology itself.

These remarks are especially pertinent in introducing Dr. Bailey's present study of Bisipara, a village in Phulbani District in Orissa in the eastern part of India. Dr. Bailey is aware that he is not studying a windowless monad, but something that has been all the time exposed to the influences emanating from the larger society. In fact, he has succeeded in describing the changes which have been brought about in the structure of Bisipara society over a hundred years of British rule. This is one of the reasons why Dr. Bailey's book constitutes an original and significant contribution to the growing body of village studies in different parts of the world.

Dr. Bailey begins by describing the economy of the peasants

of Bisipara from the point of view of a sociologist. A common phenomenon in rural India is the frequent sale of arable land by a peasant, and Dr. Bailey asks, 'Why does land come into the market?' It is not every peasant who sells his patrimony, but only those who are unable to bear the weight of what he calls 'contingent expenditure'. For instance, a bullock might die during the paddy cultivation season when prices of bullocks are at their highest. The bullock has to be replaced at once, and the only assets the peasant has are land and jewellery. When the peasant mortgages or sells any part of his land to meet a contingent expenditure like the loss of a bullock or to perform a funeral or wedding ceremony, he is dangerously close to a downward spiral that will result eventually in his parting with most of his land. The bigger the estate, the greater is the chance of its remaining intact under the pressure of contingent expenditure. But big estates are threatened from another direction: the system of inheritance decrees that each son has a vested interest in the patrimony and this means that only a succession of demographic accidents in the form of single heirs can keep an estate big over a long period of time. During the last hundred years there has been a general increase in population thanks to *Pax Brittanica*, improved communications, the creation of a famine-fighting organization, and improved public health. Two of the greatest evils of Indian agriculture, the parcelling and dispersal of holdings, are due to the increased pressure of population on arable land, and to the Hindu law of inheritance.

Dr. Bailey points out that the British administrators were in favour of the encouragement of private rights in land and that their task was made easier by the penetration of the mercantile economy which British rule brought into India. Under the new economy it was possible for one member of a joint family to be poor while another was rich. Those who supplemented their income from land with income from a subsidiary source such as employment in the administration, or in the Leaf Company or from trade, were better able to retain their land than those who relied only on land. Dr. Bailey argues that it was this economic disparity within the joint family which led people to take advantage of the Hindu law of partition. Joint families broke up and estates became smaller, and this meant the decline of clientship which in turn led to employment of labour on purely economic terms. The nature of the ties binding individuals in rural society began to change radically.

The economic forces set in motion by British rule were responsible for bringing about certain changes in the social structure of Bisipara. For instance, the confusing policy of the Government of Bengal (of which Orissa was then a part) regarding the sale of liquor resulted in the enrichment of two low castes, the Boad Distillers and the immigrant Ganjam Distillers. In pre-British Bisipara, the Warriors owned all the land, but by 1910 when prohibition was introduced, the Boad Distillers owned as much land as the Warriors while the Ganjam Distillers owned more land than anyone else. The acquisition of substantial wealth by the two Distiller castes led to investment in land: for land is still the best investment and without it a man has no prestige. They followed this by Sanskritizing their customs and ritual in order to raise their position in the caste system. It is probable that the caste system always permitted a certain amount of group mobility, and that the acquisition of political or economic power followed by the Sanskritization of custom and ritual was the best way of moving up in the system. There is no doubt, however, that mobility increased appreciably under British rule. But the system was elastic enough to 'contain' the enhanced mobility.

While Sanskritization enables most castes to raise their collective status, it seems to be unable to assist the Untouchables, though on this point the situation seems to admit of regional variation. In Bisipara, the efforts of the Boad Outcastes to raise themselves in the caste hierarchy are meeting with the opposition of not only the caste Hindus but also the other Untouchable castes, such as the Sweepers, whose economic position remains as bad as before. The Boad Outcastes are increasingly estranged from other castes in Bisipara and are seeking the help of the police and the law courts in their efforts to secure for themselves the rights which the Constitution of the Republic of India grants to them. It seems as though they are being gradually ejected from the village community of Bisipara into the political society of India. This situation is a familiar one in modern rural India, and if it proceeds unchecked, it is likely to alter the nature of the Indian village community.

Dr. Bailey has written an important and stimulating book

which ought to be read by anthropologists, economists, welfare workers and administrators.

M. N. Srinivas

Dept. of Sociology,
The Maharaja Sayajirao University of Baroda,
Baroda.

CONTENTS

PART ONE: INTRODUCTION

PART TWO: ACQUISITION OF WEALTH AND THE TRANSFER OF LAND

LIST OF CHARTS

LIST OF MAPS

LIST OF TABLES

LIST OF PLATES

ACKNOWLEDGEMENTS

WHILE I was in the field and while I wrote this book, I held a Treasury Studentship in Foreign Languages and Cultures. I thank the Committee and the various officials concerned, in particular Mr. C. R. Allen.

My wife and I wish to thank the many people who made us welcome to Orissa, especially the Chief Minister, Sri Nabakrushna Chaudhuri. From the Department of Tribal and Rural Welfare and the Department of Public Relations we received much practical help. It was our good fortune that at the time of our arrival the Deputy Commissioner in charge of Phulbani District was Dr. N. Datta-Majumdar, I.A.S., a distinguished anthropologist. From him and his successors, in particular Sri B. Venkataramam, I.A.S., who read part of this book, we received valuable help and advice. Of the many officials and private persons in Phulbani District who assisted us I mention only two : Sri S. M. Chatterji, O.B.E., and Sri Z. C. Misra. We are grateful also to the staff of the Baptist Mission at G. Udaygiri for their friendship and many acts of kindness. By Government and people alike we were received with disinterested friendliness and we count it a privilege to have enjoyed such hospitality.

I thank those who have helped me to write this book. I have been guided and stimulated by my supervisor, Professor H. M. Gluckman. Professor C. von Fürer-Haimendorf and Dr. H. H. Meinhard read and criticized the manuscript. Professor M. N. Srinivas has consented to write a Foreword. My friends Dr. E. L. Peters, Dr. T. B. Naik, and Dr. R. L. Rooksby have read the essay and given me the benefit of their criticism. I am most grateful to my wife for her assistance, in particular with quantitative data.

Publication of the book is made possible by grants from the School of Oriental and African Studies, University of London, and from the Faculty of Economic and Social Studies, University of Manchester.

Lastly, for their unlimited patience, I thank the generous people of Bisipara.

PREFATORY NOTE

IN this book I use the word 'caste' not in the sense of the four categories of Hinduism (*varna*), but to translate the Oriya word *jati*, which is an endogamous group dispersed over several villages. For those of one particular caste who reside in the same village I have reserved the term 'caste-group'. 'Sub-caste' I use to refer to endogamous divisions within what Oriyas believe once to have been an undivided caste.

The names of castes are given in English and printed in capital letters. For example, a HERDSMAN is a person of that caste: a herdsman is a man who looks after cattle. BRAHMIN and ORIYA are not given in English. 'Christian' and 'Kond' are printed in small letters, since these are not Hindu categories. But, as social groups within the village, they are in effect caste-groups. Since caste names are difficult to memorize I have set them out in Chart I in their approximate order of ritual precedence. This chart is a rough guide and must not be taken as definitive of the caste hierarchy. The reasons for this will become apparent in the course of the essay.

Those non-Hindu peoples who formerly were called 'Tribals' or 'Aboriginals' are to-day in India known as 'Adibasis'. I have employed the second and third terms. For untouchables the official designation is Scheduled Caste. I have used either term, according to the context. Where I have referred to the State (formerly Province) of Orissa, I have written 'State (Orissa)'. Otherwise 'State' is used loosely to stand for a central authority, typically in opposition to 'village'.

Since this is neither a gazetteer nor an essay in phonetics, I have felt free to write vernacular terms in ordinary Roman script. Mispronunciation will not obscure the substance of the essay. For those who wish to go to what written material exists on this area, it might be useful to know that the word which I spell as Boad, also appears as Baud, Boudh, Baudh, Bouddh, Bauddh, and Bod; Oriya occasionally is seen as Ooriah and Wodiah; Kond might be Kand, Kandho, Kondh, Khondho or Khond. In the use of place-names vernacular terms are inevitable. Elsewhere, when possible, I have translated

Oriya into English. For those familiar with the area an English-Oriya glossary is provided at the end.

It will be a help to have looked at Appendices A and B before reading Part Two of this book.

PART ONE

INTRODUCTION

B

CHAPTER I

THE ARGUMENT

IN a metaphorical sense the village communities of India were for many years beyond the frontiers of dynasties which ruled from the great cities. The administrative system controlling the cities and keeping open the lines of communication did not penetrate directly into the village. This is attested by the apparent stability of the village in the face of changes, often violent, in the larger political system. In 1832 Sir Charles Metcalfe [1] wrote :

> The village communities are little republics, having nearly everything they want within themselves, and almost independent of any foreign relations. They seem to last where nothing else lasts. Dynasty after dynasty tumbles down ; revolution succeeds revolution . . . but the village community remains the same. . . . This union of village communities, each one forming a separate little state in itself, has, I conceive, contributed more than any other cause to the preservation of the people of India, through all the revolutions and changes which they have suffered, and is in a high degree conducive to their happiness, and to the enjoyment of a great portion of freedom and independence.

The frontier of administration did not enter the villages. It stopped short of them. Until recent times the State was not concerned with the social and political organization of the rural communities, nor did it interfere with methods of exploiting the material world. The State was interested in revenue. The peasant was repaid, in some cases not at all, in most cases by the maintenance of law and order outside the villages. The functions of Government were fiscal and pacificatory and seldom reforming. Discussing Mughal times, O'Malley [2] says :

> Except for the collection of land revenue there was little State control of the villages. The activities of the State did not go further than the primary functions of defence against external enemies, the prevention of internal rebellion, and the maintenance of law and order.

[1] Quoted by M. N. Srinivas, 1951.
[2] L. S. S. O'Malley, 1941, p. 12.

The administrative machinery can scarcely be said to have extended to the villages. The civil functionaries were concentrated in the cities and larger towns ; the judicial administration was equally centralized, courts of law being established only in the same centres of population. The only contact with the villages was by the same local officials having their headquarters in the towns, who were responsible for the patrolling of the main routes, the suppression of organized crime, and the realization of the land revenue. So long as it was paid, and so long as there was no disturbance of the peace endangering the general security or outbreaks of crime preventing the safe passage of travellers and merchandise, the villages were left to manage their own affairs, with headmen and councils of elders to try their petty cases and village watchmen to prevent petty crime.

Although the great dynasties exercised no positive political function inside the village and left it to manage its own affairs, nevertheless their ruling hand lay heavily upon the cultivator. Tribute was heavy, so heavy that at times the proportion claimed by the State reduced the peasant to a level of bare subsistence. The tax-collector removed the surplus. Without a reserve in times of natural calamity, the farmer was defenceless. Indian history is marked by famines, which, although primarily acts of God, can rightly be called acts of God helped out by the scandalous exactions of the State. Even in normal times the demands of the tax-gatherer or the tax-farmer left the peasant with neither the resources nor the incentive to experiment, since increased yield meant only increased taxation.

It need not be said that this is a wide generalization and one which admits in different times, in different regions and under different rulers, of many exceptions. But it is not a caricature of the course of Indian history to say that at certain periods the State and the village were separate worlds. The single link was the dependence of the State on revenue derived from the village, and the constriction (or occasional destruction) of villages under this demand. The State rested on wealth produced by the villages. But the villages were not directly administered by the State.[1]

From another point of view, the history of the Indian village community can be seen as the progressive extension of an

[1] In a field of enquiry so wide in time and space as India and Indian history, it is not difficult to find exceptions to this generalization. The Malabar

economic frontier. It is characteristic of this frontier that it goes beyond the frontiers of administration. This is true both in the metaphorical and in the literal sense. The administrative frontiers of the State passed, metaphorically, above the villages : but its fiscal system was a factor of first importance in village economic life. In the literal sense the commercial frontier transcended political boundaries. For example, the political map of what is now western Orissa fragments in the late eighteenth and early nineteenth centuries into many independent or semi-independent hostile States. But across them all pass the trade-routes of the Brinjaris, carrying salt from the coast to the interior.

The economic frontier is not absolute. It admits of degrees. Its progressive extension to the village communities in India is not to be seen as the movement of a line on the map, so that this village is within the frontier and that village is beyond it. It is rather a frontier of commodities and transactions, and its extension is measured at first in terms of salt or kerosene or guns, and in more complex stages by migrant labour or the building of factories.

The early period of the East India Company's history as an administrator continued the traditions of earlier rulers. The Company took in revenue. It spent little and made use of existing institutions. As late as 1839 Sleeman wrote :[1]

> Beyond the boundary of our military and civil stations, we find as yet few indications of our reign or character to link us with the affections of the people. There is hardly anything to indicate our existence as a people or a government in this country ; and it is melancholy to think that in the wide extent of the country over which I have travelled there should be so few signs of that superiority

---

Kings, who derived income from trade-taxes and did not rely only on land revenue, are an example. But the generalization holds good for most periods of the Mughal Empire, particularly in such outlying provinces as Orissa. In any case, it is worth stressing this 'predatory' aspect in the relation of the State and the village in order to compare it with present 'welfare' policies, which aim to change certain features not only of the social structure of the village, but also of its economic life, in particular the techniques of agriculture. (See below, p. 251.)

[1] Quoted by L. S. S. O'Malley, 1941, p. 76.

in science and arts which we boast of, and really do possess, and ought to make conducive to the welfare and happiness of the people in every part of our dominions. The people and the face of the country are just what they might have been had they been governed by police officers, and tax-gatherers from the Sandwich Islands, capable of securing life, property, and character, and levying honestly the means of maintaining the establishments requisite for the purpose.

But even when Sleeman wrote, a process of change had begun. In Bengal and parts of Madras and the United Provinces proprietary landlords had been created. Land became a marketable commodity. After the Mutiny (1857) the pace of change was greatly accelerated. There followed fifty years of peace. Famine controls were set up. There was an immense increase in population. With the building of the railways in the second half of the nineteenth century, the frontiers of commerce were extended, and when in 1869 the Suez Canal was opened, India itself became more fully integrated in the world economy.

As the frontiers of world commerce have pushed into India and spread progressively out to the villages, so the administrative frontier has encroached further into the village community. Forest conservation is one aspect of this. Measures to control agricultural debt are another. The State intervenes to protect aboriginals, whose existence is jeopardized by economic change. These, and measures like them, are reflections of the fact that the village community was no longer a 'little republic'.

Inside the village there has been a radical change in the method by which it exploits the material world. Land was the principal form of wealth. It still is, but now land has a market value. At the same time, land has ceased to be the only source of wealth, and to a greater or lesser degree in different regions, the peasant's income is derived from and spent in the commercial economy of India and ultimately of the world.

As an outline of the history of India this account is scanty. It omits regional variations and such important factors as education, the Press, world economic conditions and so forth. But it will serve to provide a background to what follows and to introduce the concept of a moving frontier, and to show that the process later described is not unique, but is one small fragment in a large mosaic of economic history.

This book describes a village in the remote hills of western Orissa in a region which has been and still is a frontier in several senses of that word. This region is called the Kondmals.

The Kondmals are a high tableland, sharply cut off on three sides from the plains around by a precipitous range of mountains, and inhabited by an aboriginal people called Konds. These are still to-day the most numerous element in the population. But at least three hundred years ago Oriyas,[1] who are Hindus, began to push up from the plains and established fortified settlements in the hills. The region still shows many of the characteristics of a settlers' frontier. The newcomers have taken the best land. Their religion and language are different from those of the native inhabitants. They took concubines, but rarely wives. They live in separate villages. They claim superiority and derive the adjective *sita*, by which they distinguish themselves from Konds, from a word meaning 'the learned ones' or 'the knowledgeable ones'. Oriyas assert that before their coming the Konds lived like 'beasts in the jungle' and knew nothing of the proper cultivation of rice. It was the Oriyas, they say, who taught the Konds to wear clothes, while once they had gone naked. Finally, like settlers elsewhere, the Oriyas shook off metropolitan control and retained only the loosest ties with the Hindu Rajas on the plains. The relationship of the two races is still typical of a settlers' frontier. But the movement has been stopped for more than a hundred years, and although the Oriya villages throw off small suburban settlements, there is no longer a drive from the edge towards the interior of the tableland.

About a hundred years ago the political boundary of British India was extended to encompass the Kondmals. The first Oriya colonists had come from the north, but the administrators came from the south. The Administration was followed by another type of Oriya settler, who did not establish villages, but lived in the existing Oriya communities. These were the frontiersmen of commerce.

[1] A native of Orissa, of any caste, is called an 'Oriya'. His language also is 'Oriya'. In the Kondmals there is also an ORIYA caste.

It is unlikely that commerce penetrated the Kondmals to any considerable extent before the coming of the Administration. The area was not completely isolated, since it was crossed by the trade-routes of the Brinjaris, but the economy of the villages, both Oriya and Kond, could have been only minimally affected by the need to traffic with outsiders.

CHART I

APPROXIMATE HIERARCHY OF CASTE-GROUPS IN BISIPARA

A	High Hindus (*Ucho Hindumane*)	1	BRAHMIN
		2	WARRIOR
		3	HERDSMAN *or* DISTILLER *or* WRITER *or* ORIYA
		4	FISHERMAN
		5*	Kond POTTER
		6*	Kond *or* Kond HERDSMAN
		7*	Christian
		8*	Muslim
B	Low Hindus (*Nicho Hindumane*)	1	TEMPLEMAN
		2	BARBER
		3	WASHERMAN
		4	WEAVER
			Line of pollution
C	Untouchables (*Osporosoniyo jati*)	1	OUTCASTE
		2	BASKETMAKER
		3	SWEEPER

Note: (1) The word *or* indicates that caste-groups under this number dispute for precedence.

(2) Caste-groups marked with an asterisk are those considered non-Hindu. However, informants could allot them a place in a table of precedence. In the case of converts to Christianity and Islam, their rank depends on the caste of their pagan ancestors. Converted OUTCASTES, for instance, are still untouchable.

Since 1855 there has been a continuous extension of the economic frontier. The area now imports kerosene, manufactured cloth, some rice, and a variety of small manufactures, such as brass and aluminium pots, lamps, axes and hoes and so forth. It exports turmeric, hides and oilseeds. An important source of income is the paid labour of the inhabitants in the employment of the Administration.

This book seeks to analyse the changes that have come about in the internal organization of an Oriya village, as a result of the extension of the economic and administrative frontier. It is only incidentally concerned with the settlers' frontier.

Oriyas are Hindus and stratified into castes. In the original village the WARRIOR caste-group was the most important. It had the superiority of numbers. It owned the land. It was politically dominant in village affairs. It had a high position in the ritual hierarchy of caste. Land was the main source of wealth and the WARRIORS owned the land. Members of other caste-groups derived their share in the produce of the village land by virtue of a ritual and economic relationship with the WARRIORS or with the village as a whole. There were BARBERS, WASHERMEN, HERDSMEN, and SWEEPERS. There was a family of BRAHMINS. There was a large group of untouchables, called Boad OUTCASTES, who were attached to the WARRIOR joint-families as farm labourers. There was also a small group of DISTILLERS. Caste-groups other than the WARRIORS made their living not primarily by owning land but by serving the owners of the land. This arrangement was reflected in the hierarchy of caste.

The history and present composition of the village are set out in the first part of the book.

The coming of the Administration and the gradual extension of the frontiers of commerce have provided sources of income which are separate from the wealth derived from agriculture and the village land and which are not, like the land, a monopoly of the WARRIOR caste-group. This new wealth, for the last hundred years, has been altering the structure of caste-groups within the village and still is doing so.

First this new wealth has helped to break down the joint-families of the WARRIORS and to instil the habit of partition at every act of inheritance. These changes are partly the result of a growing population [1] and pressure on the land, but they are also caused by diversity of interest. As cultivators the members

[1] Owing partly to the chequered administrative history of the Kondmals and partly to an oversight, while in the field I did not seek past population figures for the village. I have since been informed that such figures are unobtainable. In the Kondmals as a whole, density per square mile increased from 83 in 1891 to 103 in 1931.

of a joint-family work as a team, but they participate in a commercial economy as individuals. Their varying degree of success and the conflict between the two interests sets up tensions which tend to break down the coparcenary. This process is described by O'Malley:[1]

> Disintegration is due to a combination of causes, chief of which is the change in economic conditions. The joint-family is an institution which had its origin in an earlier order of society, when the country was thinly peopled, the population was mainly agrarian, and cultivation was capable of expansion to meet the needs of growing families. Each family depended on its own labour and the larger it was, the greater was the number of hands available for work. It was an institution which was peculiarly dependent on a community of interests. The conditions favourable to it were those of a static society, in which the members of a family lived in the same place and followed the same pursuits from generation to generation. The economic complex has been transformed during the last hundred years. A largely increased population has caused pressure on the soil, which is acute in congested areas, where all the cultivable land has been brought under the plough and holdings are incapable of expansion. There is no longer the same uniformity of interests owing to the small size of holdings and the pressure of circumstances necessitating the adoption of different callings; one son, for example, may be an agriculturist, another a mechanic, a third a clerk.

Partition of the joint-family, since land was limited, reduced the size of estates. This, in its turn, meant that some of the land-holding peasants had to participate in the new commercial economy in order to support themselves. Also, it reduced the majority of estates to a size which could adequately be worked by the owner and his family without employing permanent servants for farm work. In this way the former servants both were attracted by the independence and possible higher rewards in commerce, and were projected into trading by economic necessity.

But the owners of the diminished estates continued in some respects to live at the rate which was customary when they or their fathers were still coparceners in a joint-family. This is particularly obvious in the expenditure on funerals and marriages. Estates below a certain size could only meet this sort of contingent expenditure by realizing capital, which usually meant

[1] L. S. S. O'Malley, 1941, p. 384.

selling land. Other estates were reduced to a level where minor crises, such as the death of plough cattle, caused land to be sold.

The commercial economy affects land-redistribution in two further ways. Firstly it slows down the transfer of land because the peasant now has an additional source of income with which to meet contingent expenses. Much of the movement of land, viewed over a period of time, is reciprocal. In one year a peasant is selling : a few years later, after a run of luck in trading, he buys land. But, secondly, there has been a drain on the land of the WARRIORS in favour of other caste-groups or of individuals in them. Individual WARRIORS, too, have prospered, but wealth is no longer the monopoly of the WARRIORS.

The greater part of those who have profited in the new economy have invested in land. This happened partly because land carries a high prestige, and partly because in a region which is only marginally on the commercial frontier and far beyond the industrial frontier, there was little productive investment other than in land. Consequently the relative wealth of the WARRIORS has been diminished not only in the new joint economy of agriculture and commerce, but also in the traditional economy of the land.

The breakdown of the original economic organization of the village, in which there was a division of labour and a division of wealth according to caste, and in which other caste-groups received their portion of wealth derived from the village lands through their relationship with the WARRIORS, is analysed in the second part of the book.

The incorporation of the Kondmals in British India has obviously had important effects in the process outlined above. The pacification of the area made easy the advance of the commercial frontier. The Administration itself provides some of the wealth which upsets the traditional economy. The subordination of the village to a larger and effective political authority gave shelter to the newly rich and prevented the WARRIORS from trying by force to re-establish their economic superiority. But the Administration did not directly interfere with the structure of authority within villages (nor within the Kondmals as a whole). The dominant position of the Oriya settlers was confirmed by employing them as the instrument of administration.

Within the Oriya villages the WARRIOR headmen were appointed Government representatives and village affairs continued to be administered by the village council. In spite of this, the change in the distribution of village wealth has more and more forced the Government to take over functions previously fulfilled by the council and the caste structure of the village. This development is nowhere spectacular. But nevertheless it is discernible.

This process, in which the State gradually subsumes the village, is analysed in the third part of the book, by considering the history of three caste-groups who gained or are gaining considerable wealth either directly in the new economy or through its secondary effects.

About 1870, in its desire to increase the Excise revenue, the Administration banned home-stills. In 1910 prohibition was enforced. But in the meantime the two DISTILLER castes had gained relatively spectacular wealth and had become the owners of large estates.

One of these DISTILLER caste-groups had been part of the original village. When prohibition was enforced, they gave up commerce and settled down as landholders and small traders. At the same time they made successful efforts to improve their status as a caste, after the traditional fashion of Hinduism. They have risen in the estimation of the village and they continue to order their lives within the traditional framework of village political organization. The disturbance set up by their new wealth is now coming to an end, and it is now possible to see that although positions within the traditional structure of the village were altered, the structure itself was unimpaired.

The other DISTILLER caste-group are part of the second wave of immigrants, who followed in the wake of the Administration. Like their fellows they profited greatly from the drink-trade, but after prohibition they continued in commerce as merchant-shopkeepers and as a group they are now more wealthy than any other in the village. The fact that they are heavily engaged in commerce means that they have many transactions and relationships outside the village. These transactions sometimes give rise to disputes, but in such disputes the traditional juridical institutions of the village have no jurisdiction. The merchants are compelled to seek justice in Government courts. This fact, and their outstanding wealth, sets them apart from the rest of the village. Although they reside within the village boundaries, and although they are a caste-group and observe all the usual restrictions, yet they are not part of the hierarchy of caste-groups which orders its affairs within the village council. Their position is equivocal and is more fully discussed later, but relatively they are citizens of the State rather than members of the village

A similar development is now taking place with that large group of untouchables who formerly were farm servants of the WARRIORS. These are the Boad OUTCASTES. In the last forty years this group has begun to profit from the protection afforded them by discriminating legislation. As a group their wealth is not large, but among them are a few very rich men. In the last few years they have begun to try to adjust their social status to their new wealth, but unlike the first DISTILLER caste they have been prevented from finding a social level appropriate to their new economic status, because they are on the wrong side of the barrier of pollution. Consequently they tend more and more to invoke the protection of the Administration, and to use their rights as citizens of the State to overcome the disabilities which the rest of the village seeks to put upon them. They patronize the Government courts. They defy the village council in its judicial function and increasingly ignore its legislative and administrative decisions. Like the second group of DISTILLERS they are passing beyond the political frontier of the village and are seeking to establish themselves as citizens of the State.

The process which brings the frontier of administration inside the village community is a complicated one. At the present day there is increasing interference with the lives of the cultivators arising from the conception of the role of government as a positive agency of welfare, rather than an evil necessity. Since Independence this function promises to be greatly magnified. But in the history of this village, welfare activities have played a small part. Here the increasing subordination of the village to the Administration has come about more through the extension of the frontiers of commerce than through the conscious direction of Administrators. Contact with the larger economy of India has been and still is minimal, if we measure it in terms of the flow of goods. Yet, in spite of this, the changes in the economic and political structure of the village are not marginal, but fundamental.

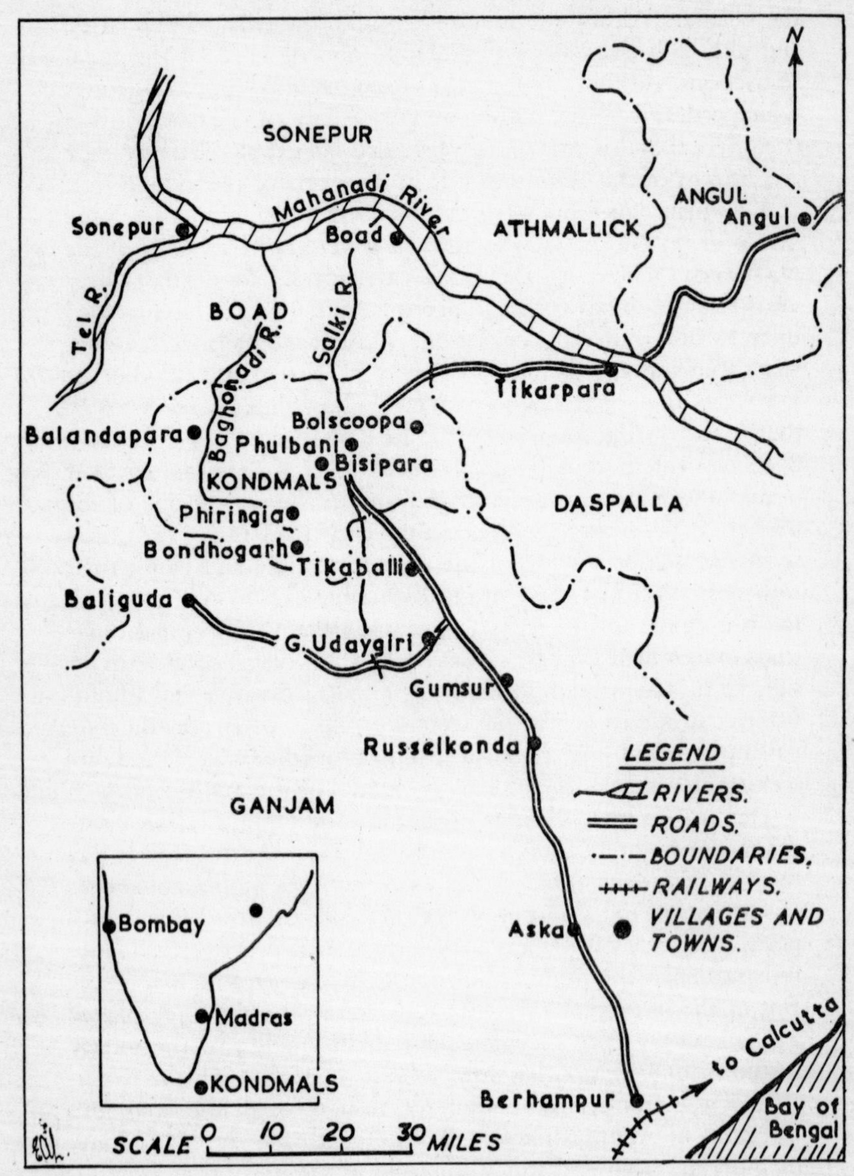

MAP 1. THE KONDMALS

CHAPTER II

THE KONDMALS

Physical Features

THE village is called Bisipara. It is populated mainly by Oriyas and it lies approximately in the centre of the Kondmals Sub-Division of Phulbani District, in western Orissa, south of the Mahanadi river.

The Kondmals, which extend over 800 square miles, lie between 20° 13′ and 21° 11′ N. and between 83° 47′ and 84° 31′ E. The area forms a rough rectangle forty miles from east to west and twenty miles from north to south. The centre of the region is approximately one hundred miles due east of Cuttack.

The Kondmals are an extension of the Eastern Ghats at the point where those mountains terminate on the southern bank of the Mahanadi river. The area consists of a plateau, between 1,500 and 1,700 feet above sea level, and broken by mountain systems which rise to about 3,000 feet. To the south and south-west the mountains continue and there is no obvious natural feature to separate the Kondmals from this country. But on the other three sides, from Ganjam in the south and south-east, through Daspalla in the east, and through Boad on the north and north-west and west, the Kondmals are girdled by precipitous mountains, which separate the area sharply from the plains around. For instance, from the south-east the road rises from about 500 feet to just over 2,000 feet within seven road miles, or about four miles as the crow flies. To the north there is a similar descent to the plains of Boad, although, since the tableland slopes gently downwards from south to north, this descent is not so spectacular.

This plateau is itself intersected by mountain systems which rise up to 1,500 feet above the level of the valleys. The valleys are innumerable and vary in size from small upland dells, a stone's throw across, to wide areas of level ground extending up to fifteen square miles. But nowhere are the mountains out of sight and nowhere, except in sections of the valley of the Salki river, is it possible to travel more than five miles in any direction without traversing a ridge of hills.

The plateau drains to the north into the Mahanadi river. There are two main streams. The Baghonadi rises in the hills near Bondhogarh and flows westward to within seven or eight miles of the western border of the Kondmals, where it turns abruptly north and after traversing the region empties into the Mahanadi in Boad. The other river, the Salki, rises in the plateau around G. Udaygiri, beyond the southern border of the Kondmals. It flows directly northwards, bisecting the Kondmals. On the middle reaches of this river lies Bisipara. Neither of these rivers are fit for navigation. In the rains they are torrents. In July 1953, at a point sixty yards from bank to bank, the Salki rose twenty feet overnight. During the dry season it is possible to walk over the river bed without getting one's feet wet, although water always can be found by digging holes in the sand. These same characteristics make the river useless for irrigation. When the river is in spate, the waters are not needed. When the water is needed, the river is all but dry and deep down below steep banks. However, the Salki is an important physical feature because its course provides a series of miniature alluvial plains, which are cultivated and relatively thickly populated, and which provide the obvious route from the south to the centre of the Kondmals. Beyond this point the valleys are narrower and the hills descend more steeply until the waters come out on the wide level plains of Boad.

Forest covers most of the hills. To the north the principal constituent is bamboo and here travel off the pathways is almost impossible. In the western part of the Kondmals there are large areas of jungle, with trees of great height and dense undergrowth. In the region around Bisipara most of the hills grow secondary jungle. The slopes have been cleared of the larger trees by men in search of wood for building, or by the axe-cultivation of the Konds. In the south, particularly around G. Udaygiri over the southern border of the Kondmals, many hills are bare except for a covering of grass and small shrubs. The forest has been killed by the woodcutters and cultivators.

The secondary jungle around Bisipara consists mostly of a dense growth up to twenty feet in height. The most common tree is *sal* (*shorea robusta*),[1] a hardwood in common use for building, for ploughs and for many other wooden implements. Occasional clumps of bamboo are found. In the upland fields, in places here and there in the jungle, and in the fields around the village itself are groves of mango (*mangifera indica*) and many isolated *mohua* (*bassia latifolia*). Both these trees are important in the economy of the people. The mangoes are gathered, dried and stored and provide a relish to be cooked and eaten with the main dish of rice for the whole twelve months of the year. The *mohua* gives flowers which either may be boiled and distilled to make liquor, or are dried and eaten. After the flowers the kernels of the *mohua* nut are gathered and pressed to provide the cheapest cooking oil obtainable in the hills. The forest is an asset in many other ways. Apart from firewood and wood for implements and house frames, and bamboos for roof frames, it provides thatching grass, fencing woods, bark string, numerous edible roots and berries, mushrooms, plants for medicines and leaves for household utensils. The Oriyas make full use of these products, but the Konds are said to be even more skilled at exploiting the forest. I have been told that if necessary they can live for three months in the year on a diet gleaned entirely from the jungle. A young Oriya man, with no particular reputation for woodlore, wrote out a list of 150 plants and trees, which grew wild and could be used in one way or another.

The fauna on the whole is unfriendly and a liability rather than an asset. Birds—the million pigeons, the jungle fowl, partridge, green pigeon, parrots, pea fowl, snipe and quail—devastate the ripening crops. Upland fields and the remoter irrigated fields are open to the depredations of the spotted deer or, more commonly, the barking deer or the rare sambhur. The wild boar is common and occasionally a herd of them will in one night destroy a complete root field or maize garden. The maize garden, indeed, is the target not only of the wild pig but also of the jackal, the hyena, and worst of all, the bear. Invariably the garden is protected by a high fence, even when it is beside the house of the cultivator, and while the crop is ripening a watchman remains in a wooden tower through the

[1] I am indebted for the botanial names of plants and trees to Sri S. Mahadeva Iyer, B.Sc., the District Agricultural Officer of Phulbani.

night, banging a pair of wooden clappers or beating an empty kerosene tin. Bears infest the jungle pathways and when surprised they attack human beings. Since the people go barefoot and move silently when alone, attacks of this sort are not uncommon. Fatalities are rare, except among women—and they do not usually travel alone—for the men can protect themselves with the battle-axe or woodman's axe, which always is carried in the jungle. However, still the most common jungle injury is to be scalped by, or to lose an eye to, the claws of a bear.

Leopards are plentiful in the vicinity of every village. Maneaters are rare, but leopards take a toll of the village cattle. They also are fond of dogs and it is not uncommon for them to enter the compounds and take off a dog which was sleeping on the verandah of a house. Hyenas, also, are known to do this. Tigers are less common than they were, but the village loses half a dozen cattle to them every year. Habitual man-eaters are very rare, but cowherds are sometimes killed when trying to protect the cattle.

Among reptiles the boa-constrictor, the cobra, the krait, Russell's viper, the whip snake and harmless grass snakes are found. But deaths from snake-bite are rare.

All these creatures are found in the vicinity of Bisipara. Away to the west of the Kondmals there are a few herds of elephant and occasional *nilgai* (*bosephalus tragocamelus*). Carnivora are more common in this area.

The climate is more extreme than that on the neighbouring plains. The hottest day in Bisipara, in 1953, offered a shade temperature of 106° F. The coldest winter night—in January—went down to 43° F. The cold weather begins in October and lasts until the end of February. From then the heat rises until the rains break about the middle of June. The climate of the Kondmals is considered most unhealthy.

The effects on a stranger may be gathered from the following remarks recorded by an Indian Medical Officer sent there on special duty. 'Its evil influences have marked every constitution, and a newcomer must pass through a trying ordeal of repeated attacks of high fever before he can find rest. His constitution by that time is thoroughly broken down ; he looks half his former self and despairs to regain his vigour and spirit as long as confined in this dreadful hole.' . . . The tract is so unhealthy that outsiders fear to visit it, and it is reported that the ordinary Oriya of the plains regards service in it as almost equivalent to a death sentence.[1]

The same fears are found to-day. A special pay allowance is given for service in this and other 'Agency' tracts. The Oriyas from the plains still find the climate injurious not only from malaria but also from the sudden changes of temperature. I did not find the climate uncomfortable, except for a short time in the hot weather, but this reputation is important since it is one more factor serving to isolate the hills from the surrounding plains.

The annual rainfall is between fifty and sixty inches. It is reliable and although the timing of different showers may materially affect the yield of the harvest, total famine through lack of rain is unknown.

The mountain barriers, the difficulty of travel within the area, the lack of water for irrigation, the comparative scarcity of land which is level enough for rice cultivation, the numbers of wild animals and not the least the climate have served to keep the Kondmals isolated to a very great degree from the neighbouring plains of Orissa.

Communications

The Kondmals, Baliguda Agency and Boad together form Phulbani District. The capital of this District is at the administrative settlement Phulbani, eight miles from Bisipara.

Two main all-weather roads are kept up in Phulbani District by the Public Works Department of Orissa. These roads are nowhere surfaced, but they are bridged and can be traversed at any time of the year. The road which comes eventually from Berhampur on the railway ascends the mountains and enters Phulbani District at a point forty miles south and slightly west of Phulbani town. At the top of the ascent, on the edge of the tableland the road branches. One route goes directly westwards and finishes at Baliguda, about sixty miles away. The other continues north to Phulbani. At this point the all-weather road stops. In the dry season and for most of the cold season another road is open leading east and north from Phulbani to descend to the plains of Boad and eventually to the Mahanadi

[1] L. S. S. O'Malley, 1908, p. 77.

ferry at Tikarpara. This road can in fact be traversed during the rains, except after a heavy shower. Instead of regular bridges, the water is carried over the road by Irish bridges and these are liable to flooding after rain.[1]

Two buses each day run from the south to Phulbani and Baliguda. A bus service is kept open from Phulbani to the Boad plains except during the rains.

Another system of roads is maintained in the Kondmals from local funds. These are called Revenue roads. They vary greatly in quality. Some stretches, for instance from a point on the main road near Bisipara to Phiringia, are bridged and can be traversed by cars throughout the year, with some difficulty. Cars can use other Revenue roads in the dry season, but the greater number are fit only for bullock carts and pedestrians. The abolition of forced labour is partly responsible, for without this there are insufficient funds to maintain the existing roads and wooden bridges. There are about 180 miles of these roads in an area of 800 square miles.

Elsewhere travelling is by tracks. These, which wind along the edges of cultivation, on the narrow banks between fields, over steep rocky defiles and through thick jungle, are passable only for pedestrians moving normally in single file. Since there are no pack animals kept in the hills—occasionally a trader comes from the plains with pack horses or pack bullocks—trade goods can reach the majority of villages only on the backs of men.

Although the Revenue roads tend to take the easiest country, that is along the valleys, and although the majority of villages are sited in valleys, yet communications are rendered difficult by the terrain and most movement and transport is at best by bullock cart and normally on foot.

The main road system connects the Kondmals with the rest of India over the southern boundary, for it is in this direction that the railway can be reached with least difficulty. Trade goods pass to and fro in this direction. There are descents from the plateau to the north and east and north-west, but these nowadays both for commerce and for administration are dead ends. To-day everything points to the south. Just over a hundred years ago this boundary was virtually closed and what com-

[1] This was written in 1954. Since that time sections of the P.W.D. roads have been surfaced.

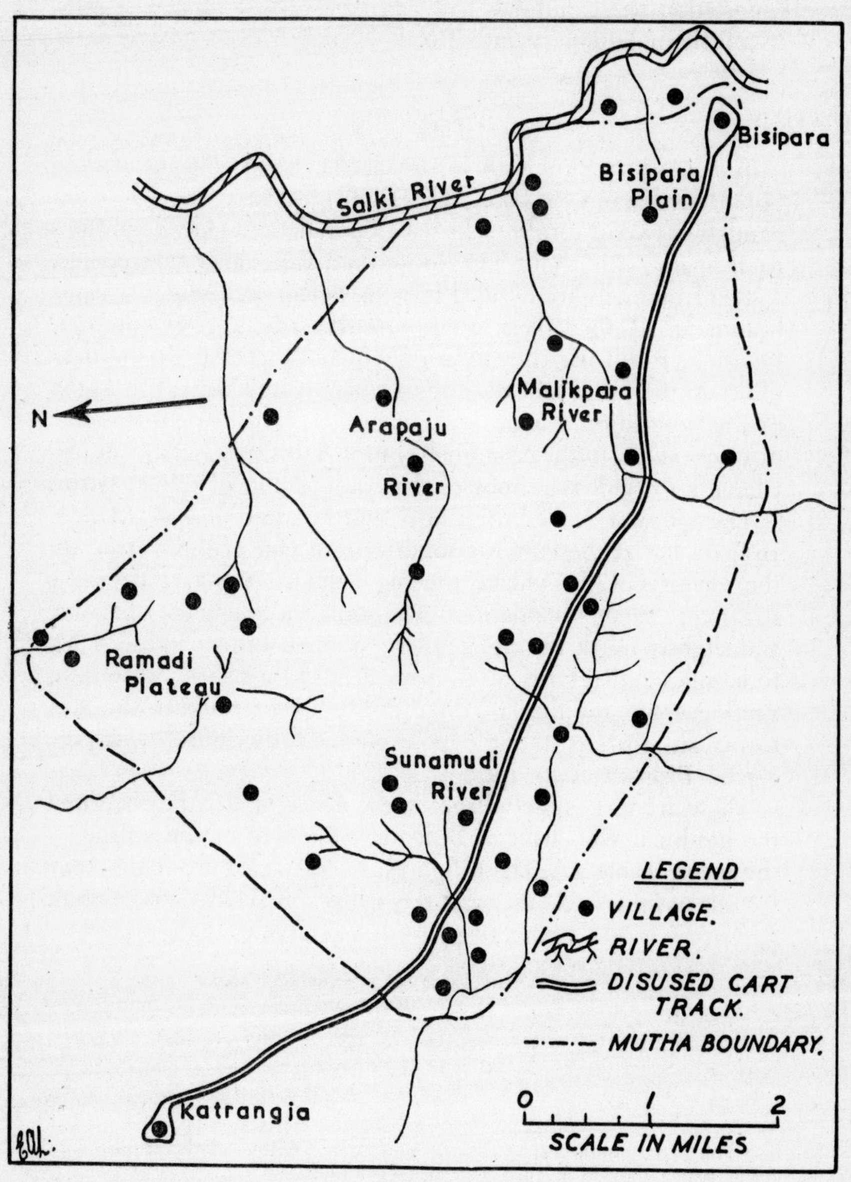

MAP 2. BESRINGIA *MUTHA*

munication the Kondmals had with the rest of India was over its northern boundary into Boad.

Population

In 800 square miles there are about 1,200 villages with a population about 80,000. These villages vary in size from hamlets of two or three houses with a population under 20 persons to Bisipara with about 180 houses and just under 700 people.

The Kondmals are divided into 50 *muthas* each under a *mutha* headman. Rather than attempt to describe the whole Sub-Division, I will use the *mutha* of which Bisipara is the head to illustrate the siting and the size of villages, and the composition of the population. This *mutha* is not necessarily representative of every *mutha* in the Kondmals, but it will serve as an example. I have no detailed account of the composition of other *muthas*.

The *mutha* is called Besringia and is illustrated in Map 2. Bisipara lies at the extreme south-eastern end of the *mutha*. In the vicinity of the village the big Salki river and a tributary stream are *mutha* boundaries. The southern boundary runs west and slightly north for eight miles : it then turns north-east for four miles and returns to Bisipara in a south-easterly direction, veering south for the last three miles. Very roughly the area forms an isosceles triangle pointing east by south, with the capital Bisipara at its apex.

There are forty-nine villages in the *mutha*, under the charge of the headman who lives at Bisipara. The size of the villages is shown in Table 1. These figures are extracted from the 1951 Census of India. At that date the *mutha* contained 3,408 persons.

Table 1

Population of Villages in Besringia *mutha*

Under 60	60–100	125	160	170	305	693*	*Total*
32	12	1	1	1	1	1	49

* This is the population of Bisipara in 1951 at the time of the census. The count which I made in 1953 gave 685 persons.

The forty-nine villages can be grouped into five areas, according to the river systems along which they are sited. This is a purely geographical grouping and is not explicitly recognized by those who live there. The areas bear names which I have given them, and although they would be intelligible to a villager, they are not in common use. The division is made because it helps to give a synoptic view of the racial composition of the *mutha* and the different size of the villages.

Geographically the *mutha* consists of a plain at the apex of the triangle, from which run three ridges of mountains to the base, and continuing beyond it. The crest of the southern ridge is the boundary of the *mutha*. About a mile north of this crest, at the foot of the hills, a disused cart track runs from Bisipara to Katrangia, which is a large village in another *mutha*. The cart track is broken down. There are no bridges and in parts the rock surface is very rough, so that while short stretches of it can be used by carts in the dry season, it is in no way a trade route for wheeled vehicles.

The track crosses a low col in the centre. Rivers flow down to the east and west, parallel to the road. Beside these rivers and their tributaries, villages are built. To the west flows the Sunamudi river, a tributary of the Baghonadi. On it and its tributaries are built 23 villages, housing 28 per cent of the population of the *mutha*. The eastern river, unnamed but here called Malikpara after a village built upon it, has 12 villages containing 22 per cent of the population. The Malikpara stream drains into the Salki river. At the eastern end of the cart track is Bisipara and one small Kond hamlet, housing between them 20 per cent of the *mutha* population. The remaining two river systems flow northwards from the central ridge of mountains, so that the villages sited there can be reached from the other three areas only by going over this ridge. This is not difficult, since the ridge is nowhere more than five hundred feet above the plain and the main river valleys : but it is jungle-covered and offers a complete obstacle to carts. The Arapaju river area has four villages housing 15 per cent of the population. The Ramadi plateau, with the same percentage of population, has eight villages. This distribution is summarized in Table 2.

The siting of the villages reflects directly the dependence on agriculture and in particular on rice cultivation. Villages everywhere are on or near streams which provide level ground, or ground which can be levelled, and which give water for

TABLE 2

GEOGRAPHICAL DISTRIBUTION OF POPULATION IN BESRINGIA *mutha*

Area	*Villages*	*Population*	*Percentage of mutha population*
			%
Bisipara plain	2	705	20
Malikpara river. . . .	12	765	22
Arapaju river	4	510	15
Ramadi plateau . . .	8	529	15
Sunamudi river. . . .	23	899	28
Total	49	3,408	100

irrigation. Except in the case of Bisipara, this factor also sets a limit on the size of the villages, for the mountains set a close limit on the area that can be levelled. Steep hill-terracing, such as is found in Assam, is here unknown. Bisipara differs from other villages in the *mutha* in that a part of its income is not derived from agriculture.

The population of the Kondmals is not homogeneous. Three categories of persons are recognized by the Administration. These are Adibasi (Konds), Scheduled Caste (untouchables) and Oriya, and they are represented in Besringia *mutha* as in Table 3.

TABLE 3

PROPORTION OF POPULATION CATEGORIES IN BESRINGIA *mutha*

Category	*Numbers*	*Percentage of population*
		%
Adibasi	2,237	66
Scheduled Castes . . .	577	17
Oriyas	594	17
Total	3,408	100

These categories are not evenly distributed. The areas more remote and with a smaller potential of cultivation tend to be populated by Adibasis. The Oriyas tend to live in Bisipara, which is nearer the lines of communication and has more level ground in its vicinity. This reflects the history of the Oriyas as conquering immigrants, and their present function as part-time traders. This is shown in Table 4. The Arapaju river and the Ramadi plateau are the remotest areas.

TABLE 4

PROPORTION OF POPULATION CATEGORIES IN AREAS OF BESRINGIA *mutha*

Category	*Bis. plain*	*Malik. river*	*Ara. river*	*Ram. plateau*	*Sun. river*
	%	%	%	%	%
Adibasi . .	22	66	94	89	70
Sch. Caste .	30	24	6	6	12
Oriya . . .	48	10	—	5	18
Total . . .	100	100	100	100	100

A similar tendency in the size of the villages shows that Adibasis are the people cultivating small areas alongside the smaller jungle streams. There is an exception in the two large villages in the remote Arapaju river area. This is shown in Table 5 and reflects again the history and status of the immigrant categories.

TABLE 5

SIZE OF VILLAGE AND POPULATION CATEGORIES

Category of village	*Under* 60 *persons*	60–100 *persons*	*over* 100 *persons*	*Total villages*
Mainly Adibasi . .	28	9	2	39
Oriya and Sch. Cast predominating . .	4	3	3	10
Total villages . . .	32	12	5	49

The significance of the figures given in these tables will be more apparent when the history of the Kondmals has been related. In the meantime they offer some general suggestions about the racial composition and pattern of residence of Besringia *mutha*. Firstly the method of cultivation has caused villages to be sited with reference to watercourses. Secondly the amount of land that can be taken under cultivation is limited by the number of streams and the possibility of widening their beds to make rice fields. Thirdly the population of the *mutha* is heterogeneous and there has been a tendency for the Oriyas to occupy the broader valleys and sites nearer communication routes. (The main tracks follow the broader valleys.) The Adibasis are driven on to land in more remote valleys. I think that this pattern of the Oriyas sitting on the 'eyes' of the land would be found over the whole of the Kondmals, although I have no figures to prove it. One would expect it from a study of their history and their present economic status. As conquerors they took the best land. As traders they occupy sites along the lines of communication.

History

There is a tradition that the land first belonged to a people called Kurmo. If a cultivator is making an offering in his fields, he usually has a long list of supernatural beings who are qualified to share in the offering—Lakmi, the spirit of the Earth, perhaps the spirit of a tree that lies beside the field, his own ancestors, the family line of extinct owners of the land, if he knows them, and always the Kurmo, 'for they first made the soil (i.e. cleared it) and the soil is theirs'. The Kurmo to-day no longer live in the Kondmals. There is said to be a remnant of them living a gipsy-like life in the foothills of Daspalla to the east.

After the Kurmo came Konds. These have their own origin myths, with which Oriyas are not concerned. They know only that the Konds came and drove the Kurmo out of the hills. The Konds were in entire possession when the Oriyas themselves arrived.

The Oriyas who live in Bisipara say that they came from a village in Athmallick, which is on the north side of the Mahanadi river, and is shown on Map 1. Many years ago they crossed the river and took service with the Raja of Boad, whose kingdom was on the south bank of the river. Some time later their ancestors began to push up from the plains of Boad into the Kond hills, first in the north-east. An early hill colony was at Bolscoopa, in the north-eastern quarter of the Kondmals. From there they spread gradually westwards and southwards, beyond the present southern boundary of the Kondmals, as far as Tikaballi (see Map 1), and to the western edge of the hills at Balandopara. A line drawn from Tikaballi through Bondhogarh to Balandopara represents very roughly the limit of the Oriya colonies which were founded from Boad and which stem eventually from states to the north of the river.

I have no accurate means of dating these events. According to genealogies the move to Bisipara was made about eleven generations ago, which would give a time of residence of between 250 and 300 years. But genealogies often are telescoped and the date of the invasion may be yet further back. I do not know. The only certain thing is that when the East India Company first penetrated the hills in the 1840s, the Oriya villages were well established.

The servants of the East India Company say that the Oriya chieftains had been sent into the hills to protect the frontier of Boad from Kond raiders. The Oriyas who live to-day in Bisipara believe that their ancestors were forced to move on by pressure of population and on the occasion of faction fighting.

There is ample evidence that the invasion was at first resisted. Subsequent relations are obscure. It seems that the majority of Oriyas and Konds have always lived in separate villages. Oriyas have taken Kond concubines. There has probably been some intermarriage although not extensively since such marriages offend the rules of caste.[1] It also is clear from records and traditions that Oriyas were fully committed in the Kond ritual of human sacrifice. Many other rites carried on in the Oriya villages to-day are in essence Kond rites. As for political power, by the time the British armies arrived after 1836, the Oriya chiefs seem to have been in a position to answer for the Konds. The tenacious fight against the British was led by men with Oriya names. This probably represents a real hegemony, but the actual influence of the Oriya chiefs may have been exaggerated because the servants of the East India Company were able to speak the Oriya language and not the language of the Konds.

[1] The evidence for these statements is contained in vague and guarded hints dropped by informants. While I lived in the village there was only one liaison between an Oriya man and an Adibasi woman, but there may have been others conducted more discreetly.

This was a frontier society and there are two important differences between its two categories of people. The first was language, and the second was religion. Oriya is a Sanskritic language and is allied to the family of North Indian Indo-Aryan tongues. Kui, the language of the Konds, is Dravidian, an offshoot of the group of South Indian languages. Oriya is written, Kui is not. The two are not in the least mutually intelligible, although there has been borrowing of odd words. Secondly, the Oriyas are Hindus. The Konds are now rapidly becoming Hindu, but, as they themselves say, formerly they were not Hindus.

These, then, were the characteristics of the Kond hills society before the arrival of the British armies in 1836. The aboriginal element were the Konds. Living among them in fortified villages, occupying the best parts of the land, of a different language and religion, superior probably in military techniques and the art of government, were Oriyas, who exercised some sort of political control over the Konds, but socially remained distinct.

This superiority of the Oriyas was confirmed, maintained and probably enhanced by events that followed.

In 1836 the Raja of Gumsur was in revolt against the East India Company. The greater part of Gumsur lay on the plains to the south of the Kondmals, in the present Ganjam District, but there were a number of villages sited in the hills and owing allegiance to the Raja. He fled and eventually died in one of these villages, but not before his hill subjects had caught and massacred a party of the Company's troops. A war followed. Hill chiefs were caught and hanged. Villages and stocks of grain were burned. The war came to an end.

For the first time during this campaign the agents of the Company had been into the hills. They learnt that the Konds were practising a rite of human sacrifice and they decided to stamp out this rite. There followed fifteen years of intermittent campaigning throughout the hills, burning villages, terrorizing, exacting promises, promising peace and good government.

It had always been supposed that the Kondmals were under the control of the Raja of Boad, who had been under treaty to the East India Company since March 1804 and whose territories were supervised as part of the South-West Frontier Agency of Bengal. In the first years of the campaign to suppress human sacrifice, it became apparent that the Raja had no control over the Kondmals, and they were taken over as part of a special Meriah Agency. ' Meriah ' is the word used for the rite of human sacrifice.

In 1855, after the rite was considered suppressed, a rebellion broke out in Gumsur and when it failed the leader fled into the Kondmals and began to recruit a following there. The Meriah Agency had by then been disbanded and the territory restored to the Boad Raja. When he proved unable to suppress the new disturbances, the Kondmals finally were annexed in February 1855.

From 1855 until 1880 the Kondmals were ruled with unexampled ferocity by Dinobandu Patnaik, holding office as Tahsildar under the Superintendent of the Tributary Mahals, who lived in Cuttack. Cuttack then was three weeks posting away, so that the Tahsildar was virtually a king in his own country, unchecked and unsupervised. At first there were troops at his disposal. Later a civil police force was established. Administration seems to have consisted of looting crops and precious metals and the Tahsildar with his family acquired a great fortune. The proper work of the administrators must have been negligible, for as late as 1888 the establishment consisted, apart from the police, of two clerks, two peons and a sweeper to look after 800 square miles. It is not surprising that there are no records or statistics surviving from those days.

The Tahsildar and his successors ruled through the Oriya hill chiefs. The effect of this, which is more fully described later, was to strengthen the controlling position of the Oriyas.

In 1891 the Kondmals became a sub-division of Angul District, an odd arrangement since the two regions were separated by the Mahanadi and then were separated as well by the independent state of Boad. In 1936, when the territory of Ganjam was transferred from the Northern Circars of Madras, the Kondmals became a sub-division under the Magistrate of Ganjam. More recently the Kondmals, together with Boad and the Baliguda Agency, were put together to form Phulbani District.

Administration

The District is in charge of a Deputy Commissioner, who also is head of the Revenue Department. Under his control are various departments, Agriculture, Forest, Welfare, Excise and so forth, whose preserve is the whole District. For each of the three Sub-Divisions of the District there is an officer with the general charge of revenue and justice, and a variety of other incidental responsibilities.

Thus, for the Kondmals, responsibility for revenue collection and justice devolves from the Deputy Collector upon the Sub-Divisional Officer. It then passes through subordinate officers in the Revenue Department and descends upon the *mutha* headmen, of whom there are fifty in the Kondmals. Those in the hierarchy above the *mutha* headmen are members of the civil services of India: the *mutha* headmen and their subordinates hold a position that is hereditary, subject to confirmation.

The Deputy Commissioner has powers to use the police to help him, but the police are responsible for their own internal organization and discipline. In the District the police are headed by a Superintendent, who has a deputy to assist him. In the Kondmals there are four police-stations. In their turn these stations control outposts. Like the Revenue Department the police also work through the hereditary *mutha* headmen and their assistants.

Language

At higher levels the language of the Administration is still English, and most of the officials, including those who are not Gazetted, speak English well. Below this Oriya is used. So far as I know there is not one senior member of any of the Civil Services who can speak Kui well, although there is a bounty offered for those who can pass an examination in Kui.

The division of language in the Kondmals persists. Roughly speaking, to the east of the Salki river everyone, including those of Kond descent, speaks Oriya. Here Oriya is the language of the home. West of the Salki river the language of the home is Kui and few women know more than one or two words of

Oriya. Most men can speak and understand Oriya, but they continue to use Kui in their villages, and it is not uncommon to find one of their number acting as interpreter for others when they are in the presence of Oriyas. Among the Oriyas of Bisipara there are about a third of the men, including the *mutha* headman—but not his son—who can speak Kui fluently.

This difference in language has given the Oriyas a marked advantage over the Konds in their dealings with the Administration. It is not surprising to find that east of the Salki river the majority of *mutha* headmen are of Kond extraction. West of the Salki most of the headmen are Oriyas.

Summary

The Kondmals have always been insulated to a very great degree against political and commercial India. This situation arises from the peculiarities of their environment. The configuration of the land at once provides a barrier to travel both into and within the region and at the same time limits the amount of cultivable land which could attract settlers. But there was some immigration and the Oriya colonists who came from Boad in the north took the best cultivating sites. The distribution of land between the two peoples in the Kondmals was altered. Meanwhile the region continued its political and economic isolation from the plains, both from the Ganjam plains to the south, which after 1803 were being opened to trade and administration by the East India Company, and from Boad in the north, which itself was relatively isolated from the rest of India.

This isolation was, on paper at least, ended by the coming of a regular Administration in the middle of the nineteenth century. Over its southern boundary the region was now connected with larger India. But in fact the contacts even now are minimal. The climate and the shortage of land above the hills have discouraged any large-scale immigration of cultivators from the south. Commerce must rely on a single road, which in fact is adequate, since the Kondmals are relatively poor and backward, have little to offer to the general economy of India, and consequently can take little from it.

For the same reasons the Administration has rested lightly on the Kondmals. This is true in spite of the systematic pillage of the first Tahsildar and in spite of the efforts of later officers to protect and develop the people and the land in their charge. These efforts, striking as some of them were, could never radically alter the poverty of the Kondmals without extensive subsidies, and this step the larger Administration was not prepared to take. The administrators had to be content to work through existing institutions, and in fact their rule tended to confirm the existing distribution of wealth and power, to the benefit of the Oriyas and the detriment of the Konds.

This book is not primarily concerned with the development of the Kond-Oriya relationship, which is a problem in itself. I intend to describe an Oriya village and the changes in its internal political structure which have followed the coming of the Administration. This chapter is offered not as an exhaustive analysis of the conflicts between Hindus and aboriginals, but as a background against which to see the political developments within an Oriya village.

CHAPTER III

BISIPARA

The Appearance of the Village

BISIPARA lies on the south-western edge of an egg-shaped plain, which is two miles from east to west and a mile from north to south. The plain is 1,750 feet above sea-level and the hills around rise between 500 and 1,000 feet higher. The Salki river runs from south to north through the plain and the village is built in a wedge of land between the Salki and a small tributary. Both these watercourses have cut deep channels, the stream about ten feet deep and the river up to thirty feet. The width of the Salki varies from about sixty yards to one hundred yards. The smaller stream, where it has not been controlled and dispersed for paddy fields, is about five yards wide.

The plain consists mainly of jungle-covered mounds, not more than fifty feet in height. On one of these Bisipara is built. To the west of the village the stream is used to water paddy fields. A mile to the north a spring rises and gives water for a wide crescent-shaped belt of fields, which curl along the north-eastern side of the village. On the east side there are levelled rain-irrigated paddy fields. The edges of the mound, clearings on other mounds and on the gentle slope that runs to the foot of the mountains, and the sides of nullahs, are used for dry cultivation of rice and other crops. Around the edge of the village and interspersed in the cultivation are groves of mango and jackfruit, valued for their produce and the shade they give in summer. Trees of many kinds grow everywhere, and viewed from the mountain-side, the houses of the village are submerged in a sea of foliage.

In a direct line the village is a mile and a half from the road which comes from Berhampur, at a point about six miles distant from Phulbani. During the summer there is a pathway directly from the village to join the big road. During the rains the traveller must go three miles round, following a track which leaves the village and joins the Phiringia-Phulbani road near a big bridge over the Salki. Until the middle of 1953, when the rains washed away an old stone bridge, it was possible to drive a car into Bisipara. To the north-west a disused cart-track leads down the length of Besringia *mutha* to the village of Katrangia. To the north and east a multitude of narrow footpaths pick their way through the paddy fields to other hamlets on the plain, both in Besringia and Bhetimendi *mutha*, and in the hills beyond. To the west a single precipitous track climbs to a wild plateau, which is sparsely inhabited.

The History of the Village

Bisipara was colonized by Oriyas, who are Hindus and divided into endogamous castes. These castes were WARRIOR, Boad BRAHMIN, BARBER, WASHERMAN, HERDSMAN, Boad DISTILLER and Boad OUTCASTE. They were not a heterogeneous aggregate of ritual groups, but together they formed an agricultural community. The BRAHMIN, BARBER, WASHERMAN, HERDSMAN and DISTILLER each had specialist tasks in the economic and ritual organization of the village. The WARRIORS, who were more numerous than any of the other caste-groups, except perhaps the Boad OUTCASTES, were the cultivators and owners of the land. The Boad OUTCASTES were their farm servants. All these groups came from Boad in the north.

At some time late in the eighteenth or early in the nineteenth century this community was joined by a caste said to be sprung from the union of a man of the Oriya POTTER caste with a Kond woman. They are called Kond POTTERS. It is probable that other small groups attached themselves to the village from time to time, and later moved on or died out, but this is the only group of those who came after the founding of the village and before the days of the Administration, about whom I have information. They also are the only group now in the village whose ancestors came during that period.

Among the Kond POTTERS in Bisipara the first to come were the Kohoro family. They first were in Boad [i.e. the northern part of the Kondmals, and not the state of Boad]. They wandered from a place in Boad called Nosoghoro and first settled in Malabhui. From there one of their ancestors came and settled in Bisipara. These are the real Kond POTTERS. Being Kond POTTERS they made the

(*a*)

(*a*) KOND POTTER STREET

This is the eastern half of the street. The western end, which adjoins Market Street, is of about the same length. The street is narrow and crowded, and is to be contrasted with WARRIOR Street, which is shown in Plate II.

(*b*)

(*b*) BOAD OUTCASTE STREET

The street is narrow, congested and disorderly (see page 215). It is to be contrasted with WARRIOR Street.

Earth offerings in Bisipara. They came to do it and other sacrifices. According to what the old men say, Dhuba Kohoro is the name they know. Dhuba's great grandfather was the one who first came to Bisipara. Dhuba's son was Onusoro. Onusoro's sons are . . .

But since the Kohoro family did not perform the rite well, the Bisois [the name of the WARRIOR lineage at present ruling the village] summoned a Dehuri family from Koinjoro. The first one of them to come was Phogu Dehuri's father. Phogu was one of four brothers. Gradually all of them came. Phogu's son was Petu and Petu's son was. . . .

After the Dehuri family came the Behera family. Two daughters of the Dehuri family, sisters, married two brothers from Lainpara, Rao and Sunderosingh, who settled in Bisipara, coming as sons-in-law. Rao had three sons . . .

After everyone else came the Maliks. First came Gujjara Malik from Malabhui. He came as a son-in-law, married to a daughter of Rao Behera. His brother Kuti married another of Rao's daughters and came here. Gujjara's son was Anadi . . .

Namo Behera married Sukru Dehuri's father's sister and came here from Rotungo. Namo's son was Oja and Oja's son . . .

This is the order in which the Kond POTTER families settled down in Bisipara. Apart from this, no Kond POTTER history is known.

According to this story the Kond POTTERS first came to the village in order to perform a function which was denied to the Oriyas—namely the proper service of the Kond deities, in particular the Earth. This may mean that Kond POTTERS came much earlier than the end of the eighteenth century, since it is likely that Bisipara was colonized before that date. It may equally mean that previously the Oriyas had served the Earth using their own specialist and their own form of ritual. It may also mean that other aboriginals had performed this function for them. However, there is only one priest of the Earth —an office still held by a Kond POTTER of the Dehuri family— and those who came as sons-in-law must have been attracted by other economic opportunities. I think it probable that like the Boad OUTCASTES they entered into the service of the WARRIORS as clients. There is to-day the tradition of such a link between one of the Kond POTTER families and a WARRIOR. It is unlikely that they acquired any substantial share of the land.

If the genealogies are correct, the last two families whose names occur in the story of the Kond POTTERS arrived in Bisipara after the Kondmals had been annexed. This annexation is the next landmark in the history of the village, for Bisipara was chosen by the first Tahsildar as his headquarters. It remained so from about 1855 until 1904, when A. J. Ollenbach, Sub-Divisional Officer at the time, moved to a new site at Phulbani, because Bisipara was too unhealthy. Before that time the courthouse, the gaol, the Magistrate's house, police lines and so forth were located in Bisipara. All the buildings were of wood and there is now not a trace of them. Nor is there any Civil Servant living in the village.

But the period when Bisipara was the capital of the Kondmals has left its mark on the composition of the village, for it then attracted immigrants from the south and to some extent from the north-west in the region of Sonepur (see Map 1). These men came to exploit the new economic situation, either directly by taking a job in the Administration or by trading. Those who came at this time from Ganjam in the south were Ganjam DISTILLERS, Ganjam BRAHMINS, Ganjam OUTCASTES, a HERDSMAN family, and Christians. From the north came WEAVERS, a TEMPLEMAN, a man whose caste is called ORIYA, and FISHERMEN.

This accounts for all the caste-groups at present found in the village except the SWEEPERS, the BASKETMAKERS, Konds, Kond HERDSMEN, WRITER and a woman whose caste is indeterminate.

The BASKETMAKERS are non-Hindu aboriginal people, who now are reckoned among the untouchable castes. I consider that they have been in the hills for many years but that they probably came to the village after 1855. Neither they nor anyone else knew. The SWEEPERS are employed all over the Kondmals as watchmen for the Government bungalows and rest-houses, and some people asserted that they came to the village in the service of the Administration. Others say that they were among the founding caste-groups. I cannot say which view is correct.

All the Konds and Kond HERDSMEN have come to the village, mainly to serve as farm labourers, within the last fifty years. The WRITER, who comes from Russelkonda in Ganjam, opened a shop at the western end of the street of the WARRIORS, five years ago.

The woman whose caste is in doubt is the widow of a Pathan

and therefore appears on the official lists as a Muslim. She is a native of the Kond hills, but no-one knew what previously was her caste. She is not known to have any relatives.

TABLE 6

ORDER OF ARRIVAL OF CASTE-GROUPS IN BISIPARA

Time	*Place of origin*	*Name of caste-group*	*Percentage of present population.**
Founding caste-groups . . .	Boad	WARRIOR	19·3
		Boad DISTILLER	6·7
		Boad BRAHMIN	1
		HERDSMAN	3·4
		BARBER	1
		WASHERMAN	1
		Boad OUTCASTE	21·7
? *c.* 1800. . . .	Kond hills	Kond POTTER	16·5
After 1855 . . .	Ganjam	Ganjam DISTILLER	2
		Ganjam BRAHMIN	1
		Christian	0·8
		WRITER	0·2
		Ganjam OUTCASTE	6
	Kond hills	BASKETMAKER	1
		Kond	3·8
		Kond HERDSMAN	2·7
	Sonepur area	ORIYA	0·8
		WEAVER	4·6
		TEMPLEMAN	1
		FISHERMAN	1·4
Uncertain . . .	Unknown	SWEEPER	2·6
		Muslim	0·1
			Total 98·6

* The method of reckoning this figure is discussed in Appendix A.

The information given in this section appears in Table 6. This table is intended to give a rough synoptic view of the order in which the different caste-groups arrived in the village, and the proportion they form of the present village. In presenting it certain complexities have been ignored. For instance there is reason to believe that the HERDSMAN family which came at the time of the founding of the village has since died out, and

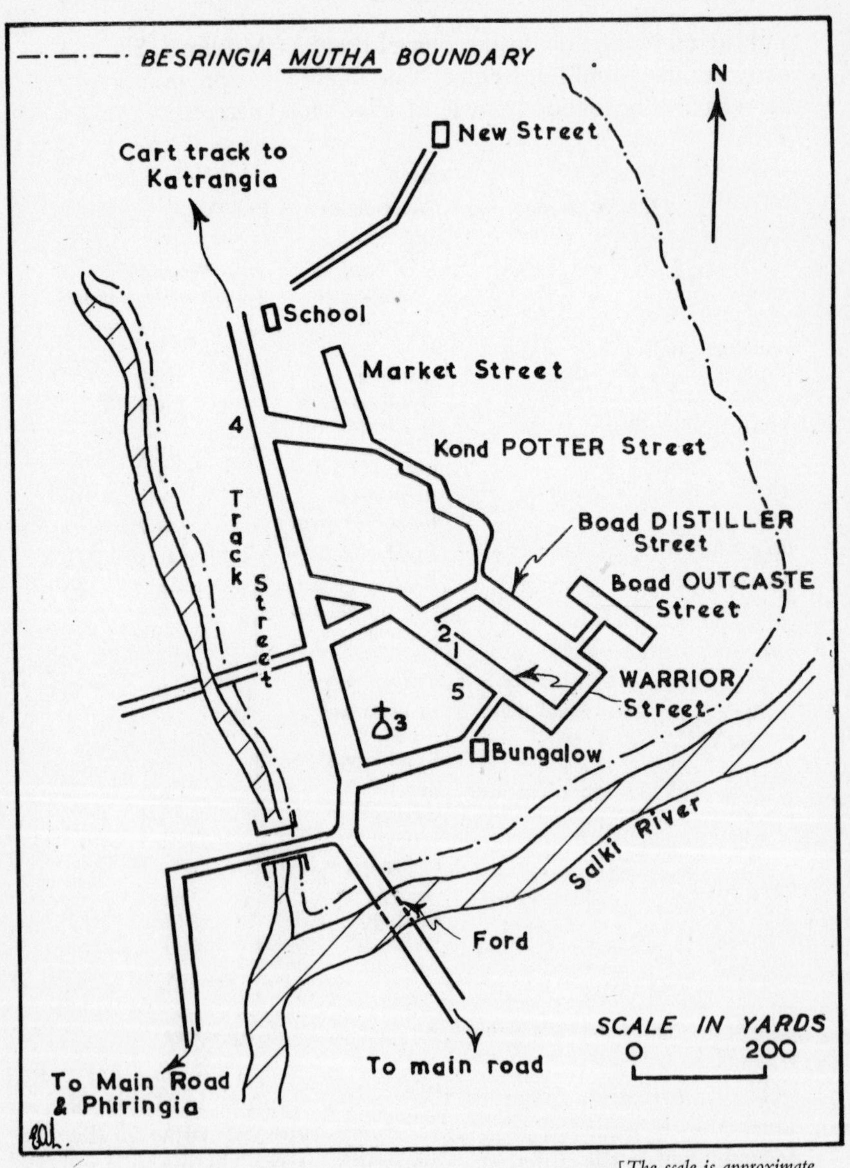

[The scale is approximate

1. Meeting house. 2. Village temple. 3. Kondmals temple.
4. Stockman Centre. 5. Headman's house.

MAP 3. BISIPARA

I know for certain that one of the present HERDSMEN's ancestors came from the south after 1855. However, it would be false to present him as a separate caste-group in the way that the Boad DISTILLERS and the Ganjam DISTILLERS are separate caste-groups, since for some years his lineage has been accepted fully as a member of the group of Boad HERDSMEN. So far as I know, there are no other distortions involved in Table 6.

The Pattern of Residence

This history is reflected in the way in which the village houses are sited to-day. The village consists of a number of streets, which are shown on Map 3. The streets are WARRIOR Street, Boad DISTILLER Street, Boad OUTCASTE Street, Kond POTTER Street, Market Street and New Street. In addition there is an aggregate of households of various castes spread around the cart track to the west of the village. This is not a street, neither geographically nor socially, in the sense that the others are, but since in certain circumstances it is comparable with them, I must give it a name. The names of the other streets are in common use. This one I will call Track Street.

The first four streets named share certain characteristics: firstly, a pattern of house sites; and secondly, a majority of persons of the eponymous caste.

Before the coming of the Administration a village had to protect itself both from enemies and from the attacks of wild animals during the night. Consequently the early villages were stockaded. Houses were built attached to one another in two parallel lines. Behind the houses were gardens and at the end of the gardens ran a stockade. At each end of the street the stockade fences were brought to a point, leaving a narrow entrance which could be closed at night. From the way the houses lie at present it is clear that this was the manner in which WARRIOR Street, Boad DISTILLER Street, Boad OUTCASTE Street and Kond POTTER Street were built. It seems likely, then, that these four streets existed before the Administration came.

In contrast to this the houses of Market Street are grouped in a rough square beside the site of the market, which operated before the capital was moved away from Bisipara. There is no sign that they were fortified after the traditional pattern. This is to be expected since the street was built after the market was opened, that is, after the arrival of the Administration. In the same way in New Street, which contains the overflow from WARRIOR Street and Kond POTTER Street and was built within the last twenty-five years, although the houses stand in straight lines, yet they are detached, each standing in its own garden. The householders have been able to give first importance to their garden and were not compelled to bunch for defence, as in the old streets. In Track Street the furthest houses are as much as half-a-mile apart.

Secondly the older streets tend to show a majority of the

PLATE II

(*a*) WARRIOR STREET

The photograph is taken from the eastern end of the street. Notice the width of the street in comparison with the streets shown in Plate I.

The photograph was taken from the roof of a concrete house which belongs to a Christian. The large roof beyond that in the left foreground belongs to a HERDSMAN. The small roof beyond that belongs to a poor WARRIOR. The large roof in the left middleground belongs to the headman. In the distance on the left, houses which are set slightly in to the centre belong to the WASHERMAN and to some HERDSMAN families.

In the centre of the street, the open roof beneath which can be seen white-clothed men, is that of the Meeting House. Beyond it, slightly to the right in the trees, can be seen the roof of the WRITER's shop. In front of the Meeting House is an erection of poles and saplings to provide shade. In front of that is a similar smaller erection, now abandoned.

Both the headman's house and the house in the right middleground have a double roof. The house itself is roofed with timbers and mud : above that is a thatch fly-roof. This arrangement is a protection against fire and an effective insulation against heat.

The gap beyond the house in the right middleground is the site of a house which is being rebuilt (see page 82).

The distance from the roof in the foreground to the shop is about two hundred yards.

(*b*) WOODCUTTING

The photograph was taken in WARRIOR street, in front of the house of the headman. who is standing on the left, stripped to the waist.

The man next to him is splitting logs, ready for burning on the kitchen fire. This man is a Boad OUTCASTE and is the client of the headman (see page 216). The shirted man in the foreground is the leader of the schoolmaster-policeman faction among the Boad OUTCASTES (see page 224). All the other persons are Boad OUTCASTES, with the exception of the small figure in the background, who is half-brother to the headman.

(*a*)

(*b*)

PLATE II

eponymous caste, while the newer streets are mixed. Warrior Street, for instance, is composed of:

	%
WARRIOR households . . .	65
Christian	7·5
HERDSMEN	12·5
BARBER	5
WASHERMAN	2·5
WRITER	2·5
Boad BRAHMIN	5
Total	100

This caste homogeneity is emphasized by the siting of the houses. The WARRIOR households form a compact block in the centre of the street, and households of other castes are tacked on at each end of the street. Similar figures are given in Table 7 for the other three old streets.

TABLE 7*

EPONYMOUS HOUSEHOLDS IN THE OLD STREETS OF BISIPARA

Street	*Eponymous caste*	*Others*	*Total*
	%	%	%
WARRIOR Street	65	35	100
Kond POTTER Street . . .	87	13	100
Boad DISTILLER Street . . .	84	16	100
Boad OUTCASTE Street . . .	100	—	100

* Calculations in Table 7 and Table 8 are made on the basis of households, irrespective of their size. Accordingly they show slight differences from tables calculated by the method given in Appendix A.

This is to be contrasted with an analogous table for Market Street and Track Street. Their composition is distinctly heterogeneous and no one caste predominates as markedly as in the older streets. This reflects the fact that they have come into existence not as part of the original community of agriculturists but as individual immigrant households coming to exploit mainly the non-agricultural economic opportunities which emerged after the arrival of the Administration.

There are, then, two kinds of streets in the village, distinguished from each other by age and by the relative sizes of the caste-groups within them. Speaking approximately, those streets

TABLE 8

CASTE COMPOSITION OF MARKET STREET AND TRACK STREET IN BISIPARA

Market Street	%	*Track Street*	%
Ganjam DISTILLERS	22	SWEEPERS	18
FISHERMEN	6	Ganjam OUTCASTES	36
Ganjam BRAHMINS	5	HERDSMEN	4·6
HERDSMEN	17	Kond	32
WEAVERS	50	Ganjam BRAHMINS	4·6
		BASKETMAKERS	4·6
Total	100	Total	99·8

which are relatively homogeneous are also older and were part of the original agricultural village. The heterogeneous streets, on the other hand, have come into existence since the arrival of the Administration.

OUTLINE OF THE ARGUMENT FOLLOWING

While the coming of the Administration has tended to confirm the distribution of wealth and political power between the Konds and the Oriyas, it has nevertheless wrought considerable, if unintended, changes in Bisipara.

A new population has arrived since 1855 and new streets have been built, which differ from the streets of the old agricultural village.

The arrival of the Administration has brought the village into the larger economy of India and from this time a new process of change began. The method by which the village as a whole exploited the material world was altered. The traditional economy rested on agriculture. Wealth still is largely derived from the land, but this is no longer the only source. There are also the profits of trading and the work on behalf of the Administration. The economy no longer is exclusively agricultural. It now also is mercantile.

In the new economy wealth can be got by other means than owning land. This led to the breakdown of joint-families. Estates were reduced in size by constant partitioning until some of them became uneconomic and land was sold. The land was bought by those who had profited in the new economy.

Individuals both among the newcomers and among the old

residents have profited in this way. But there has been a tendency for the WARRIOR caste-group, who formerly monopolized the land, to lose property in favour of the other castes, particularly the two groups of DISTILLERS and more recently the Boad OUTCASTES.

This change in the distribution of wealth has brought about an adjustment, which still is taking place, in the traditional political structure of the village.

Part II describes the way in which land comes into the market, and how the new mercantile economy operates. Part III is concerned with political adjustments.

PART TWO

ACQUISITION OF WEALTH AND THE TRANSFER OF LAND

CHAPTER IV

WHY DOES LAND COME INTO THE MARKET?

The Problem

In the past hundred years the population of the village has been increased by a large number of immigrants. This influx coincided with, and was made possible by, the coming of the Administration. Formerly land was for practical purposes the one source of wealth. But the arrival of the administrators and the subsequent integration of the area in the larger economy of India opened new sources of wealth, which the immigrants came to exploit. At one time there must have been two distinct socio-economic categories: the old residents who owned the land; and the newcomers who had no land but derived their wealth from commerce. Subsequently some of the newcomers became landowners and some of the old residents went in for trade.

This picture is, of course, simplified, since the immigration took place over fifty years and by the end of that time most of the earlier immigrants would have obtained land and the old residents would have learned to exploit the new economic opportunities. It would be wrong to imply that the newcomers were a corporate socio-economic group to be set off against the old corporate village. They were not: they came mostly in single households, which is significant for the study of their subsequent integration into the village.

The environment and the technique of agriculture set a limit to the amount of land in the vicinity of the village that can be cultivated. There is no evidence that in the last hundred years new lands have been brought under cultivation on a large scale, so that the newcomers have had land mainly by buying it from the old residents.

This poses the problem: Why did the residents sell land? A similar phenomenon—businessmen acquiring land and peasants becoming labourers—is encountered all over India and particularly in aboriginal areas. It usually is explained in terms of the dishonesty of the merchant and the helplessness of an illiterate peasant who cannot see the implications of rates of interest.[1] On the whole this is a fair description, particularly of those cases which are reported to Commissions of Enquiry, and it is good propaganda for the peasant. But the question still remains: Why do the peasants sell? The persuasiveness of the money-lender, no matter how compelling, cannot in itself be an efficient cause. His character and his chicanery are an aggravating and marginal factor in a process which has more fundamental prime causes.

Whatever be the case in other areas, in Bisipara land came, and still comes, into the market because estates of less than a certain size cannot survive the normal contingencies of their owner's lifetime. In other words, the owner incurs costs which can be met only by realizing capital, and in certain income categories this means selling land. The most important single cause bringing estates down to this danger-level is the system of inheritance—partition of the estate between all sons at the death of the holder.

When lands come up for sale they are bought by persons who have a source of income other than cultivation alone. This has led to a considerable redistribution of land in Bisipara, but since almost everyone finds opportunities of making money by other means than owning land, peasants are often able to recover lost fields. While it is true that many of the sales represent a drift of estates towards the large landholders, many others are transactions between peasants. The opportunity of the small man to make money, and the vulnerability of even the largest estate in the village to division at inheritance, combine to prevent the land drifting permanently into the hands of the same few owners.

The present distribution of land between caste-groups is summarized in Table 9, and will serve to indicate roughly the magnitude of the transfer of land from the old residents to the newcomers, and from the WARRIORS to other original caste-groups.

At present the original caste-groups—WARRIORS, Boad DISTILLERS, Boad OUTCASTES, etc.—hold 61 per cent of the land compared with 39 per cent held by the later comers. A little

[1] See, for instance, W. Grigson, 1949, p. 384.

TABLE 9

DISTRIBUTION OF VILLAGE LAND BETWEEN CASTES IN 1953

Caste name	*Share of total income from land owned, taken in pledge or share-cropped*	*Average annual income per head in units of paddy*	*Percentage of village population*
	%		%
WARRIOR	28·2	21·7	19·3
Boad DISTILLER . . .	10	21·5	6·7
Ganjam DISTILLER . .	12·5	96	2
Boad BRAHMIN . . .	1·7	28	1
Ganjam BRAHMIN . .	0·8	13	1
HERDSMAN	1·25	6	3·4
BARBER	nil	nil	1
WASHERMAN	0·13	1·6	1
WEAVER	1	3·4	4·6
TEMPLEMAN	1	13	1
FISHERMAN	0·75	7·5	1·4
ORIYA	1	18·7	0·8
Christian	2·6	51	0·8
SWEEPER	0·6	3·3	2·6
BASKETMAKER	0·5	7·6	1
Boad OUTCASTE . . .	20·5	13	21·7
Ganjam OUTCASTE . .	3	6·8	6
Kond	0·75	3	3·8
Kond HERDSMAN . .	0·25	1·7	2·7
Kond POTTER . . .	12·2	11	16·5
WRITER	nil	nil	0·2
Muslim	nil	nil	0·1
Total	98·7		98·6

Note: (1) In the population figure allowance is made for the differing needs of adult and child. See Appendix A.
(2) The method of calculating income from village land is given in Appendix B.

of this 39 per cent is made up of land bought from Konds and lying in other villages, but most of it is land bought from the older residents of Bisipara.

The WARRIORS now have only 28 per cent of the land and must be considered the principal losers. What evidence there is indicates that before 1885 WARRIORS owned all the land. That is (if I may give a rough quantitative background to the discussion), the other original castes have acquired 33 per cent of the land and the newcomers have acquired 39 per cent.

The account that follows is based on fieldwork done 1952–4. There are no quantitative surveys of household expenditure or mercantile wealth—to take two topics—made before this time, either in this or any other village in the Kond hills. Therefore the mechanics of a process that has been going on for nearly one hundred years have largely to be inferred from what is happening to-day, if the argument is to be based on quantities. Whether or not this is legitimate can be judged after the argument has been presented.

Estate Management and Normal Expenditure

When an estate is below a certain size it can only meet contingent expenses (for example the costs of a marriage or a funeral) by selling land. But every estate, large and small, must provide for certain regular items of expense, both to support the owner and his family and to meet the costs of its cultivation.

To illustrate this I have taken two estates as examples. I describe the technique of cultivation, the methods of management, and the use to which the products of these two estates are put. In order to round off the account I have included certain items of income (salaried occupations and trading) which are discussed more fully in later chapters. I call these two householders X and Y.

Title to an estate is normally held by one man. He is the head of a household, consisting of his wife and his unmarried children, occasionally a married son, and sometimes an aged parent. This group works the estate and consumes the produce. Although some land is held by adult married brothers, the joint-family administering its estate through a senior member as manager is not found in the village. The absence of this institution is important, since it is the constant partitioning in prolific lineages that brings estates to the margin where they are liable to be sold.

X is by caste a HERDSMAN. There are three males in the household: X's father, a widower of sixty, X himself, and his son of nine. Besides X's wife there was in 1953 a divorced sister of X living with them. X has two infant daughters.

X's grandfather came from Ganjam as a policeman. Scorning the local HERDSMEN he kept apart and married a BRAHMIN woman. He died while his only child, X's father, was an infant. The mother kept the house going by labouring on other people's farms and trading in Kond villages. She was related to another BRAHMIN woman who had married a Christian, a clerk in the Administration. This man helped the young HERDSMAN to train as a schoolmaster. From his salary X's father saved enough to give a feast and have himself accepted by the local HERDSMEN, and he took a wife from a HERDSMAN family at the other end of the street of the WARRIORS from that at which his father had built. Over the course of years he saved enough money to acquire land, which now gives them in an average year about 90 units [1] of paddy.

Apart from their land his household has two sources of regular income: X's father is still a schoolmaster and gets a salary of Rs.31 [2] and a pension from a previous appointment of Rs.6 each month; X worked for me, but before that he was assistant and guide to a Veterinary Assistant whose office was in the village, at a salary of Rs.30 a month.

X has 17 plots of land. In fact they are registered still in the name of X's father, but X manages them. Only two of these plots adjoin. These two are stream-irrigated fields giving approximately half the family's total income from land. There are eight rain-irrigated fields giving the other half of their income. Both types of irrigated fields grow rice alone. In the six dry fields and the garden near the house both rice and other crops are grown. For reasons given later (see Appendix B) these crops are unimportant in considering household budgets.

In village thought the year begins after the first harvest is eaten, but for purpose of budgets I found it convenient to begin when the first rain falls in June and the soil becomes soft enough for the plough. Then every field must be ploughed, and the farmer is out from dawn until midday with his yoke of oxen. Rice nurseries are planted, the dry fields are sown with rice or

[1] 'Unit' and 'Measure' stand for Oriya words. See Appendix A.

[2] There are sixteen annas in the rupee, which at the moment is worth approximately one shilling and sixpence.

another crop, and some of the wet fields are sown over their whole area with rice. The remaining wet fields are thoroughly ploughed and prepared until they are an absolutely level bed of liquid mud, a foot or more deep. When the seedlings in the rice nurseries are nine or ten inches high, about the middle of August onwards, they are lifted and planted by hand in the prepared fields. Most of the planting is finished by the end of August. After three or four weeks these planted fields, and occasionally a sown field, are weeded of grass, which seems to grow in spite of the fact that wet fields are three to four inches deep in water. Care must be taken to see that the banks are in good order. About the third week in September the rice sown in dry fields is harvested and it is after this harvest that the new year officially begins. The main harvest takes place in the first two weeks of December. The crop is then threshed. From that time until midway through March the year's work peters out in spasmodic ploughing of stubble, until the sun bakes the soil iron-hard.

X organized the labour on the land, but neither his father nor he himself worked. According to daily records of hours of work spent on this estate from the first rain in June 1953 until the second week in January 1954, the work was divided as follows:

	%
X's family	13
Casual labour (*mulya*)	45
Farm servant (*holya*)	42

The member of the family who did most of the work was X's sister. In other years his wife had worked, but for the first half of the season she was heavily pregnant and in the second half was occupied in looking after the house and two infants. Casual labourers are recruited day by day and paid according to a rate fixed by the village. The farm servant is hired for the season, given two meals a day, two cloths and Rs.10 in the course of nine months' work.

The cost of his labour is high, measured against the total product. It was as follows:

	Rs.	
Labourers	21/13	7 units 4 measures of paddy
Farm servant	15	13 units
Total	36/13	20 units 4 measures

Taking the average price of paddy spread over the year the cash payment was equivalent approximately to 11 units of paddy, making the total cost in labour 31 units or just under 40 per cent of the crop of the fields cultivated under X's direct management.

The cost of seed, taking into account some seedlings bought for cash, amounted to about 5 units of paddy, bringing the total costs of cultivation up to 46 per cent.

X gave out two of the rain-irrigated fields to share-croppers and received at the rate of fifty-fifty a net return of 6 units of paddy.

For purposes of comparison with other cultivators this is sufficient, but as an absolute record of the profits of cultivation it is on the gloomy side since it does not include the vegetable and lentil crops, which are eaten with rice, nor does it include a small income of paddy from the dry fields. The latter amounted to a maximum of 10 units.

The income of the household, then, consists of salaries amounting to Rs.67 per month and a yearly gross income of 90 units of paddy.

The regular normal outgoings of the household in the course of a year will be considered under the following headings: food; capital equipment other than on land; purchases from the shop; and the expenses of cultivation.

According to the wage fixed by the village as sufficient for a casual labourer (see Appendix A) X and his family require each year 80 units solely to feed themselves. The figure is, of course, rough. None of the family consider themselves heavy eaters. No allowance is made for the morning snack of parched rice, and the figure represents the need only for rice.

Under the heading of capital equipment I have included only such things as are necessary to sustain life at the standard enjoyed in the village. These consist, almost entirely, of the house and the equipment required for housekeeping. Agricultural equipment is considered later. Jewellery is significant in another context and is not here included. The depreciation of this household equipment is calculated by dividing the number of years which it is expected to last into the cost. The method works well enough for such short-lived things as sleeping-mats or bamboo baskets or winnowing-fans, but with a big brass water pot which lasts twenty years, it would be desirable to take into account changes in the value of money. Since these changes were not systematically recorded the problem has been solved in cavalier fashion by considering everything at present-day value. Finally, as in considering the costs of cultivation, goods which can and commonly are made within the household are not taken into account, since the need for them will not cause a man to realize capital. Examples of goods which are purchased—not necessarily by X—to equip X's household are brass and bell-metal cooking and eating dishes, bamboo baskets for storing grain, a bed, sleeping-mats, an image of Lakmi the goddess of wealth, axes, hurricane lanterns, umbrellas, etc. (Some of these things, in particular the brass and bell-metal vessels which are the most costly items, come as part of a dowry. For the calculation I assume that X and his father have spent as much on presents as they received—in other words, that these items cancel out.) Counting the actual things in X's house at the moment, the annual cost of replacement comes to about Rs.40. There is no need to say that this is an approximate figure.

Purchases from the shop is a residual category and varies very much from house to house. In X's case the figure is high since he has to purchase about half the food his household requires. To feed his family X must buy at least 30 units of paddy a year, and dal or vegetables to the value of at least Rs.50. Some of the other items can be standardized. The minimum need for clothes, for example, can be ascertained. X and his father, who both are better dressed than most men in the village, reckon to spend each Rs.20 a year on clothes. The boy, who still is young enough to go naked most of the time, costs them Rs.4 a year. The wife's clothes cost Rs.25 a year. On kerosene, oils for hair and washing, salt, tea, sugar and spices he spends about Rs.8 each month. To be included in this category is the tithe (*jejemani*) which X pays yearly to the village servants, amounting roughly to 4 units of paddy.

The upkeep of the house and kitchen—purchase of thatching grass and bamboos and employment of labourers—costs about Rs.8 a year.

The capital equipment used on the land comprises hoes of

various sizes, at least two ploughs, a scoop for shifting and a plank for levelling earth, and the plough cattle. The material objects have a limited life and a rough estimate can be made of their annual value—about Rs.8. The depreciation on a yoke of oxen is low—about Rs.10 a year—but this, so to speak, is a calculation for the 'economic ox' which like the economic man is a fiction. On the one hand the beast might have been born in the owner's house and cost him nothing. On the other hand many oxen die before their time—of cold in winter or a tiger takes them. Purchase of plough cattle is frequently named as a reason for realizing land-capital.

In the budget set out below all figures for paddy have been converted into cash at the average rate of paddy for the year (Rs.3/5 per unit).

Income	Rs.	*Expenditure*	Rs.
Wages	804	Cultivation . . .	120
Land	300	Food	316
		Household . . .	40
		Buildings . . .	8
		Shop and tithe . .	203
		Farm equipment . .	18
		Balance . . .	399
	1,104		1,104

Thus X's family at the moment enjoys a surplus of Rs.399 each year to meet such contingencies as illness, funerals and so forth.

Y is of the WARRIOR caste. His household consists, besides himself, of his wife, two sons (aged eleven and five) and an infant daughter. So far as he knows he and his sons are the only living males in his lineage. He knew the name of his grandfather and beyond that could say only that his family had lived in Bisipara since the Oriyas came. His land brings in about 80 units of paddy a year. Other sources of income are bi-weekly trading in the markets bringing a maximum of Rs.2 a week and seasonal trading in turmeric and liquor-flowers, the income from which is very uncertain, but may be estimated not to exceed Rs.60 a year.

Y had 18 plots of land. Five are stream-irrigated fields giving 50 out of his 80 units. There are five rain-irrigated fields producing 28 units ; six dry fields in two of which he grew various crops, among which was 2 units of paddy ; and two gardens.

Y and his wife hired labour only at the time of transplanting and for the harvest. By records kept for the same period as the HERDSMAN X, the work was divided as follows :

	%
Y and his family	80
Casual labour	20

The costs of labour were consequently much smaller than X's and amounted only to 6 units of paddy. The cost of seed was 4 units. This makes the total cost of cultivation 10 units or 12 per cent of the total yield.

Y's income therefore is 80 units of paddy and cash not more than Rs.160. Y's expenditure follows a pattern very different from that of X. To feed his family each year he needs 54 units of paddy. The equipment of his house is not inferior to that of X, and although I did not survey it systematically (it took a long time to win his confidence), its annual value is probably about the same as X's—Rs.40. In his daily life he lives much more simply than X. The family has fewer new clothes, are not systematic tea drinkers, use molasses instead of sugar and cruder oils for washing themselves, and grow practically all the dal, etc., which they consume. His clothes cost him about Rs.12 a year, those of his wife Rs.15, and those of his sons Rs.2. His tithe payments amount to 4 units of paddy. His day-to-day purchases from the shop are not made with cash but with paddy and he was pointed out to me as a typical *kheja khina loko* —a buyer with food. Every day his son went twice to the shop : in the morning to buy crude oil for washing, molasses and snuff ; in the evening to get the small wick lantern filled with kerosene, and to buy again molasses, snuff and sometimes tea. This rate of buying would cost him about 6 units of paddy a year. He and his wife do all the repairs to their house. All the wooden instruments used on his land he makes himself and the annual value of his purchases under this heading does not exceed Rs.2. For cattle the annual cost is Rs.10.

Y's annual budget is set out below :

Income		*Expenditure*	
	Rs.		Rs.
Land	266	Cultivation	33
Trade	160	Food	180
		Household	40
		Shop and tithe	62
		Farm equipment	12
		Balance	99
	426		426

Y's surplus for contingencies is thus Rs.99 each year.

The first thing to be noticed about these budgets (apart from their all-too-obvious proneness to error) is that they are not records of what is actually spent in one particular year. They are concerned with what might be called basic spending—on food, on growing food, on clothing, and on shelter and household necessities. Other spending—equally unavoidable in the social context—will be discussed later.

Secondly, no-one—not even the systematic orderly X—thinks in terms of annual depreciation, setting aside for example Rs.1/1 a year so that in twenty years they can trade in the remains of their old brass water jar for a new one. Depreciation allowances are not a feature of housekeeping anywhere in the world. When one thing is worn out another is bought, if the money is at hand.

The produce of an estate must meet certain regular inevitable costs each year. These are the costs of cultivation, mainly seed and the hire of labour ; food ; purchases from the shop, which include such basic items as kerosene, molasses, clothes and so forth ; equipment and maintenance of the household and the house itself ; and a small amount on farm equipment. Obviously these costs vary according to the size of the household and the style at which it chooses to live. But some expenditure is inevitable. The household must have food. If it has enough land to feed itself, it cannot cultivate without hiring labour. Clothes must be bought. If, through sickness, the household needs to employ more labour, or if the harvest is bad, the net yield of the estate in that year may fail to meet its needs for that year. Yet since these needs must be met, the peasant disposes of capital and this might mean disposing of land. In other words, although this sort of expenditure is regular and to some extent predictable, yet there is always the chance that it may be turned into contingent expenditure, which requires the sale of land.

Occasions for Selling Land

The first step in finding out why land came into the market was to enquire about particular sales. The results of this enquiry are set out in Table 10.

Table 10

Reasons for Selling Land

Reasons given	*Number of sales*
To pay for mortuary rites	11
To bring a bride	15
To send a bride	4
To buy plough cattle	9
To make good damage to a field	1
To buy food	7
Miscellaneous ritual expenses	3
To fight a case	1
As a result of trading losses	1
For convenience of cultivation	2
To build a new house	1
To pay for bringing a doctor	1
With the intention of leaving the village	1
Total	57

Without the examination of particular cases this table reveals little more than the nature of the events that lead to the sale of land. It tells us nothing about the frequency of these contingencies as operative causes for land coming into the market, since the event named may be only the end of a chain of such events. It does, however, establish the first point in the argument, that land comes into the market because the seller needs cash, and at his initiative and not through the financial wiles of a moneylender. In the sample only three sales took place for reasons not primarily connected with the seller's need : one field was sold because it lay alongside the street of the Boad OUTCASTES and the owner lost most of the harvest to thieves ; one because the owner lived eight miles away; the third was sold because the owner intended to leave the village. In only two cases was the sale the result of borrowing money. These are shown in the table as 'trading losses': a man (the same in both cases) took an advance of money to trade in turmeric and lost Rs.20, and then left his debt standing five years with the shopkeeper until the principal and interest amounted to Rs.60. To meet this debt he sold a field to the shopkeeper. In all but these two cases the initiative came from the seller.

The fact that this is a buyer's market means that by any reckoning the price is low. If an ox drops dead in the middle of the ploughing season, when no-one wants to lend or hire their cattle, and if the peasant must sell land to buy a new ox, he is in no position to drive a hard bargain. In general the market of buyers is restricted to his own village, where everyone knows his predicament. The same can be said of the cost of mortuary rites which must be concluded within at the most twelve days. There is not the same immediacy about sales to provide for a marriage or to build a house, but the price is still kept low because the prospective buyers know that the time which the seller can spend bargaining is limited.

These facts are pointed by the immense range of prices recorded in the sale of land. For a sample recorded for 1947, the price paid per unit of expected yield varies from Rs.1/12 to Rs.20; in 1948 from Rs.4 to Rs.20; in 1949 from Rs.2/8 to Rs.17/3; and in 1950 from Rs.1/5 to Rs.8. Since the average price through the year for a unit of paddy is Rs.3/5, those who bought land producing this much for Rs.1/5, even allowing for the costs of cultivation, struck a very hard bargain: and the man who paid Rs.20 did not strike a very bad bargain. Even at the high price of Rs.20 per unit of expected yield, on land pledged this represents an annual interest rate of 16 per cent less the costs of cultivation; at Rs.1/5 it is an annual interest of 250 per cent less the cost of cultivation.[1]

[1] When A pledges a field to B, A receives a sum of money and B has the use of the land for at least one harvest and for all subsequent years until A repays the money. The debt may last through generations. In this analysis the difference between sale and pledge is not relevant, for a pledge redeemed can be counted as sale and re-purchase. In a list of 'sales' over the last four years there was no regular variation in prices paid between the two types of transaction. See also p. 283.

But the buyer's market—the eagerness of the seller and the almost ludicrous display of indifference by the buyer—would not alone account for the variation in price. If this were the only factor prices should be low and relatively uniform. Partly the variation must be caused by the varying eagerness and bargaining skill of the buyers : partly it may be the result of misinformation in the yields of land and the prices paid : partly—and this is a tautology—it appears because there is no 'market-price' for land, against which the seller can measure the bargain he is about to strike. Although both the seller and buyer know the yield and history of the field in question, and although they know the price of paddy throughout the year, the seller at least does not seem to weigh his bargain in the light of this knowledge. He does not say : 'This field will give you about 10 units of paddy each year. Give me at least Rs.60 for it.' Rather he thinks : 'I need Rs.40 in the next week. Who has Rs.40 and what field is he likely to want for it ?' Again, since there is no possibility of selling only part of a field, a man's smallest field may be much more valuable, in our reckoning of price per unit, than the amount of money he needs, an amount which the buyer is quite capable of estimating. Yet if land is his only capital resource, he must sell this field, and since the factors in bargaining are so much in favour of the buyer, it is likely that the seller will get no more than he needs.

The way in which the seller is induced to part with his land at an uneconomic price has been discussed in detail since it is an important factor in the continued survival of the seller as a landowner, in that even small needs represent a relatively heavy drain on capital. A man who is already on the margin where he has to sell land to meet a small contingency is not long able to pay what is in effect an annual interest of 250 per cent without realizing further capital before a long time has passed. The low prices for land sold is not, of course, a primary cause for land coming into the market, but it is an aggravating cause.

The process is illustrated in the two following cases. In each case the informant was asked to say what land he had bought, sold or redeemed since his father's death, and the results are set down in Table 11 and Table 12.

Since 1949 the man whose history is given in Table 11 has sold no more land. He has no oxen, but gives his fields to share-

TABLE 11

SELLING OF LAND. CASE 1

Year	*Price, shown as Rs. per unit of paddy produced annually*	*Reasons for selling and comments*
	Rs.	
1913	not known	To pay for father's mortuary rites
1933	12	Cost of bringing first wife who was later divorced
1938	6/10	To pay for mother's mortuary rites
1939	2/4	With the intention of leaving the village
1948	10	Cost of bringing second wife
1948	6/10	Cost of bringing second wife
1949	8	To buy food

croppers and gets yearly 15 units of paddy. The household needs 40 units for food alone, and most of this is provided by the young wife who labours in the houses and fields of others. Apart from the first entry in Table 11, on which information is lacking, the annual value of all the fields sold is Rs.192 : their sale fetched Rs.250, which is little more than the value of one year's crops.

A sure sign that an estate is in the process of breaking up is a series of sales the purpose of which is to buy food, for this means that the man sells not to meet a contingency, which with any luck will not come again for some time, but in order to meet a constant and unremitting need. This is shown in Table 12.

TABLE 12

SELLING OF LAND. CASE 2

Year	*Price, shown as Rs. per unit of paddy produced annually*	*Reasons for selling and comments*
	Rs.	
1933	5	Debt resulting from a trading loss
1937	2/6	— ditto —
1938	3	To pay for wife's mortuary rites
1941	3	To buy food
1943	2/8	To buy oxen
1943	1/10	To buy food
1945	1/2	To buy food

All this man's land is gone and he supports himself by trading in Kond villages. He is a widower and has no dependants.

To sum up, the occasion for land being put up for sale is usually given by an informant as personal necessity for cash, arising from some contingency. On this information it is not possible to estimate the frequency of each type of event, since their effect is cumulative and to distinguish one as more important than another would be misleading. For example, the death of an ox and the expense of a mortuary ceremony for a relative coming both in the same year might cause a man to sell land. To attempt to allocate priority would not be sensible, since it may be their coincidence that forces the man to realize capital. Land offered for sale in this way comes into a buyer's market and goes for very low prices, measuring the fields in terms of the value of their annual yield. This, other things being equal, makes the estate-holder more vulnerable next time a contingency arises.

In the analysis that follows this section a model is used as an expository device. The centre of this model is the landowner, considered in abstraction from whatever other sources of income actual landlords have. When discussing expenses I have used expense accounts of events occurring 1952–4. But when these are stated actually to have led to the sale of land, it must be remembered that there were probably other contributory causes both for and against the sale, operating in economic systems other than agriculture.

Cost of Marriages and Deaths

A man is obliged on occasions to spend more than his income will permit him. From the nature of some of these occasions—funerals and marriages—it is clear that the imperative is a social one and that social obligations are allowed to override economic prudence. How has this dilemma come about? That is a question which can be answered only in the light of larger economic forces and will be taken up later. Here I am concerned only to discuss some of the pressures operating and to give a rough idea of the costs involved.

A death is expensive because certain rituals are required to rid the agnates of pollution and to set the dead man among his fellow ancestors. The expense lies not so much in the rites themselves but in the feast that follows.

The expense of the feast and the rites is normally borne by the heir of the dead man, out of the estate which he has just inherited. But this obligation does not arise out of the inheritance, since the ceremonies must be performed no matter how little is inherited. Responsibility for the proper performance of the ceremony devolves, in the absence of an heir, on the dead man's caste-fellows, since they alone can touch the corpse.

The corpse is washed and as soon as sufficient men are assembled it is taken off to the jungle and burned. If there are not sufficient men available to fetch wood, then it will be buried beside the river, or, in the dry season, in the river bed. The party then washes and returns to eat a purificatory meal. The entire lineage may not cook, and meals are prepared for them by members of another lineage of the same caste. On the third day after the death a ceremony called *brahminopani* takes place, by which all the lineage except the household of the dead man are freed to do their own cooking. (If, as in some small castes, there is no other lineage available, then a daughter of the house may cook. A woman who has married in may not cook on these occasions.)

On the tenth day the *dosa* takes place. It is performed at the bathing ghat by male agnates of the dead man and followed by a feast attended not only by them but also by uterine and affinal kin. In the evening an offering is made for the dead man at a place outside the village where his corpse was set down, while the cremation party was assembling.

On the eleventh day is the *sudho*. This is attended by all the relatives and is followed by a feast.

On the twelfth day there is another feast (*baropotro*). When it is dark the heir and a group of male kin go out and capture a glow-worm, which is placed in a corner of the main room of the house. With that the dead man is among the ancestors. On the following day all the visitors return to their own villages.[1]

It is obvious that the expenses of these rituals vary with the number of persons whose duty it is to attend the funeral. There

[1] This is the basic pattern of a funeral rite among all castes in Bisipara, other than the Kond. For the Konds, the most important, and the most expensive rite may be postponed up to two years after a death.

is an approximate justice in that the death of a rich man of high prestige will attract more people than a poor one, so that funeral expenses are to some extent correlated with the size of the estate that is paying for them. But this is not an invariable or necessary correlation. There are a few men whose castes are not populous and whose wealth has not been used to attract a following. On the other hand there are poor men who are members of large agnatic groups, all of whom are expected to attend.

I have the expenses for one such WARRIOR funeral. The dead man had no land : his younger brother's son, who was the heir, had none. The agnatic group to which they belong numbers twenty-seven households. The accounts of his funeral are set out in Table 13.

TABLE 13

EXPENSE ACCOUNT OF A FUNERAL

	Income Rs.	*Expenditure* Rs.
brahminopani	nil	12
dosa	nil	8/2
sudho goods worth about .	15/11	28/14
baropotro	nil	5
Balance to find . .	38/5	
Total	54	54

Both the dead man's household and his nephew's were supported by petty trading. To meet the expenses of the rituals they produced about Rs.16. The remaining Rs.23 were obtained by pledging the garden of their house to the village temple in return for paddy to be eaten at the *sudho*, and by borrowing paddy from two other households.

The great bulk of this expense was on food. The BRAHMIN priest received about Rs.3, taken partly in cloth and rice. A further Rs.2 were spent on buying ritual presents for the persons of other lineages who came to help at one time or another—towels at about As.8 each.

This account is about the lowest expense the death of a WARRIOR of adult ritual status could occasion. This caste is of particular interest in that it is they who have lost most land. Other castes, if they are poor and not numerous, can observe the same full ritual at a much lower cost. It is the fact that they belong to a lineage of 27 households that makes WARRIOR funerals costly, although faction has divided this into two equal-sized groups and one group is obliged to provide food for the other only at the *sudho* stage of the rites.

In the case given above the only outsiders were four men affinally related to the dead man, and three men from a section of the lineage resident in a neighbouring hamlet. All the other participants belonged to the village.

This is to be contrasted with the funeral of a man of the same caste which took place a few months before the one described above. This man could trace no connection with the large lineage in the village, but since he had allied himself with the headman's faction, they observed pollution for him as if he had been known to be of their lineage. (They said : 'He is really one of us. But the connection was long ago and has been forgotten.') This man was rich. He had married twice. A selection of those who came to his *sudho* is : two representatives of the house of the father of his second wife ; his grand-daughter's husband ; a sister's son ; a daughter ; a sister and her two sons ; and five persons whom the grandson called *sanga*, i.e. 'person whose relative has married my relative'. This is by no means the full total, since many of those who came were of standing in their own villages and brought two or three companions with them. I did not record the expenses of the *brahminopani* or the *baropotro*, but the cost of the other two rituals was Rs.176. Rs.8 of this was for the ritual present of cloth : the remainder was the cost of food, including the price of seven goats. On the income side three goats and rice to the value of Rs.48 was brought by the visitors or given by the people of the village. The widow received cloths of various kinds worth in all Rs.42, but this is not a contribution to the expenses of the mortuary rites. The balance of Rs.128 was met entirely out of the estate, and no land was sold or loans raised.

These two were WARRIOR funerals. I tried to get similar information about two funerals among untouchables, one SWEEPER and one Boad OUTCASTE. For the latter I could not get a consistent account of the expenditure, perhaps because this was not in fact known. The *sudho* happened to be held on the same day as a fair at a village four miles away and many people seemed to have dropped in on their way to the fair to see what they could pick up at the feast. It was a much more chaotic affair than other funerals I witnessed. In the SWEEPER funeral the accounts given—not written for me, but kept by one of the family—were internally contradictory. But I do know that the family pledged a field worth annually Rs.36 for only Rs.20 and that they had Rs.10 worth of rice on credit from a shop. Both these funerals attracted large numbers of guests.

This expenditure is compelled by social pressure. When I asked why it is incurred, and pressed for an answer, I was told that the purpose of the rites is to put the dead man among (the word they use means 'equal to' or 'level with') the rest of the ancestors. If he is not there, he is liable to hang around the homestead or the paths outside the village as a ghost, making a nuisance of himself. They add that this would open the way to disaster and sickness in the house, if the proper rites are omitted. This belief is certainly there, and is strong among the untouchables, in particular the SWEEPERS. But the needs of the dead man are in fact met in the relatively inexpensive rites. The money goes in the feast which is eaten after the ritual and very often eaten by three or four times as many people as have taken part in the rites. In short the obligation which costs most is

---

PLATE III

(*a*) GOAT SACRIFICED AT A FUNERAL

The sacrifice took place at the *sudho* ceremony of a SWEEPER. The goat, an exceptionally large animal, was worth about Rs.30, and the family found it necessary to pledge a field in order to pay the cost of these rites.

The traditional weapon of the hills, the battle-axe, with which all sacrifices are performed, can be seen in the right foreground. The stroke is just completed and the head of the goat is falling. All three persons are of the SWEEPER caste.

(*b*) SACRIFICE AT A WEDDING

The photograph was taken at the western end of WARRIOR street, during the wedding of a HERDSMAN youth.

The head of the goat has been severed, and the carcase is lifted to allow blood to spray over the drums, the decorative horns of which can be seen in the foreground.

The man holding the goat and the man at his side are HERDSMEN, relatives of the bride. On the left, the man with a child on his hip is a Kond HERDSMAN, the plough-servant of the *mutha* headman. The man on the right, who is playing a drum adorned with peacock feathers, is a Ganjam OUTCASTE.

The stockade of the WRITER's shop can be seen in the background on the right.

(*a*)

(*b*)

PLATE III

not a ritual obligation to the dead man and to the ancestors in general, but rather is to be seen in the social ties of household, lineage, caste and village. The more extensive the ties of the bereaved household in the kinship system or the caste system, the more is the bereavement likely to cost it : and although the extent of a man's ties are influenced to some extent by his wealth, poverty does not cut out ties within a certain social distance. The rich WARRIOR's mortuary rite attracted affinal and uterine kin in numbers and some from relatively great distances : but the poverty of the other WARRIOR did not excuse his heir the obligation to provide appropriate feasts for a group of agnates as large as that of the rich WARRIOR. One does not count the cost of the obligation of death in rupees—at least not until after the obligation is fulfilled.

While it is imperative to perform the rites and give appropriate feasts within twelve days of a death, plans for a marriage can usually be made some time in advance. Within certain limits marriage rituals can be postponed or advanced according to the prosperity of the giver. Secondly, while mortuary rituals for adults are approximately the same in all instances, there are many forms and stages of marriage from which to choose, giving a much larger range of expense. Thirdly, mortuary rites concern the living and the dead, a relationship which lacks the continuing point of friction between two living groups of affinal relatives. A frequent source of expense is the mishandling by either party of this relationship.

The relevance of the possibility of planning can be documented in several ways. The father of HERDSMAN X was left the sole male member of his lineage, which had no land, while still an infant. He put off his marriage until he had saved enough money. An orphan child adopted into a SWEEPER family married only at the late age of forty, after he had worked a year for me. Note that in any case neither of these people had land or other forms of capital by the sale of which to raise money. Again there are several instances where it is clear that a plan has been upset or planning made difficult. In Table 10 among those who sold land to bring a bride or send a sister in marriage are several who were young men at the time and had just taken charge of the estate and were still labouring under the debts arising from the father's mortuary rites. Of course, this is not true in all cases of selling land for a marriage. Planning means, in effect, saving out of income to pay for the marriage: and if there is not a surplus of income no saving or planning is possible. Thus there are several instances of men marrying comparatively late, when they had for many years managed the estate, and still pledging land to meet their expenses.

Every girl of clean caste—and some of the untouchables are now following the rule—must be married before she reaches puberty. If a girl who has not been married menstruates for the first time in her father's house, then she puts it in great ritual danger and the proper course is to expel her, leaving her to roam in the jungle until she dies or is killed by wild animals. The classic way of meeting these demands is for the girl to be married as a child, usually when she is eight or nine. The ceremony might better be described as betrothal, since she stays in her father's house and does not join her husband until the second or third marriage season after she has menstruated. But ritually and legally she belongs to the house of her husband, in that they must observe pollution for her if she dies, as they do for women who had already come to their lineage, and legally in that if she defaults and runs away with another man, they may bring a case before the courts against her agnates. A child marriage of this sort is expensive and is falling into disuse, because the long interval between marriage and arrival in her husband's house is a risk. She may die: she may grow up diseased or ugly or lazy. On the other hand the groom might take a fancy to another girl, and if this happens her agnates have little redress.

More commonly little girls are put through a form of marriage which varies from caste to caste. HERDSMAN girls are married to a sword. WARRIOR girls marry an old man, who receives a present but incurs no responsibility or rights by this marriage. BRAHMIN girls are married, as the villagers say, to a prayer (*mantra*), which I take to mean that they are married simply by the rite without using a symbol for the groom.

The expenses of such a marriage are trifling. The BRAHMIN who performs the ceremony gets a fee which is fixed by haggling, but does not seem to exceed Rs.3. The girl (and in the case of the WARRIORS the groom) will get a new cloth, both of which can be provided for Rs.5. A feast is given to the caste-group within the village. Two or three girls might be married at the same ceremony. The feast need not be large and seldom is lavish, since if a man wishes to make his mark he will hope for a child marriage in place of the token marriage, or else postpone his display until the girl is betrothed to her future husband.

Except for the token marriage, the initiative in making marriage arrangements must come officially—and usually does in fact—from the lineage of the groom. If there has not been a child marriage, then the young man's father looks for a girl who is about the age of menstruation. The point in doing this is that by then she is capable of doing all the duties of the household and a good idea of her character and capabilities can be had. Questions of 'State'—the relations between the two lineages concerned—are also relevant, but these do not overrule the concern with finding a girl who is industrious, good-looking and of a comfortable disposition. If she is suitable and her lineage is willing, she is then married and in the same or the following season she departs for 'her mother-in-law's house', as the villagers put it.

The costs of marrying a girl and sending her to her husband, or of finding a wife for a boy and receiving her, vary with the opinion which the agnatic group has of its own status. This correlates to some extent with their economic status, but, as with deaths, below a certain standard one does not count the cost. Again, as in the case of death, the cost will vary with the number of persons who expect to be invited to the feasts—and since there are two parties concerned the cycle of wedding feasts tends to cost more than mortuary feasts. Another difference is that there are other large items beside feasting: for the girl, providing a dowry; for a boy, providing the brideprice.

These general statements can be sharpened by looking at the range of costs in each of the four cases: betrothing a boy; bringing a bride; betrothing a girl; and sending a bride to the house of her mother-in-law.

When the groom's people think they have located a suitable girl they find out through a go-between whether their suit will be acceptable. If it is, the horoscopes of the pair are matched, and if this comes out rightly, then a party goes from the groom's house to attend the betrothal ceremony. In the case of a

HERDSMAN boy of a family of moderate means, a party of nineteen men from his village went to the bride's village. They handed over Rs.45 as brideprice and a set of glass bangles, which are the tokens of the married state, and a new sari. The bangles cost under one rupee. The sari cost about Rs.15. A fee of R.1 was paid to the headman of the bride's village to witness the transactions. Add to this the cost of feeding the party (a goat and some rice) and the expenses of the groom's agnatic group came to about Rs.85.

The betrothal ceremony of a poor WARRIOR boy cost his family about Rs.70. They did not provide a goat for the party. But the WARRIOR brideprice is Rs.50/4.

Each of those Kondmals castes which hold a biennial or triennial meeting[1] threaten severe penalties for fathers who demand more than the stated brideprice for their daughters and for those who agree to pay more. The trouble seems to be most acute in the smaller castes, particularly in the HERDSMAN caste, within which there is a shortage of women. I cannot account for this shortage, but there are clear signs that it exists. The brother of the HERDSMAN mentioned above is paying nearly Rs.100 for his bride and her father is still putting off the betrothal ceremony. In another HERDSMAN family a girl of renowned bad temper, who was divorced after four childless years, has been sought by six different groups since she returned to her father's home. Formerly it would have been true to say that for most of the Kondmals castes the brideprice was a small part of the expenses of a boy's marriage. In some castes, notably the HERDSMAN and the OILMAN,[2] there are signs that this no longer is true.

The remaining expenses, in particular the presents for the bride, can be very much greater than those set out in the two cases above. In 1952 the son of the WARRIOR *mutha* headman was betrothed. About 120 men of clean caste went to the ceremony. I have no accounts, but the cost of feeding them must have been between Rs.100 and Rs.150. When they arrived they handed over, besides the brideprice of Rs. 50/4, a silk sari which had cost Rs.70 and four gold bangles worth Rs.200.

[1] See p. 103.

[2] This caste is not represented in Bisipara.

The corresponding expense in the girl's household at a betrothal ceremony is relatively small. Her father must provide a cloth to be sent to the boy, which will not cost more than Rs.5 : and he gives a generous meal to the visitors and to a few people from his own village.

When the bride is brought to her husband's house, the positions are reversed. His people provide a feast both for the visitors and their own castemen and villagers. Roughly the same remarks apply to this feast as to the *sudho* mortuary ritual feast. The scale of feasting and the expense are roughly correlated with the social status of the giver. He receives gifts in kind and contributions in cash from all households in the village and the members of these households come to eat at his house, if the caste relation is appropriate, or else receive food to be cooked and eaten in their own street. But the expenses of the girl's house are much greater, for they must provide her with a dowry consisting of jewellery and of brass and bell-metal household utensils. In the wedding of the poor WARRIOR mentioned above, the whole expense of the groom's household came to Rs.106 for feasting and Rs.2 for the BRAHMIN. The girl brought with her ornaments and dishes to the value of about Rs.300.

It is this last item which makes daughters so much more expensive than sons. The villagers say that daughters make a man poor. A boy costs his family the expenses of a bride-price, a betrothal party and a feast when the girl comes. The father of a girl must entertain the betrothal party and provide the dowry. Furthermore, any presents which the groom's side gives at betrothal come back to them when the girl arrives.

That is the normal and respectable method of marrying. Within it there are considerable variations in the schemes of expenditure, but some items cannot be avoided even by the poorest if they are to make a normal marriage. These are : for the boy, the brideprice and the expenses at betrothal and the feast when the girl comes ; for the girl, entertaining the betrothal party and providing the dowry.

A recognized marriage giving status in society to the children issuing from it can be contracted without incurring these expenses. Unions made in other ways than that described above do occur, and need not necessarily bring disgrace, but they are rare. A young HERDSMAN married a poor girl by giving her mother—the father and all his lineage were dead—Rs.10 and a sari for the girl. After a year the girl ran away. The girl was of the right caste and had children been born, they would have been under no disability. A second way is to inherit the wife of a dead elder brother. Such an event is marked by no feast or ritual. The younger brother simply moves into the place of his dead brother. Thirdly there are said to be cases where a very poor man elopes with a girl whose father has opposed the match. They go off to a remote Kond village and come back after two or three months. Technically the father has redress before the caste court or the Government court, but informants said there would be no point in his bringing the case, since the young man would have no money to pay damages, and might go to prison, and thus leave him with a daughter no longer fit for the marriage market. The young man would try to regularize his position by paying something towards the brideprice.

Elopement to a Kond village usually occurs when the couple are of different castes. Seizing a bride with her connivance and against her father's will is more common. It has happened twice in the last four years in the WARRIOR group in Bisipara, but in each case the girl was brought to the man's home and married by the proper ritual. Having outwitted her father, attempts are then made to placate him and to seek approval before the caste court. In neither case was the boy driven to this expedient by economic necessity.

Potentially the most costly form of marriage is to steal another man's wife. A WARRIOR woman was married to a drunkard and after some years ran back to her father's house. He did not raise the matter before the caste court, but let her go off with another man. Her husband's family brought a case in the Government court against her father and the new husband, and they were awarded Rs.300. A less dramatic case took place in 1953. A Kond POTTER girl, who was betrothed, took a dislike to her prospective husband who had a loathsome skin disease and persuaded her father to let her go to another man. The case was thrashed out between the three groups concerned and other lineages of the same caste, and resulted in the return of the brideprice and a payment of Rs.25 each from the father of the girl and her new father-in-law 'for the honour' of those who had lost her.

To sum up, I have discussed some of the occasions on which social obligations cause land to be sold. At the top end of the scale a limit can be set to expenditure according to economic means: but at the lower end, both in mortuary rituals and marriages, there is a standard below which few care to drop, if they can avoid it by realizing capital.

ECONOMIC CAUSES FOR THE SALE OF LAND

Continuing to think in terms of economic models rather than actual histories, one could construct a scale showing the sizes of estates vulnerable to particular contingencies, if the frequency of these contingencies were known. Thus estate A, which has just lost a field to pay for a girl's dowry, would have remained intact if the demand had been merely for a pair of oxen. The owner of estate B, who has pledged a field to buy a yoke of oxen, never had to borrow paddy. The owner of the smaller estate C is able to borrow enough paddy to tide him over a bad harvest. But no-one will lend paddy to the owner of estate D because his fields are so few that they doubt their chances of getting repayment. This, in the model, represents the significance of those particular contingencies, which are normal occurrences. Uncommon expenses, such as a law case, might break estates richer than A, but I am concerned only with the more frequent contingencies. Among these it is those contingencies which involve social obligations which cost the most.

In this section I discuss estates at the secondary level of disintegration—those called B, C and D above—which are unable to meet economic contingencies. *A fortiori* they are unable, thinking in terms of the model, to meet contingencies arising from social obligations.

In fact, of course, other things are not equal and one is unable to apply the model directly to particular cases owing to the complicating facts that troubles often do not come singly and that few people depend on the land alone. These two factors will be introduced into the analysis at a later stage.

At this level much the most devastating single event is the loss of an ox (or plough buffalo). This is quite a common event. The village cattle are pastured in two large herds, which go off by day to the scrub jungle or even up the mountainside into the deeper jungle where there is better grazing. The single cowherd brings them back and when they have dispersed to the different houses the loss is discovered. The owner and his friends and the cowherd go out to search but the area is large and it is counted a piece of luck if the beast is found before nightfall. If it stays out all night it may fall into a ravine or be killed by a tiger or leopard. Wild beasts even raid the herds while they are under the cowherd's charge. Again, oxen cannot stand the cold weather and the rain. Buffaloes are not healthy in the hot weather and both types suffer then from lack of pasturage.

The seriousness of the loss depends on when it happens. Prices are highest from the end of May until about December. They are lowest in March. This fluctuation in price—there is a regular market for cattle—is correlated partly with the degree of agricultural activity at the time and partly with the availability of feeding stuffs. Towards the end of the hot season, when the flowers of the *mohua* tree are lying on the ground, the price begins to rise because the beasts are in good condition after feeding on *mohua*. The price level continues high until planting is finished. It then declines, as the need for ploughing gets less urgent and the difficult hot season approaches. Thus, if the beast dies just before or during planting time, the owner is doubly unfortunate. He has no time to look around and strike a good bargain : and he has to buy in a seller's market.

The largest individual herd in Bisipara comprises 14 head of cattle, but not all of these are available for the plough. Some are calves. There are four other herds of over ten beasts, but most people are limited to a single yoke of oxen. This means that if a beast dies, it must be replaced within a limited time since land cannot be cultivated without the use of a plough. As a temporary measure, an ox might be borrowed from a relative, or a yoke of cattle and a ploughman might be hired at R.1 a day; but during the planting season, when the need is greatest, most people are too busy to hire out or lend cattle.

About five years ago there was a cattle plague which carried off many beasts. Prices rose. Then, as cattle have become more plentiful, there has been a steady decline in the price. The price of an ox is highest when it is three years old. At that time, informants said, providing it was cared for, a beast would give ten years' service and such animals were costing around Rs.50 in the planting season of 1953. In the dry season a bargain might be struck around Rs.30. As the beast gets older, so the price declines, but even for an aged animal with one or two more seasons before it, the price will not fall below Rs.12 to Rs.15. The fact that price is not evenly correlated with expectation of work—the price for a beast with ten years in it is four times as much as the price for a beast with two years work before it—is accounted for in actuarial terms. The expectation of working life is not reckoned solely in terms of age and care, but also in terms of accident.[1]

In terms of the model (that is to say, ignoring the possibility of income from sources other than land) anyone who is forced to sell land for any contingency is on a descending spiral from which there is no escape. Each sale decreases the yield from his estate and makes him progressively more vulnerable to less expensive contingencies. As things work out in practice, most people can draw on a second source of income and stay the rot, or even recover lost land, so long as they are in categories A, B or C. But both in the model and in life, when a man is selling fields just to feed himself, his career as a landowner is close to the end. For, so long as he has a chance of recovery, he will be able to borrow paddy, since the lender has first call on the next harvest. To sell land in these circumstances is an admission of defeat.

Alternative Methods of Raising Money

Still treating the landowner as if he had no other regular income, what sources of money are available in times of contingency, other than selling land? There are two resources: one

[1] While I had no difficulty in getting a consensus of opinion about the prices of cattle of various types and ages, informants were surprisingly vague about the working life of an ox. One man, whom in other situations I had found scrupulous and exact, considered that the working-life of an ox, 'if cared for', might be up to thirty years. This, perhaps, is a further indication that in fact few cattle do die of old age.

is to sell other forms of capital goods ; the other is to borrow, either as a straightforward economic transaction or by using kinship or quasi-kinship ties. The other forms of capital—mostly jewellery—are unproductive and therefore tend to be sold in preference to parting with land. Therefore the likelihood of an estate-owner losing his land depends, among other factors, on the amount of jewellery he possesses. Providing the estate will produce a surplus over normal consumption, the ability to sell jewellery gives the landowner a breathing-space and in effect lets him spread the cost of contingencies over a number of years. Borrowing, on the other hand, is likely to bring the landowner nearer the margin of sale, since he has to pay interest. The severity of the rates of interest depends on the borrower's relationship with the lender, and shades down from outright economic transactions at a rate of 25 per cent or more, through transactions between kinsmen, where the borrower's sole obligation is simple reciprocity (a tacit agreement to do the same for the lender where he is in difficulties), to a simple gift when both sides know that the possibility of return is remote.

In this section I discuss the sources, value and methods of realizing jewellery ; transactions with the moneylender ; and the significance of various types and degrees of kinship in the context of economic assistance.

Jewellery is acquired in two ways : by buying it whenever there is spare cash in the household ; and in the form of a dowry which comes with a bride. The ultimate source, of course, is always purchase. But from the point of view of the householder there are the pieces which he or other persons have bought for his daughters and there is the collection which his wife brought from her house.

Men invest in jewellery for several reasons. They like to see their wives and daughters brilliantly attired at festivals. But apart from this there is a definite economic motive. Jewellery is a reserve, a form of saving against hard times. Men do not save in cash and do not use it productively by investing in the Post Office Savings Bank, although there is a Post Office in the village and another in the headquarters eight miles away. They are unfamiliar with the procedure and suspicious of Government agencies. (A further reason, to anticipate the argument for the moment, is that anyone who has the *savoir-faire* to use the Post Office Bank can get much higher rates of interest by lending money or using it as capital for trading.) Nor do men usually hoard cash. This is done, but it is not the common or the approved method of saving. Cash is recognized to have two great disadvantages: it is too liquid, and it depreciates. Villagers are very conscious of the difficulty of keeping cash intact, especially when they are not far above the margin of normal consumption. The money is frittered away in day-to-day luxuries. This was brought home to me by several of those whom I employed insisting that I should keep their wages until the time came for me to leave. Rupees are soon spent: but jewellery is less liquid, partly because of the resistance of the women folk, who wear it, and partly because often it can be realized only at a loss. Therefore, as a means of saving, it is preferred to cash. The fact that money depreciates is not perhaps so immediate a motive for investing in jewellery but it is recognized as an economic phenomenon. A young WARRIOR's father worked as a schoolmaster for Rs.8 a month: the son, also a schoolmaster, gets Rs.31. Yet, he says, his father was rich and he is poor: and he goes on to retail the amount of paddy that could be bought for one rupee when his father was a boy. Yet gold and silver have to some extent kept their value. I have no adequate figures, but a man from the village who hawked gold in nugget form around Kond villages told me that twenty years ago, when first he began to work with his father, they were selling for Rs.40 what they now sell for Rs.100.

Apart from jewellery having the right degree of liquidity and resistance to depreciation, an important incentive to buying it is not only that this is saving, but it is saving for a purpose. Every piece of jewellery in the house is one piece less to be bought when the daughter goes in marriage.

This dowry is the second source of jewellery for a householder. As one would expect, values vary enormously. Out of five dowries which I recorded the variation in the combined value of ornaments and brass vessels was from Rs.130 to Rs.1065. The remaining figures are set out in Table 14. Many factors are involved in causing this variation. It is sufficient to say here that the first and third marriages were between moderately well-off families and went according to plan. The dowry of

TABLE 14

THE VALUE OF SOME DOWRIES

Caste	*Value*	*Comments*
	Rs.	
HERDSMAN	430	—
HERDSMAN	130	—
HERDSMAN	514	—
WARRIOR	200	—
WARRIOR	1065	Add to this 8 head of cattle the value of which is approximately Rs.300

Rs.130 was brought by a poor girl who came as second wife. The fourth dowry went with a girl whose household was at the time in great difficulty through the coincidence of several deaths and a bad harvest. The last dowry was given with a girl, who was the only child of a widow, and it represents the widow's efforts to transfer as much wealth to her daughter as she could without trespassing on the right of her husband's collateral agnates to the land.

Ownership of the dowry is important, since it affects the right of the landowner to realize the dowry in times of distress. In theory the dowry belongs to the girl's father until she bears a child, male or female. Then it is the property of the child. This means that if the woman dies before bearing the child, or if she dies in childbirth and later the child dies, then the dowry returns to her father. In practice the dowry is often treated exactly like other ornaments and the husband does not scruple to sell it or pledge it, even before a child is born. The first example in Table 14 was a dowry for a girl who was divorced four years later. By then her husband had sold everything except the things she habitually wore—the nose-rings and ear-rings: these alone came back to her father. Her family are indignant, but think that it would be useless to sue, since the man would have nothing to give as damages. Normally, if the husband has some grounds for asserting that he is acting in the best interests of his household, then no-one would object to him selling the jewellery. His right to do so is tacitly recognized and I have never heard of a case where the father-in-law objected.

A man often accumulates jewellery with the specific purpose of providing dowries for his daughters, but this hoard is always at his disposal for sale or pledging, except in one circumstance. If the father dies before the girl is married, it is the normal thing to divide wealth which pertains to women in equal parts between the daughters, to be taken by them as dowry when they marry. The nucleus of this should be the dowry which their mother brought and whatever acquisitions have since been made. The division is made and witnessed by the headman and elders of the village. The goods then go back into general use in the household, but everyone knows what is the share of each girl. The sons have the ornaments and dishes which their wives have brought, and may not touch their sisters' wealth in order to meet contingencies. The right of the girl to this wealth is not *sui generis* but is to be considered a part of her general claim against the estate of her father for the expenses of her marriage.

Before describing the method and significance of realizing jewellery, I will show in Table 15 the cost of purchasing various pieces at the present day. Most of these are of roughly standard size, except the gold necklace which might go up to Rs.240. This fairly wide range of price is significant in that the seller can adjust the amount of capital he liquidates according to his need, while if he sells land he cannot as easily do so.

Table 15

Ornaments and their Cost

		Rs.
Upper forearm bracelets, silver	pair	20
Wrist bracelets, silver	pair	25
Thin silver bracelets	pair	5/8
Rings, silver	each	1/4
Collar, silver	each	12
Hair comb, silver	each	10
Modesty belt, silver	each	22
Gold necklace	each	120
Large nose-rings, gold	pair	50
Gold rings for the top of the ear	pair	40
Gold ear-studs	pair	8
Gold ear-rings	pair	20
Small nose-rings, gold	pair	6
Nose-pendant, gold	each	15

There are two ways of realizing capital in the form of ornaments: one is outright sale, the other is to use the ornament as security for a loan.

The market for jewellery is a buyer's market, but not so much as is the market for land. The initiative is taken always by the seller, and buyers know that jewellery is sold only when there is an urgent need for cash. Consequently, unless the seller had bought the piece from someone in similar difficulties, he seldom can get back what he paid for it. But the loss is never very much, for there are three factors operating against the buyer. Firstly the value of gold and silver depends directly on their weight and the buyer, knowing this, usually sets a limit below which he will not go. Secondly, he can do this, much more than he can for land, because the market of buyers of ornaments is much wider than the market of land-buyers. Items of jewellery are easily transported and if the seller cannot strike a bargain to suit him in his own village, he may travel to other villages and to the markets to find a better price. Thirdly, if a good bargain cannot be struck, the seller may use the ornament as security for a cash loan. For these three reasons it is uncommon to find anyone parting with jewellery at rates much below the market price, except when they default on a debt and lose their security.

If the seller does strike a reasonable bargain, he is in a much better position than if he has had to sell land. Firstly, for reasons given above, he gets a fair price. Secondly, he can raise cash in amounts proportionate to his needs and to the amount of capital he liquidates. It is not the practice to sell half a field. But quite small sums can be raised by the sale of less valuable ornaments. Thirdly—and most importantly—since jewellery is not productive, the sale does not diminish his annual income, as does the sale of land.

This last advantage is to some extent nullified if the ornament is used for security on a cash loan, since interest at a rate never less than 25 per cent is charged and this can be met only out of annual income. There are no big professional moneylenders, with this as their sole occupation, in the district. This commerce is usually combined with shopkeeping, although there are a few rich men who lend money and who are not shopkeepers. The interest charged will depend a little on the relationship of the lender and the borrower, but mainly on the use to which the money is to be put. A HERDSMAN schoolmaster borrowed Rs.25 free of interest from the Schoolmasters' Poor Fund and another Rs.25 at 16 per cent from a rich man in another village, with whom he had ties of ritual friendship (*maitro*). In neither case was a security demanded. If the money is to be used productively it may be given free of interest and it is common to find sums up to Rs.500 advanced to traders for a specific expedition, without interest and without security. But this is more like a transaction between agent and employer than between borrower and lender. In a loan to meet an emergency interest always is charged and security always is demanded. As one would expect the value of the security greatly exceeds the amount of money advanced. For example, a WARRIOR put down as security a gold necklace worth Rs.120 for a loan of Rs.80 at 25 per cent per annum interest.

This institution of loans at a high security serves to prevent 'debt enslavement'. In other parts of India rural debt is a problem. A large part of the cultivator's harvest goes to the moneylender. It is common to find the grandson paying the interest on debts contracted by his grandfather. But here it is unknown. The ultimate reason for the absence of this type of moneylending is probably the relative poverty of the hill regions [1] combined with preventive legislation. The mechanism by which debts are wiped out is clear enough. The lender levies a distress on the security, if he thinks he is going to have trouble collecting further interest.

One form of loan is not given in cash and can be had by reputable people without security, but at a high rate of interest. There are about a dozen people in the village who lend paddy. Paddy in the husk can be kept easily for two years : with care it can be stored for four years and still be good to eat. With this duration it becomes a capital good, which can be used for investment. Houses at the margin of self-sufficiency, or other houses in years when they have had heavy demands on their stocks of paddy, will begin to run out of grain, usually in the planting season when labourers must be paid in paddy. They may then borrow, returning the loan and interest at 50 per cent when their harvest is brought home three months later. If they have been improvident enough to eat their seed paddy, which can be stored only for two years, the interest rate is 100 per cent.

[1] For the connection between prosperity and debt see M. Darling, 1925, Ch. XII.

These loans are given to landowners and to village servants who are in receipt of a tithe, and only if it is certain that the harvest or tithe payments will be big enough to meet the loan. The significance of paddy-lending for the problem of realization of land-capital, is that it enables the cultivator to tide over a bad harvest without selling land or needing cash.

If a man raises money or gets help in kind either free of interest or at preferential rates, it will usually be because there is more than the purely economic relationship between the borrower and the lender.

To the costs of funerals and marriages there is always a contribution from relatives and fellow villagers—from village-brothers, as they are called in the vernacular. The contribution from the last-named and from caste-brothers not closely related is called by the same name whether for a wedding or a funeral—*boroni*. It is *de rigeur* and is regarded as a reciprocal gift for a share in the subsequent feast, but it is seldom large. It certainly goes little way towards diminishing the heavy expenses of these occasions. Collateral agnates and such key uterine relations as the mother's brother make a bigger gift, particularly for a boy's wedding, but again their contribution goes a small way to defraying the total cost.

On the other hand substantial help often is given when the emergency is a purely economic one, but this help does not come from agnates in collateral lines so much as from the mother's brother's house or from the wife's house. A particularly good example of this was a WARRIOR widow whose house was falling down. When houses reach a certain age the wall timbers have been eaten away at the bottom by white ants and the walls begin to hang outwards. Then the house must be taken down, the timbers reset and trimmed and replaced where necessary, and the house built up again. It is man's work, and the widow with her two daughters and small son could not have done it alone. She—through her dead husband—belonged to that large group of WARRIORS which numbered 27 households, but none of them, not even members of the faction with which her husband had sided, came forward to help her. She and her elder daughter cut straw for thatch. (Straw in the field is there for the taking, unless the owner of the field puts up a mark indicating that he wishes to keep it for his own use.) The work was done by her brother from another village and a friend who came to help him. Her husband's agnatic kin gave no help whatsoever.

Another example is a WARRIOR who suffered a series of calamities. His father died : then his grandmother died : his younger sister was ill : and in the same year the harvest was poor. He fell into debt and pledged three fields. Then, at the beginning of the next ploughing season an ox died. Instead of letting more land go, he went to the house into which his elder sister was betrothed and borrowed from them sufficient money to help buy an ox. The money was lent without interest. He, too, belonged to the large WARRIOR lineage, and although they gave more generously than usual when the time came to send this sister in marriage, yet he did not feel able to ask them for money. It was this same WARRIOR who quoted a proverb : 'Your brother is your enemy.'

A final example of disinterested help by uterine kin is this. A WARRIOR who was the only adult male in his lineage died leaving two girls and a small boy to be cared for by the widow. At every crisis in the life of that family, the widow's father and then her brother have come forward to help. They financed the wedding of the two girls. When the boy grew up they helped to find him a wife—from their own village—and they helped build a new big house. The man is now grown with children of his own, but his mother's people still come to help him and he is a frequent visitor at their house.

Two questions arise. Why is not more help given at the contingencies which arise from social obligations—weddings and funerals—since these are often the most costly ? Secondly, why are agnatic kin on the whole more backward than uterine and affinal kin in giving help ?

It is difficult to find a convincing answer to the first question. At a funeral particularly, and to a lesser extent at a wedding, one does not count the cost. The obligation of kin of both sorts is to give ritual aid in a ritual emergency by their presence and by prescribed ritual gifts—cloth, a contribution to the feast, or a small sum of money. A characteristic of a prescribed contribution is that it is not exceeded. But perhaps more important is a kind of myopia which limits attention on the social and ritual implications of the event to the exclusion of finance. In the situation of a wedding or funeral, behaviour towards both sets of kin is prescribed, because these are events which concern them. On the other hand, when an ox dies, the owner is not bound to a particular pattern of behaviour nor are his kindred. Therefore he is free to use his initiative and, if he likes, try to exploit his maternal and affinal ties of kinship.

But why does he not seek for help from his agnatic kin in these economic emergencies? The reason is perhaps contained in the proverb which says that the brother is the enemy. There is at least potential hostility between brothers arising out of the difficulties of dividing the father's estate. This does not mean that all brothers hate one another: they often co-operate in the fields; they often live amicably in the same compound; in sickness or other ritual crises they rush to help one another. But these are not economic situations. It is as if partition sets the pattern for their future economic relationship. In sickness, or against outsiders, the brother is an ally and a friend. But if he mismanages his part of the estate, then let him look after himself. On the other hand there is no land to make rivalry between a man and his mother's brother or a man and his wife's brother. Further, in the latter case, if the man is in distress, then so is their sister, and they are the more likely to give help. These reasons, of course, will not apply to every case since there are often factors of personality operating. But they do seem to account for the different behaviour of collateral agnates on the one hand, and uterine and affinal kin on the other hand, when a man is in financial difficulties.

A man who is bound to give help in all contingencies, both those arising from social obligations and those which are purely economic, is the ritual friend, the *maitro*. This is a relationship entered into during boyhood or adolescence with a person of another caste. It is a solemn bond, contracted before a BRAHMIN and cemented and publicized by a feast, but the reasons for picking a particular person are often trifling. The most frequent one is coincidence of name. Some of these friendships pass away, but many endure through the life of the partners and sometimes through their children's lives. The ritual friend helps in every situation. At weddings or funerals his is the most generous contribution. At times of sickness he comes or sends help. If he can, he will help with money. But I have noticed that the ritual friend relationships which endure, are usually those between persons of approximately equal economic status, and it may be that they endure because one partner is not obliged to make continued demands on the other, and because their gifts can be reciprocal. This fact diminishes the ritual friend as a source of money in hard times.

To sum up, the landowner has several resources to help him over emergencies without selling land. He might have other forms of capital—usually gold and silver ornaments. If he can find a buyer at a reasonable price this is the best solution for him, since he is not losing productive capital. For this and other reasons jewellery is a favoured form of investment. If he cannot find a buyer he might borrow money using jewellery as a security. But the rates of interest are heavy and the security may be forfeited. Finally he might receive gratuitous help from kinsmen, usually from uterine or affinal kin.

Inheritance

In the last five sections I have suggested that land has come and still is coming into the market because there are estates of a certain size which cannot meet the cost of the common contingencies of a lifetime, out of income. Land is then sold. For purposes of exposition I used a model of a cultivator who had no source of income other than his land and described the nature of his responsibilities at times of crises, and the methods he could employ to meet their cost. Implicitly used was a concept of estates at the margin of disintegration.

It is obvious that this is a very wide and variable concept, since the necessity to sell land to meet contingent costs (which is what is meant by land at the margin) will be regulated not only by the annual surplus produced by the estate, but also by the frequency of the contingencies; and furthermore, the model cannot be translated into reality until the effect of mercantile sources of income has been considered. Prediction about the size of disintegrating estates is not possible. All that can be made is a general statement that estates do disintegrate continually, and that, other things being equal, the larger the estate the less likely it is to disintegrate.

If this were the whole story the future of landholding in Bisipara could be predicted. We would expect to find, in examining the techniques of cultivation and farm management, that economies of scale were possible. The costs of running a small estate would be higher proportionately than the costs of running a large estate. Small estates at the margin would disintegrate and be bought up by the larger cultivators, who with each purchase would be rendered more secure against the contingencies which afflict smaller estate-holders and would profit steadily from the economies of scale. Land would drift into the hands of a few large landholders.

In fact there are two completely effective checks on this process. From the one side the ability to make money outside the landholding system prevents many farms from coming into the market. From the other side the system of inheritance has a devastating effect on the wealth of a lineage. If a man has four sons, then his estate is divided into four parts at his death. The chances are that these four estates will be at the margin of disintegration. Multiple inheritance and the low degree of probability of getting a long line of only sons prevent wealth from remaining for more than two or three generations with one lineage. This extreme impermanence of wealth has had important effects in helping to prevent the formation of economic classes.

The system of inheritance is not the only thing which brings estates down to the margin of disintegration. A run of bad luck can break up an estate which might have survived under a less malignant star (this is the Oriya idiom). Spectacular mismanagement can do the same. But it is the system of multiple inheritance which in the end lays flat the ramparts of wealth.

The principle of agnation regulates the inheritance of land. When a man dies his eldest son may choose one field. The rest of the land is divided into equal parts between all the sons, including the eldest. The house, and sometimes the garden, belong to the youngest son. Movable property is divided in the same way, equally between the sons of a dead man.

If there are no direct male heirs, then the property goes to collateral lines in the lineage (*bonso*), to whichever person is nearest genealogically to the dead man. If there are two persons of the same propinquity, then the property is divided between them. But the nearer agnate excludes all more distant from the dead man. The right of collateral agnates is not to a general share-out of land falling without heir, but only to a place in a hierarchy of reversionary heirs. Ultimately land escheats to the Government.

Women born into the lineage have a right to maintenance and to the expenses of their marriage against the estate of their father. If the father dies when they are still in his house, then their claim persists and it is the duty of whoever inherits the father's land to see to the care and marriage of his daughters. The daughters have no claim at law for more than this. The division of movable property at the death of the father often includes the daughters : but this is not their right, for such gifts go only to unmarried daughters and are an instalment towards their dowry.

The widow of a man has a right to maintenance from his estate until her death, so long as she remains in his household and does not remarry. Her right is to maintenance alone and she may not sell the land. If she tries to do so, then the agnates of her late husband may take her to court. If she marries and goes to another village then she loses all rights in her former husband's land. She is permitted to become the wife of a younger brother of her late husband, actual or classificatory. If she does so, then no land from her late husband's estate is reserved for her, since her maintenance now falls on her new husband.

These are the rules of inheritance. In practice there are many variations tending both to mitigate and to sharpen the difficulties of the heir.

Although division of the land at the death of the father is, in a sense, the normal proceeding, men regard themselves more as coparceners than as heirs. In fact the division may be postponed for some years after the death of the father, or it may take place while he is still alive.

When the eldest son marries and brings a wife to his father's house, they almost always get a room to themselves, but it is normal for the girl to begin working under her mother-in-law in the household. After a month or two she will take charge of the cooking. The reason, Oriyas say, is that of all woman's work, cooking is the lightest and they do not wish to overstrain a young girl or get themselves into trouble with her father and brothers. But the older woman continues to supervise and to be manager of the household. The father, mother, son and his wife form one household, both as producers and consumers.

Some households go on like this for quite a long time, but most seem to break up within six months. The trouble starts within the kitchen and the girl demands a separate cooking-place. She may get just this, but usually she gets her own share of the harvest as well as her own fire, since girls do not like having a daily ration given to them by the mother-in-law. This is the second stage of the process by which the eldest son breaks away from his father. They are still working the land in common under the management of the father. But when the harvest is gathered and threshed, the grain is divided between the kitchens of the mother-in-law and daughter-in-law.

Then the two households quarrel about the division of the grain, particularly if one woman is a better manager than the other and makes her store last longer. The final break comes and the son takes his share of the fields. The size of the share will depend on the number of sons who will inherit and it is usual for the father to take the opportunity to settle once for all which field will go to which son and which he will retain for himself and his wife. He may call in other members of the lineage to help make the decision. He will probably call in the village headman and selected elders to feast on a goat and to witness the arrangement.

When such an anticipatory division is made it is usual for the father to allow for the expenses of marrying off daughters in the share which he keeps for himself, and to divide the brass vessels and jewellery into dowry-lots.

Although a father at his eldest son's request divides the land between all sons, he usually retains the management of the land of the unmarried sons. In the same way, if the land is divided at the father's death and the younger sons are unmarried, then a married brother will manage the estate. A widow too will manage land for her small sons. This is important, since it means that the effects of sub-division are not rigorously effective until all the sons are married and mature. Thus although an estate may be divided into five anticipatory parts, only the surplus of that one-fifth which belongs to the brother who has partitioned will not be available to meet contingencies. Four-fifths of the annual surplus will be at hand.

The word applied to land owned and managed in common is *soja*. Such estates are exceptional. Only close relatives, like full-brothers or a father and his married sons hold such estates, and there are few examples even of these. Only one group of brothers comes near to holding all its land in common. In other cases only a part of the land is held in common and this land either lies in some distant village and is worked by share-croppers, or there is something to make it different from the rest of the estate. In one case the eldest of three brothers died and the two younger men, instead of dividing the land, worked it jointly and assumed joint title to this land. In every case joint landholders are moderately or very rich and the joint land is commonly kept not for personal needs but to run as a business enterprise. The income from the land is at the disposal of the coparceners sitting as a council and not, as in the traditional Bengali joint-family, under the direction of a manager. In fact, of course, a man of strong personality will often control the council, but the form of partnership is at least there. The funds are used to meet contingencies or are invested either by lending paddy or by using them to enlarge the estate.

Why is land retained in this form and not divided? The first reason is that in two of the three cases in which a large amount of land is jointly held, all the coparceners have enough land of their own comfortably to meet everyday needs. Their wives are not putting pressure on them, as they do when they need more rice and think they can get it by making their husband manage the land himself instead of leaving it with the coparcenry. Indeed, when the land is in another village and is share-cropped this would not be possible. Secondly, on the positive side, the coparceners admit the advantages of the system. The surplus is large enough to be used productively. It forms a useful reserve. If the joint estate were divided then the smaller surpluses would be likely to be frittered away on everyday needs or small luxuries.

The number of households benefiting from this system is small. Of 179 households in the village, 132 own some land.

There are only two coparcenries for whole estates, one consisting of the households of three brothers, and the other of the households of a man and his dead elder brother's son. In this way 127 households manage their own estates. Among these there are two coparcenaries holding some land in common : one is a group of five brothers, the bulk of whose joint estate lies in other villages; the other consists of two brothers and the adult son of one of them who keep in common the estate of a dead elder brother.

Of the five richest men in the village, four were sole heir or have become sole heir by the death of brothers. The fifth benefited from a special arrangement.

The fifth person is the *mutha* headman. He has four half-brothers. When the father died the eldest son took over an estate five times as large as that of each of his brothers, who received only enough to keep them. I do not know how in law this was done, but the arrangements could have been effected by a will. Informants are quite frank about the significance of sub-division and the connection between wealth and political power. They say that such a division was necessary to enable the headman to perform his duties. He has many expenses which a poor man could not afford, and it would have been foolish to divide the property equally. The present headman's eldest son insists that his younger brother—also, as it happens, a half-brother—will get only as much as he needs to live. I thought perhaps that the land was attached to the headmanship, but it is not. Headmen receive a proportion of the revenue which they collect and not a grant of land.

Another of these rich men is making special arrangements to prevent the estate breaking up after his death. He has four sons. The second son helps on the farm and eventually will inherit it. The eldest and the two youngest sons will be educated so that they can find a position in service and their share of the estate will be spent on their education. One son is on the point of finding a job. The other two are young. If they succeed at school—the second son failed—then the father will make a will leaving all the land to his second son.

Not every rich man is interested in seeing his estate survive intact and the will may be used to pass land to daughters. One of the five rich men has no sons. He belongs to an extensive and powerful lineage among whom there are many people qualified to take the land as reversionary heirs. Some years ago he took the nearest of these into his house intending that he should be in place of a son. But they quarrelled and the young man left. Then the old man sold much of the land and gave the money to his daughters and their sons. In 1953 he made a will dividing what was left of his land into four equal parts: one each for his two married daughters; one for his widow to revert after her death to the lineage; and one part for the person nearest him in the lineage who will perform his funeral rites.

In summary, the system of multiple inheritance serves to prevent the continued existence of large estates, because it is improbable that there will be a sole heir for more than two generations. Males alone are eligible to take property, whether movable or immovable, but women have rights to maintenance and among them daughters have a right to the expenses of their marriage. The division commonly starts with quarrels between women in the household and may begin before the father dies. But, although the shares may have been marked out for many years, the division is not completed until the youngest son is married. Strictly, the expenses of all the girls' marriages and of the parents' mortuary rites are put to one side before the estate is divided, so that a young man should not have to pay for the marriage of his sisters or brothers or the funeral of his parents out of his share alone. Whether or not he will have to do so in fact depends on the wealth of the family.

A will may be used to retain the estate intact, or to break it up, according to the wish of the owner. In fact, whether by chance or irregular inheritance, all the richest men in the village have been sole heir to the estates which descended to them.

Did this Happen in the Past?

I think it is unlikely that the WARRIORS were losing much land before 1855. I have no knowledge of how common was the practice of selling land in the Kingdom of Boad, the isolated district from which they came, but it was normal in the districts which the British administered. However, in the hills it is difficult to see who could be the purchasers of land before 1855.

Most of the land has in fact gone to the DISTILLER castes and now is going to Boad OUTCASTES. But the last-named have begun to acquire large estates only within the last twenty or thirty years. The Ganjam DISTILLERS were not in the village before 1870. There is no evidence that the Boad DISTILLERS were landowners in the original village. Circumstantial evidence points the other way.

If there was no-one to buy land from the WARRIORS, how were they able to meet such contingent costs as deaths, marriages or the need to buy plough cattle without selling land ? The most probable explanation—assuming that rites, which are the main expense, were conducted on the same scale—is that estates were not reduced to the margin of disintegration, not because everyone was richer in the old days, but because the joint-family was still a flourishing institution. So long as partition does not take place, the devastating effect of multiple inheritance is avoided and contingent costs fall upon estates of a size sufficient to meet them. The principle is the same as when a slump may eliminate a small business and be survived by a big business.

Why, then, has partition become normal and the joint family the exception ? While the family are agriculturists pure and simple, family economics can be efficiently managed by one man. Whatever the rivalries and tensions between brothers their economic interest is directed to the same end—making the estate produce as much as possible. But when one brother gets an income from trade and another is a policeman and a third is a carter and the fourth and fifth remain on the land ; and when the trader and the policeman and the carter refuse to put their earnings into the common pool, as they are permitted to do in certain conditions ; and when they demand a share of the estate so that they may sell it and use the money to finance other undertakings—then all the brothers are glad to partition and go their own way. The joint-family cannot survive divergent interests and disparate incomes among its members.

Opportunities to make money in fields other than agriculture caused joint-families to be partitioned. Many of these smaller estates, especially when partition has become a habit, cannot meet the costs of contingencies, which occur in everyone's lifetime, without selling land. The same change in the economic environment has provided funds which are invested in land and has attracted to the village a new population which shares in the redistribution of land.[1]

In the following chapters I shall examine the various sources of mercantile wealth and see how far they have been responsible for the land-transfer that has taken place.

[1] An increase of population is, of course, an important contributory factor to the splitting of joint families. See page 9 and page 234.

CHAPTER V

MERCANTILE WEALTH: SERVICES AND TRADING

WORKING one's own land is not the only source of income, and no household in the village depends on this alone. Indeed many estates are kept intact only because the owner has a second source of income. Conversely, those with money earned by other activities can buy land when it comes into the market. There is a very rough correlation between the size of an estate and the amount of money earned from other sources. Those who have the biggest outside income tend to have the biggest estates, partly because their fields are not lost under pressure of contingent expenditure and partly because they enjoy a surplus which can be invested.

In this and subsequent chapters I shall describe various activities, and try to estimate the average income obtained from them, since by no means all are profitable enough to give a surplus for investment in land. Secondly, for each activity I shall ask how far it is restricted to certain groups or categories of persons either by legislation or by concepts of pollution or by acquired skills. Much of the transfer of land that takes place to-day and presumably took place in the last hundred years was the result of chance. X sold a field after a run of bad luck to Y, who had completed a good year's trading. Five years later Y was selling land and X was buying. Land went to and fro and no trend could be discerned. But in other cases some groups received much land and lost little: others lost heavily and regained little. When such a trend is noticeable, it is because the buyers of land have had special opportunities to exploit an economic opportunity wholly or partly denied to others.

I have defined mercantile[1] activities rather widely but the definition need cause no confusion. I include under this heading all activities which bring an income in cash or kind, other than

[1] 'Mercantile' here is used as the adjective of 'merchant', and the meaning is extended, as is explained in the text. It has nothing to do with 'Mercantilism' as an economic theory.

work on one's own land or work on one's own behalf in the jungle, such as collecting bamboos to make a roof. Grouped together as mercantile are such varied activities as keeping a shop, casual labour on farms, schoolmastering, crafts, barbering and so forth.

The Village Servants

The village employs three BRAHMINS, two BARBERS, a WASHERMAN, two HERDSMEN for cattle, a HERDSMAN for goats, a TEMPLEMAN, and two SWEEPERS.

All these occupations are restricted to the appropriate caste, except that of herding cattle. This restriction is qualified in two ways. Firstly anyone can perform any of these activities, except the BRAHMIN's and the TEMPLEMAN's, for himself. The housewife sweeps her courtyard. Men, or more often their young sons, herd the family's cattle and goats. A woman can and does wash her own and her husband's clothes. But no woman of clean caste will wash the clothes of another household, nor sweep the street. Neither can anyone cut hair among the clean castes for payment except the BARBER. But individuals or even groups of households can employ a man or boy to herd cattle, whatever the caste. There are few HERDSMEN and this may be the reason. But, in spite of the scarcity, it is rare to find a *village* cowherd who is not a HERDSMAN. In the streets of the clean castes one never finds a man cutting hair who is not of BARBER caste, nor a woman sweeping the street who is not of SWEEPER caste, nor a washerman who is not also of the WASHERMAN caste. The second qualification arises from the refusal of the village servants to attend unclean castes. Therefore untouchables must either do the work for themselves or make one of their own number into a specialist. They cut each other's hair. If the street is swept at all, the work is done by the housewives. They have their own herdsman. They can cope with all the ritual crises of life without the service of a BRAHMIN, but, if they pay enough, the BRAHMIN is willing to perform rites which do not bring him into close contact. He might read a horoscope or divine for the cause of an illness. But he will not attend their marriages or their funerals.

In Hindu theory, every caste has an hereditary occupation.

But in this section I am considering only those who are in regular employment in the village at their hereditary occupation and whose market is principally in the village. The WEAVER caste (the work is done also by Boad OUTCASTES) are discussed in a later section since they have no contractual relationship with households in the village, but produce their pieces entirely for sale in a cash market. Musicians are not here considered since their work is occasional and is not a significant source of wealth which might have affected the redistribution of land. Again, such perquisites as the right of the SWEEPER or OUTCASTE to take the hide and eat the meat of dead cattle are disregarded for the same reasons. Trade in cattle hides, an important source of wealth, is considered later.

Not every person works at his traditional occupation. The DISTILLERS do not touch liquor. The Kond POTTERS do not know how to make pots. The FISHERMEN do not fish. The WARRIORS are cultivators. Even where there is scope for practising an hereditary occupation, not all members of the appropriate caste engage in the work (see Table 16).

TABLE 16

NUMBER OF HOUSEHOLDS IN EACH CASTE EMPLOYED AS VILLAGE SERVANTS

Caste	*Number of households in village*	*Employed by village*
BRAHMIN	5	3*
BARBER	2	2
WASHERMAN	1	1
HERDSMAN	9	3
TEMPLEMAN	2	1
SWEEPER	4	2†
Total	23	12

* One of these is the widow, who lives in effect on a pension.
† A third SWEEPER household is employed in a nearby Kond village.

Since there are in all 179 households in the village, those households which have regular employment in the service of the village number 12, or 6 per cent of the total.

Among these the BARBERS, the WASHERMAN, the three HERDSMEN and one of the SWEEPERS have no farm land. The sizes of the estates of the rest are shown in Table 17.

There seems to be no tendency in the village for other castes

TABLE 17

SIZE OF ESTATES OWNED BY VILLAGE SERVANTS

Owner	*Gross value of annual paddy crop*	*Remarks*
	Rs.	
BRAHMIN A . . .	333	Now boycotted
A's brother . . .	100	—
BRAHMIN B . . .	150	—
BRAHMIN C . . .	50	—
TEMPLEMAN . . .	250	—
SWEEPER A . . .	66	—

to trespass into these hereditary preserves. This is partly the result of concepts of pollution. For instance, a caste lower than the BARBER could not take to barbering because they would have no customers. A man of higher caste cannot cut hair without implicitly lowering himself. It also is the result of superior skill passed on from generation to generation. It takes many years to learn all that a BRAHMIN must know, and there was one BRAHMIN in the village who was too stupid to learn. To a lesser extent this applies to cutting hair and washing clothes, and is even true of herding cattle. One HERDSMAN, whose father and uncle were killed by tigers, tends to remain close to the village and his cattle are always getting into the crops, or straying up the mountain-side in search of better grazing. The other is bolder and takes the herd away into the jungle.

The BARBERS, BRAHMINS, WASHERMAN, TEMPLEMAN and SWEEPERS are paid by a tithe system (*jejemani*). After the main harvest is gathered they receive from each house, which is in the system, a payment of paddy. Then, when their services are required, they get another payment, usually in rice. For the SWEEPERS this takes the form of a handful of cooked rice from each house each day. The TEMPLEMAN receives only the annual payment, since ordinarily he has no day-to-day activity for the different households. The HERDSMEN and the woman of the same caste-group who looks after goats are paid in paddy after the harvest, the amount from each household depending on the number of cattle it sends to the herd. The cowherds and the goatherd collect a handful of cooked rice every day from the houses whose cattle they take.

Not every household pays tithe to the village servants. OUTCASTES, of course, are excluded. But among the clean castes there is a division between those who pay tithe and those who pay cash. The division runs roughly between the original castes and those who have come later. The BARBER, for instance, receives tithe from all WARRIORS, Boad DISTILLERS, HERDSMEN, BRAHMINS and the two FISHERMEN households. From the Kond POTTERS, the Ganjam DISTILLERS, the WEAVERS and so forth, he takes cash at each transaction.

The BRAHMIN and the BARBER have tithe relationships with households in a few neighbouring villages where Oriyas have settled. They also work for cash in Kond villages, where the BRAHMIN can be persuaded to perform the full Hindu ritual for a funeral, if he is paid about twenty times the fee he charges to Oriyas. The BARBER also goes every week to work in the market-place.

Do these people earn enough to keep themselves and their families? Do they make a surplus? Is there sufficient profit to be made to attract other specialists to the village?

The clientele of the village is divided between two BARBERS, a man and his elder brother's son, here called BARBER X and BARBER Y respectively. Their annual income is estimated in Table 18. For food alone BARBER X needs a minimum income of

---

PLATE IV

(*a*) BRAHMINS PERFORMING THE 'DOSA'

The photograph was taken on the bank of the Salki River, which can be seen in the right background through the trees.

This was the *dosa* ceremony for a rich WARRIOR who had died. The man squatting in the left background is a relative of the dead man. The youth whose head is shaved is the heir. The youth on the right is the son of a BRAHMIN who was invited to perform the ceremony, but who had an attack of fever on the day. The older BRAHMIN on the left happened to be visiting the village, and he gave assistance, since the young man was not fully trained. Both these persons belong to other villages. Bisipara's own BRAHMIN was not asked to perform the rite (see page 104).

(*b*) BARBER AT WORK

The photograph was taken in WARRIOR street on the veranda of the house of Postmaster, which appears in the right middleground of Plate II (*a*).

The man on the left is the BARBER (in the text called BARBER X). He is shaving a WARRIOR. Another WARRIOR squats in the background.

The morning is cold and all three are wrapped in heavy cotton shawls. They have chosen this veranda because it catches the sun.

The neat finish to the mud walls of a house, mentioned at page 116, appears in the photograph.

(*a*)

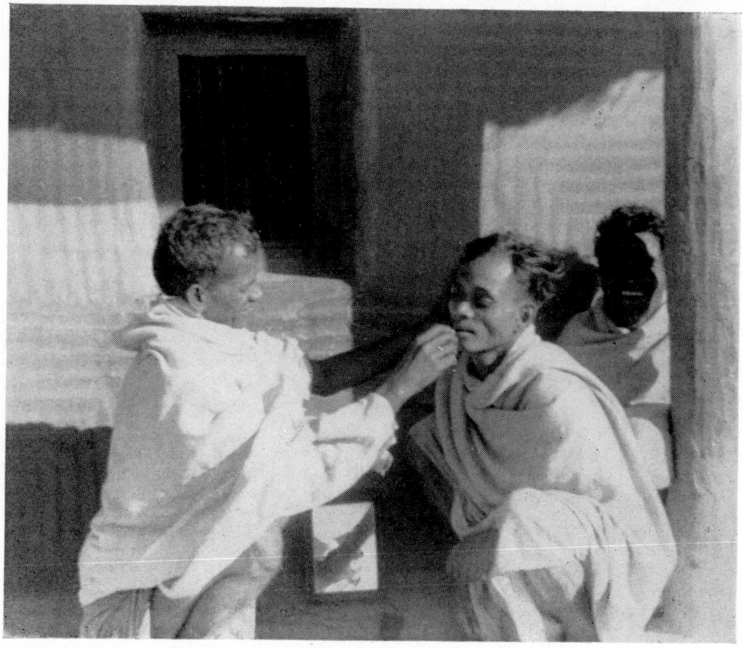

(*b*)

PLATE IV

Table 18

Minimum Annual Income of Barbers

Source	*Barber X* Rs.	*Barber Y* Rs.
Tithe and occasional payments from own and other villages : paddy worth	100	226
Cash payments from own and other villages to the value of	47	37
Total	147	263

Rs.135 : BARBER Y needs Rs.180. In fact the table indicates the minimum income of the two men, since I could find no reliable way of estimating their takings in the market-place nor the amount of casual payments received for their services at weddings nor from such miscellaneous sources as shaving the hair off goats. (When a goat is cut for sale, the carcase is not skinned, but the hide is sold attached to the pieces of meat. Therefore it is first shaved.) In fact both BARBERS are more comfortably off than a comparison of their needs with the income shown in Table 18 would lead one to suppose. But neither of them shows signs of wealth. They and their women are badly dressed : their houses are modest : neither own land, except the garden behind their house : and both every year are reduced to borrowing paddy before their tithe payments come in.

The WASHERMAN is considered very rich. His family is large and to feed them he needs the equivalent in paddy of Rs.360 a year. From washing the clothes of his own village and half-a-dozen houses in neighbouring hamlets, he gets paddy equivalent to Rs.273 and cash about Rs.12. He owns no land except his garden, but he share-crops a few fields. His sons and daughters work these fields and hire themselves out as labourers on other men's farms. For some years he made ends meet in this way. But for the last two or three years his eldest son has been washing the clothes of a large Oriya village about five miles away. I could not discover how much they earned in this village, since I did not know its composition, but the villagers say he gets as much from there as from his own village. He has not used the money to buy land, perhaps because he is afraid to show his wealth and because the village has been trying to get money out of him on one pretext or another for the past twelve months.

The village employs two cowherds, one of the Oriya HERDSMAN caste and the other a Kond HERDSMAN. For nine months in the year, from about the middle of June to the middle of March, when there are crops growing in the fields, the cowherds take the cattle out beyond the village boundaries. They wait around until mid-day, when oxen which have been yoked are brought out to them. Then they wander further afield, perhaps up the mountain if they are bold. In the evening they bring the herd back again. During the three hottest months of the year, when there are no crops, oxen are turned loose and buffaloes are sent out with small boys, since, unlike oxen, buffaloes cannot be trusted to come home at night. For the season the cowherds are paid for an ox or a sterile cow paddy to the value of R.1 ; for a cow that has calved paddy to the value of Rs.1/3 ; for a buffalo Rs.1/10. No charge is made for animals that are not mature. In addition the cowherd gets a daily handful of cooked rice from each household which sends out cattle. If the household is of lower caste than the herdsman, they give him paddy to the approximate value of As.3 a week. The Oriya HERDSMAN is young and not yet married and requires to feed himself each year paddy worth only Rs.60. His income is paddy worth Rs.155. He pastures the cattle of the street of the WARRIORS. The Kond HERDSMAN takes the cattle of the remaining clean streets, Kond POTTER Street, Boad DISTILLER Street, Market Street and New Street. His annual need for food is paddy to the value of Rs.180 : his income is worth Rs.233. One HERDSMAN achieves a bigger surplus than the BARBER but neither HERDSMAN appears to be very rich. Neither owns land : neither dresses well. The surplus is not so big as the figures indicate, since out of it must be provided clothes, kerosene, lentils to go with rice, and so forth.

There are three sub-castes of BRAHMINS in the village, each represented by one lineage. The oldest (A) came from Boad and is ritually highest in status and professionally the most skilled. This sub-caste alone knows the rites for a marriage and a funeral. It also had charge of the village temple, although the other sub-castes would be competent to do this. The other two BRAHMIN sub-castes and the TEMPLEMEN are concerned with the Kondmals temple which was built on the edge of the village by the first Tahsildar. He brought from Ganjam a BRAHMIN family to care for the temple and this family is now represented only by a widow (B). The father of this woman brought the TEMPLEMAN, who was then a boy of five, from Boad. The temple is now managed partly by the TEMPLEMAN and partly by another BRAHMIN (C) of a third sub-caste, which came originally to the village to care for a temple built in Market Street by a rich WEAVER. Originally A looked after the village temple and all household rituals which require a BRAHMIN : C's father looked after the Market temple : B's father and his assistant the TEMPLEMAN looked after the Kondmals temple. Now C works in and derives an income from all three temples. B and the TEMPLEMAN share the profits of the Kondmals temple with C. BRAHMIN A performs some of the family rituals in other villages, but in his own village he is boycotted. Towards the end of 1953 his younger brother began to do some family rituals in the village : other people hired BRAHMINS from other villages.

For the village temple the BRAHMIN in charge, C, gets paddy to the value of As.6 from each clean house every year. This is clear profit, since the materials for the daily rite are supplied by each house in turn. The Market Street temple is endowed with two fields. The profit from this is not great since the fields are share-cropped and the BRAHMIN himself must provide the material for the daily rite. The total profit from the Kondmals temple is high, since, in theory at least, every house in the Kondmals contributes paddy worth As.6 each year. The right to collect is usually farmed out to Boad OUTCASTES in return for a cash payment. Some years the TEMPLEMAN himself collects from the near villages. In 1953 the income was cash Rs.300 and paddy to the value of Rs.100. The TEMPLEMAN takes Rs.200 : C gets Rs.100 : and B gets Rs.100. The temple has property of its own bringing in annually paddy to the value of Rs.83. In addition scarcely a day passes without a suppliant coming to the temple with an offering of rice, fruit and coconuts. In theory all this income belongs to the temple. In fact it is divided between the priests, the greater part going to the TEMPLEMAN, and no accounts are kept.

It is possible to make a very rough minimum estimate of the profits of B, C and the TEMPLEMAN from ritual activities and prerogatives. C, who needs for food paddy worth Rs.120, gets at least Rs.165. The TEMPLEMAN, who needs Rs.250 worth of food, gets at least Rs.240. B, the widow, needs food worth Rs.60 and gets at least Rs.120. The TEMPLEMAN and B each have enough land to feed themselves so that their income from ritual sources gives them a considerable surplus.

Formerly A received tithe payments to the value of Rs.40 from his own village. From other villages he still gets paddy to the value of Rs.80 and Rs.3 in cash. In addition he received a payment each time he performed a rite, the total value of which it is impossible to estimate. A's land provides two-thirds as much again as he needs to feed himself, so that his whole income from his profession as a BRAHMIN represents a surplus for investment.

The street of the WARRIORS employs one SWEEPER (P). The remaining streets, Kond POTTER, Boad DISTILLER, Market Street and New Street, employ another (Q). One old SWEEPER woman works for a Kond village about two miles away. P gets a tithe of paddy worth about Rs.12 and daily food worth in a year about Rs.100, a total income just a little under what is required to feed two persons. Q gets an income of paddy equivalent to Rs.240 to meet a household requirement of about Rs.135. The income of the third SWEEPER could not be estimated, since I do not know the composition of the village which she served.

The village as a whole employs one goatherd, a woman of the HERDSMAN caste and her twelve-year-old son. Like the cowherd they receive food each day and a yearly tithe based on the number of goats sent to the herd. The family needs each year paddy to the value of Rs.100 for food alone. Their income from goatherding is worth about Rs.148 a year.

Apart from the TEMPLEMAN, who strictly is not the servant of the village, but of the whole Kondmals, none of these jobs, *in themselves*, offer striking opportunities for making money. They are adjusted roughly to meet the needs of a man and his wife and their small children. If the incumbent's household happens to be smaller than this, then he or she may be able to show a profit, like the Oriya HERDSMAN or the goatherd. But this profit will vanish when the cowherd or the son of the goatherd marry and have children. BARBER Y, who supports a widowed mother, a wife and an infant son, is going to find it increasingly difficult to make ends meet, although he has a larger share of the local clientele than his uncle.

The cowherds, the goatherd, the BARBERS, SWEEPER Q and BRAHMIN C have no significant source of income outside their profession. Pasturing goats and cattle, and cutting hair, are full-time jobs. SWEEPER Q's household consists of herself, her divorced daughter and her infant grand-daughter, and their work takes the two women most of the day. BRAHMIN C, who suffers both from consumption and congenital syphilis, just sits around when he is not working.

The cowherds and the goatherds and the BARBERS and SWEEPER Q have no time for other work; but the other village servants have. Sweeping the street of the WARRIORS takes about an hour a day and collecting the cooked rice takes about another hour. Furthermore the work is done by women, so that the men of the household are left free to do other things. The daily rites in any of the temples never lasts more than two hours unless there is a festival. Washing takes the whole day, but now that the WASHERMAN's family contains four children old enough to work, the father has plenty of time to himself.

Therefore, although village service is not in itself a source of spectacular wealth, some types of service—especially priestly service—are in effect part-time activities and allow the incumbent to make money in other ways. In fact the TEMPLEMAN and two of the BRAHMIN households are maintained from other sources and the reward of their priestly activities represents a surplus for investment.

Every Oriya village in the hills has some or all of these specialist castes, and each caste spreads over a number of villages. They are endogamous units and occasionally they meet to hear complaints. But only the HERDSMEN caste have a regular council meeting every two or three years to regulate conduct and hear disputes. I have never heard of the BRAHMINS, WASHERMEN, SWEEPERS, BARBERS or TEMPLEMEN holding a full council. If there is a flagrant transgression the members of the caste in two or three neighbouring villages may get together and expel the offender, but they never meet to make positive rules about conduct, as do the WARRIORS and the Boad DISTILLERS and the HERDSMEN.

In other parts of India observers have seen a resemblance between specialist castes and a craft guild or a trade union. They have noticed corporate economic action by the specialist castes to raise their pay or improve the conditions in which they work.[1] Cities sometimes are thrown into confusion by a strike of SWEEPERS; but this does not happen in the village. The village is master and in past years has successfully disciplined its servants. The specialist castes take no corporate measures to protect themselves or to make a better bargain, even when, like the HERDSMEN, they have a functioning council.

They have tried. Many years ago, when the elder of the two BARBERS, X, was a boy, he was playing in the street with some other boys when he fell, struck his head on a stone and was knocked unconscious. His elder brother, Y's father, who is now dead, protested to the headman and demanded compensation. The headman said it was an affair of boys and they should forget about it. The BARBER went on strike and said that he would only work again when the village council had listened to his case. The village refused and went to market to be shaved and get their hair cut. (Most men shave two or three times a month.) In the end X's father climbed down.

More significant, since it was economically motivated, was the action of BRAHMIN A. Two years ago he had charge of the village temple and received the tithe for performing family rituals. Many years before, BRAHMIN B's father had received two fields as payment for caring for the Kondmals temple. BRAHMIN A, already a rich man, proposed that he should receive two fields for his work in the village temple. He demanded two fields as well from a rich old WARRIOR, in whose house he performed the same rite as in the village temple. The old man gave the fields. The village refused and said he must be content with his tithes. The BRAHMIN replied that if he did not get the fields he would not perform the rite. The village promptly called in BRAHMIN C to look after the village temple and at the same time decreed that A should no longer get the tithe for family rituals. For eighteen months, when there was a death or a wedding, the householders called in a BRAHMIN from a neighbouring village and paid him cash and rice. They would have used C, but he did not know the rites well enough. BRAHMIN A has made several attempts

[1] Cf. M. Opler and R. Datt Singh, 1950, p. 490.

to climb down. On the eve of the annual fifteen-day festival in honour of the god who inhabits the village temple he made a long appeal to be allowed to resume the work. 'This is my work. Give it to me!' The village refused and said that he could prompt C, who is not experienced, and C should give him a small quantity of paddy. Some weeks later, when the old wooden temple was being pulled down and the foundation stone of a new building was laid, A asked again to be allowed to do 'his' work, especially as C had not the least idea of the correct rites. Again the village refused and called in a BRAHMIN of the same sub-caste as A, who could be trusted to know what to do. This visitor was assisted by C. Brahmin A looked on and prompted them from time to time. Six months ago A's younger brother quarrelled with his mother's brother, in whose house he was living, and returned to Bisipara. He now has taken his brother's place and receives the tithe for family rituals, which he is competent to perform. At the harvest of 1954 he was paid at half the usual rates, since he had worked only for six months. The elder brother A appealed again to be allowed to resume the care of the village temple and the family rituals. The village council replied politely that they would keep him in mind if either of the present incumbents let the village down, but in the meantime they were satisfied and saw no reason to move either of them.

In these two cases both the BARBER and the BRAHMIN were at the mercy of the village, since their castes are quite unorganized for joint militant action. There is no concept of loyalty to the caste or caste-fellows, which is sufficiently strong to make a man think twice about breaking a strike. There are plenty of BRAHMINS willing to come for Rs.2 and do what is required at a wedding. If the BARBER goes on strike, then there is a whole row of barbers waiting every week in the market-place. The WASHERMAN cannot act against the village, since he is in competition with the WASHERMAN from a village across the river, half a mile away, who can use an iron and is anxious to build up a business in Bisipara.

More than this, the village has ideas on what are the proper rewards for its servants. For many years the specialist castes received dues (*mamul*). At a wedding the BARBER kept the old cloth, when he had helped to dress the groom in his new cloth. He had a right to certain parts of animals slaughtered for a wedding-feast. When a girl menstruated for the first time, the WASHERMAN had a right to keep the cloth she was wearing. He could keep the cloth in which a woman had died, or in which she had born a child. In 1953 the village council decided that the WASHERMAN and the other specialist castes should lose the greater part of these perquisites. The servants have protested. At the first wedding in 1954 the BARBER X said that they would not play their part unless they got their dues: but in fact they did the work and did not get their dues. The WASHERMAN, who had been in trouble in other ways, is threatening to leave the village. Recalcitrant specialists protest and threaten and try to bully individuals into disregarding the decision of the council, but in the last resort they are helpless. They are, in fact, public servants.

The village rationalizes these decrees against its servants not by saying that the servants are getting too rich, but by claiming that they, the masters, are getting poorer and can no longer afford to pay dues. But at least part of the reason is a dislike of seeing village servants getting rich. This particularly applies to the WASHERMAN since his eldest son has been working. He has been fined two or three times for letting his buffaloes stray into other men's gardens, and the fine has been demanded in cash while other offenders are penalized only by admonition or a demand for a small amount of paddy in compensation.

The belief in the power of spirits enables the community to attack the newly-rich. There are two aids to getting rich. One is the worship of Lakmi, an entirely respectable cult. The other is to keep a spirit (*devata*), who will bring wealth but whose presence is to be concealed, since spirits sometimes break out and harm other people. Spirits are kept in the house, or in the cowshed, or under a tree at the bottom of the garden. Sooner or later someone stumbles on the man while he is making the daily offering of rice and liquor to the spirit, and realizes what he is doing. But keeping a spirit is not in itself a crime and nothing is said or done. At the beginning of 1953 five people were known to possess this form of spirit. Three other men, diviners, kept good spirits to help them with their work. As well as this, almost every tree and rock and bend in the river has its own spirit.

In May, a six-year old HERDSMAN boy who lived in the next house to the WASHERMAN died suddenly in the night, having first awakened and called out the name of his playmate, the WASHERMAN's small daughter. The boy was buried and nothing much was said. Children under ten years of age are liable to die very suddenly.[1] Two days later a fifteen-year old girl of a WARRIOR family which lived next but one to the WASHERMAN went into a fit and died twenty-four hours later, after she had been taken to hospital. It was said that a spirit had caused these two deaths and people at once accused the WASHERMAN of keeping a harmful spirit. A levy of R.1 was taken from each house and an important diviner was called in. In the course of a day he had located all the spirits in the village, friendly, malignant and indifferent, and performed rites to drive the malignant spirits out of the village. The council, which may be attended by all the heads of clean households in the village, then met to decide punishment. First all had to take an oath that they would abide by the council's decision and not call in outside authority in order to evade punishment if they were found guilty. The oath called for supernatural penalties and was reinforced by a secular threat of ostracism. Four of those who kept malignant spirits were then told that they would be fined Rs.2 each : the WASHERMAN whose spirit had done the damage was to pay Rs.10. That night the WASHERMAN and three others (including BRAHMIN A, who was still trying to get back into village service) met together and decided to complain to the police. Next morning the conspiracy was revealed to the headman and council by the brother of one of the conspirators. The council renewed the threat of ostracism and successfully extracted a fine of Rs.5 from three of the conspirators. From the WASHERMAN they demanded Rs.100. He threatened to leave the village, pleaded poverty, and then, after some weeks of haggling, paid up Rs.60. For two months following the death of the girl the WASHERMAN did no work, but I was not able to discover how much of this was due to his own obstinacy and how much to a village boycott. When the time came to pay his tithe, the council met and reduced his fee to correspond to the ten months during which he had actually worked.

[1] Cerebral malaria is commonly the cause of such deaths.

Throughout these disputes, the contestants were the village and the BRAHMIN, or the village and the BARBER, or the village and the WASHERMAN. But it would be wrong to regard the village as an amorphous unorganized public opinion acting in defence of moral values. This is too great a simplification. They were led, and the opposition to the village servants was organized, by the headman. His motive was not to defend moral values, but to squash people whom he thought were getting too rich. I cannot say whether he did so out of simple envy, or whether also his undoubtedly acute political instinct told him that too much wealth in the servant castes threatened his political power. It also is true that the unanimity with which the village opposed its servants was due in part to fear of offending the headman. There were one or two sceptics who saw the situation in a different light. A rich Boad DISTILLER asked me, ' Well ? In your country do spirits eat people ? Do *you* think spirits eat people ? What's the cause of all this ? Him ! ', and he waved his hand towards the headman's house.

The headman may have acted out of personal malice. But he was in fact backed by the village, since the campaign against the village servants kept down the cost of living.

The campaign now is turning against the TEMPLEMAN. The Kondmals temple, which is built of stone, needs re-plastering and a fresh coat of whitewash. While the British were in charge, this temple was kept in good repair by forced labour (*bheti*), which now has been abolished. In fact the village council still organizes unpaid labour parties for its own needs. A dam serving the irrigation system was repaired in this way. The village temple is being rebuilt by this form of labour. Those who absent themselves are fined by the council. On the whole the work is not resented, since it is for the direct benefit of the village. But the big temple belongs to all the Kondmals. Why should the village alone repair it ? The logical step would be to call for a working-party from all the Kondmals, but the village council decided to save itself the trouble of trying to impose voluntary labour on those who are outside the range of its sanctions. It has decided that the TEMPLEMAN and BRAHMIN C, who in fact consume the temple income, should pay for its upkeep. First they refused. Then they agreed, but said that they could not afford the work. In January 1954 they were still delaying, but sooner or later they will have to pay up or be dismissed. No servant is indispensable.

Although the specialist occupations of the village servants are restricted to the appropriate caste, they are not monopolies. Monopoly is impossible since the castes concerned are not organized for economic ends, neither to improve their economic position in the villages nor to restrict competition.

The economic relation is between the individual specialist and the village for which he works. The village sets the scale of wages. These wages on the whole enable a man and his family to live moderately but do not in themselves provide a large surplus which could be invested in land. Where village servants have in fact become extensive landowners, they have another source of wealth and their specialist activity is a part-time activity. Among them the priests seem to make most money.

When a village servant shows signs of getting a lot of money, the village seems to resent this and penalizes him. In the dispute that follows, victory goes always to the village, since the specialist castes are not organized to protect their members against these attacks.

The community controls its servants, and money made in village service has not been a factor in the redistribution of village land.

Crafts

None of the craftsmen—carpenters, weavers, doctors, diviners, goldsmiths and others—are village servants. None of them have a tithe relationship with their fellow-villagers. Their products or their skilled services are bought as the need arises and they are paid, usually in cash, sometimes in rice or paddy.

Some of these crafts are wholly or partially restricted to one caste. In the Kondmals carpenters, doctors and diviners are found in all castes, from the highest to the lowest. There is a caste of GOLDSMITHS, but in the village a SWEEPER family makes and repairs gold and silver ornaments. The elaborate decorated cloth for women is made by the WEAVER caste. Lengths of plain white cloth and cotton shawls are made by Boad OUTCASTES.

The materials which a weaver uses are not polluting. Castes higher than the WEAVER, which is just above the margin of the unclean, could handle the loom without degradation, but would be degraded by association with the WEAVERS. In any case, the question does not arise, since weaving requires some capital and a long training and does not offer spectacular profits. The restriction arises not so much through pollution concepts as through the high degree of skill required. It is not a craft that a young man can pick up by just watching. In effect, he needs to be born in a house where there is a loom. He must know the markets and the prices to pay for various sorts of cotton and dyes. His womenfolk must be able to spin cotton. Natural weavers might be born, but the talent is lost unless they are born into a household of WEAVERS.

On the other hand a man can pick up carpentry, doctoring or divining, because to some extent every man is his own carpenter, doctor and diviner. If he turns out to have an aptitude for one of these crafts, then his talent can grow and he can begin to work for others. Caste has no direct or indirect influence on entry into these trades.

There are eight looms in the village, all worked by men of the WEAVER caste, who live either in Market Street or at the end of Kond POTTER Street which adjoins the former market-place. In a nearby hamlet two Boad OUTCASTES have looms. All the WEAVERS were born in the village, but their fathers came from other places—from around Sonepur and Sambalpur (Map 1). The eight looms are divided between five lineages thus: a father and son, one each (A); three brothers, one each (B); three other men (C, D, and E). Among these the B group owns a shop and a cart and has a joint estate worth Rs.150 a year. E has land worth Rs.116 a year. The rest depend on their weaving to make a living.

Of the twenty-eight parts of a loom, the weaver makes for himself all but six, the total cost of which is Rs.25. These parts are bought from skilled craftsmen in Sonepur. In fact the maintenance of a loom does not exceed Rs.10 in a year. The weaver works five days in the week and goes to market on the other two days. Working these full five days, they produce cloth which sells for between Rs.10 and Rs.15 more than the cost of the cotton from which it is made. Out of this must come the cost of the dye and depreciation of the loom. Nor do the weavers work at full stretch all the time. Nor are they always certain of disposing of their cloths. If all is in his favour and he works hard, a weaver might show an annual profit of about Rs.400, enough to provide food for six adults. In fact, judging by the appearance of their houses and their style of living, weavers work hard enough to live comfortably, but not hard enough to produce a surplus for investment.

The weaver's market is competitive, not so much between weaver and weaver, since the prices of different kinds of cloth are fixed by tradition, but between weaver and the factory. The market, in fact, has been restricted largely to decorated cloths of local patterns, which are not produced in the factories. The plain white cloth for everyday use is generally factory-made. The weaver can make a living. But there is now no room for more people in the trade.

The WEAVER family B is rich. But their wealth comes from the shop and not from weaving. E was once one of the richest men in the village, but his wealth was got by trading and financing and was founded, so the story goes, not on the profits of his loom, but on the finding of a pot full of gold coins in the ground, where he was building a new house.

It is not possible for one man to combine weaving with other activities. His whole family is occupied. There is no slack season. E, when he was rich, neglected his loom and has returned to it only since his downfall. Of the group B, one brother looks after the shop, and leaves his loom : another divides his time between carting and weaving : the third is a full-time weaver.

The village carpenters, on the other hand, are part-time carpenters and have other sources of income. Their work consists in making ploughs, fitting the share, making door frames and doors, making house frames, and constructing two wooden agricultural implements, the plank and the scoop. Some of them can make beds. Some make wooden stools.

There is hardly a cultivator in the village who cannot do all these tasks for himself, except make a door frame, and many can do that. All the tools needed are an axe, an adze and a chisel.

For the finer work needed on a bed, a drill and a plane are required. It is the possession of these two instruments that marks off the carpenter from the layman. But there is not a great demand for joiners. A moderately well-off man, or a man fully occupied elsewhere, might ask a carpenter to make the frame of a new house. A few cultivators will commission a plough at As.12 or R.1. Looms need occasional repair. Cart wheels have to be reset every four or five years. Apart from this there is little to be done.

In the village there are eight men qualifying for the title of carpenter (*mystri*, a word used in India for anyone with any sort of expertize). Three are WARRIORS, one is a Kond POTTER, three are Boad DISTILLERS and one is a Kond. All but the Kond own farm land. None of them depend for their livelihood on their craft. The most skilled and the one who found the most employment was a WARRIOR, a relative of the headman. During the twelve months from November 1953 to November 1954 he undertook ten major tasks, for which he says that he received payment amounting to Rs.130 for a total of 55 days' work. The Government pay local carpenters Rs.2/8 a day, but the village people drive a harder bargain. The other carpenters did less work and earned less money, but I do not know how much.

It is clear that while carpentry might provide a useful income for individuals, it is not a means of acquiring a surplus for investment in land, and it is not a cause of the transfer of land from one group to another. It might provide a little—the

TABLE 19

SIZE OF ESTATES OWNED BY CARPENTERS

Person	*Gross value of annual paddy crop*
	Rs.
WARRIOR A	216
WARRIOR B	300
Kond POTTER	150
Boad DISTILLER A	50
BOAD DISTILLER B	33
Kond	—
Boad DISTILLER C	50
WARRIOR C	50

WARRIOR whose year's income is given above is increasing his holding of land—but it is not a source of conspicuous wealth.

The size of estates owned by carpenters is shown in Table 19.

Most people know a little about herbal medicines. The headman has a manuscript written by his grandfather and enlarged by his father, listing leaves and roots and the method of preparing them for different illnesses. An alternative is to call in a ritual specialist, either a BRAHMIN, who uses Sanskritic lore to find the cause of the sickness, or a diviner who is aided by a spirit. A few people from the village will go to the dispensary eight miles away, where there is a qualified doctor, but even the boldest usually wait until they think they are at the point of death. Those who are rich enough might visit or even summon the Ayurvedic doctor, who lives in Phulbani.

There is always sickness in the village. Everyone suffers from malaria. In the winter there are few who do not get an unpleasant cold, and in this season elderly people die from pneumonia. Dysentery, both amoebic and bacillary, is common, and children often suffer from failure of the liver, an alarming disease which causes the body to swell to unbelievable proportions. Many people are in a state of chronic disability resulting from hookworm anaemia. Scabies is common and runs its course until the sores turn septic and kill off the infecting agent. Cuts from an axe or pricks in the foot with a thorn result in purulent sores. Children and young men fall from mango trees. Women get their fingers caught in the grain pounder. Any disease or accident is aggravated by a diet that is deficient in everything except starch.

Yet there is only one man in the village who is a doctor (*baidyo*). When there is sickness, he is called in along with the BRAHMIN and the diviners and they all do what they can. The doctor expects a fee of a glass or two of rice—about As.5—but he does not haggle and hold out for more as do the BRAHMINS and the diviners. Possibly prestige is his main reward. The financial reward is not great.

Why are there not more doctors, when there is such an obvious need? The reason partly is that although there is a need there is not a great demand for doctors. All events are ordained beforehand, and if it is your fate to recover, you will recover. If it is your fate to call in a doctor, then you will call him in, but the issue depends not on what he does but on what is laid down for you. This attitude of acceptance is deeply rooted in the village mind, and I have heard a schoolmaster excuse misconduct with a girl whom he subsequently married on the grounds that he was doing what he was fated to do and there was no use in other people complaining. A second reason is that the field of curing is largely a ritual field and the market for secular specialists is limited. The present doctor can meet all the cases needing herbal medicines, which the householder cannot treat for himself. A doctor with a different technique —European or Ayurvedic—in whom the village has confidence would find a large market.

The doctor is of the WARRIOR caste. He and his elder brother's son have a joint estate, the annual value of which is Rs.400. His craft is very much a sideline and not a prominent source of wealth.

The diviner has a larger field than the doctor, since he can treat any sort of misfortune. A wealthy WARRIOR bought a shotgun. He had an early success and brought home a buck, the meat of which he sold. Then, for a year, he missed with every shot. The final humiliation came when he was out one night shooting at rabbits in the paddy nurseries. A large rabbit, mesmerized by the light, sat three yards from the end of his gun. He fired. But the cartridge which he had bought in the bazaar failed to go off. He cursed loudly and the rabbit fled. The next day he called in a diviner to investigate the gun. A fowl was sacrificed over it, but the diviner pronounced the gun blameless and said that the misfortune was caused by the man selling the meat of the buck, instead of distributing it, a little piece to all the houses, as other sportsmen do.

Again, the doctor caters for individuals, while the diviner can treat whole communities. If the community is his own, he is not always paid for the work. If he is called in by another community, he can name his fee and diviners with a high reputation make plenty of money. Even when they work for their own community, the diviners usually get most of the foodstuffs which are used in the ceremony. Between November 1952 and May 1953, three out-of-the-ordinary ritual divinations were held. In December, a rite was performed to drive away an insect (*Lepto-corisa SPP*) which was attacking the ripe paddy. One of the village diviners (a Kond POTTER) organized and presided over the ceremony. Then, in May, an expert (a WARRIOR) was called in from another village to find the spirits that were harming Bisipara. He worked the whole day and at night drove nails into the paths at the four corners of the village to keep out the spirits which he had expelled. The village then went on to the secular measures related above. A fortnight later a WARRIOR woman was seized with a fit, which did her no harm. But in the middle of it she rushed off screaming accusations against the WASHERMAN and saying that his spirit was eating her. The WASHERMAN was on the point of paying his fine and no further action was taken against him. Instead, one of the village's own diviners (another Kond POTTER) was asked to perform another type of rite to drive out the spirits.

There are two diviners among the clean caste-groups of the village. Both are of the Kond POTTER caste. A diviner works with the aid of a friendly spirit and he can only qualify as a diviner by giving proof of the possesssion of this spirit. He goes into a trance, reveals the name of the spirit which is in him, and afterwards provides the spirit with a resting-place in his house or his garden, and gives her [1] nourishment. All these spirits are Kond and the diviner addresses them in a mixture of the Oriya and Kui languages. He is quite open about their presence, unlike the man who keeps a malignant spirit for the sole purpose of making money.

Judging by results it is more profitable to keep a good spirit than just a money-making spirit. Both diviners, from a very poor beginning, are building up estates. The older, in particular, a good showman, is doing well since he organizes all the Kond-type rituals which are performed in the village, in particular the cult of the Earth spirit and the cult of the Mountain spirit. A woman has a bad dream, a man's foot is poisoned, someone cuts down a tree and then realizes that there might have been a spirit dwelling in that tree—all this is work for the diviner. The older man has an estate, the annual income from which is Rs.166, of which about Rs.60 comes from land he has bought since he took over the farm from his father. The

[1] A spirit is always invoked as 'Mother !'.

younger man's estate is worth annually Rs.50, of which Rs.40 comes from fields bought or taken in pledge in the last five years.

There are other experts in the village. A little apart from the other houses lives a family of BASKETMAKERS, who produce for the market. I was unable to discover anything about their income, but the only land they possess is a grant given many years ago by the Government in return for making screens of bamboo in Government buildings. Their work seems to support them, but apparently they are not making great profits, nor have they bought land.

Another expert is a man, a Boad DISTILLER, who makes strong rope, which is required for a carrying-sling or for lashing the plough-pole. One woman, a WARRIOR, is skilled at tattooing. Several others are in demand to put a fine finish to the mud walls of a house. Several men can make bamboo fish baskets and partridge traps. Much of this work—except rope-making and basket-making—is done for a favour. None is very profitable.

Some of the crafts, like basket-making and weaving, occupy the craftsman all the time. He has no chance to indulge in any other economic activity, unless he abandons his craft. The profits of this work are sufficiently large to maintain the craftsman and his family in moderate comfort, but not large enough to give him a surplus, or to attract competition. In the case of the weaver, entry into the trade is limited, because the skills are not easily acquired and because the market is limited by competition from factory cloth. In both basket-making and weaving, the materials handled are not polluting, but higher castes would be reluctant to do the work, even if they could learn the techniques, since they would be degraded by association with the WEAVERS and BASKETMAKERS. The profits offered are not outstanding and have not been a significant influence on the transfer of land.

On the other hand, crafts like the carpenter's, the goldsmith's, the doctor's and the diviner's are significant for the problem. The profits made from them although seldom large enough to provide a surplus for investment in land (except perhaps for the diviners), do provide an additional revenue for the cultivator, which might prevent him selling land. Their importance, as against weaving and basket-making, lies in the fact that they are part-time activities.

When we are discussing the fate of individual estate-holders, the ability to practise one of these crafts is important. But since the craftsmen are not numerous, and since they are not confined to any particular caste, income from crafts discussed in this chapter has not influenced the way in which land has moved from one group to another.

Agricultural Work

There are three ways by which a person can earn an income from agriculture other than by owning land. (Land taken in pledge is throughout counted as land owned, although strictly the property belongs to the pledger and not the pledgee.) These three are share-cropping, plough-service, and casual labour.

A man gives his land to a share-cropper because he is unable to work it himself. Very occasionally a rich man will allow a poorer man as a favour to share-crop a field, but usually it is necessity which drives the owner to let someone else do the work. A well-to-do man commonly allows to be share-cropped only those fields which lie in villages too distant for cultivation by himself and his servants. There is not a great deal of such land. I have a set of figures showing land owned in other villages, but since it is based solely on information from the owners and not checked by a survey of the ground,[1] it is not worth giving here. Other men, who have work which occupies them a large part of the time, or causes them to live away from the village, will allow their fields adjacent to the village to be share-cropped. In this category are a small number of fields, the value of the annual crop of which is about Rs.100. (The annual value of the total rice harvest of the village is approximately Rs.23,300, calculating from the average price for the year.) Others who are incapable of managing an estate will share-crop the land rather than supervise a plough-servant. A widow with young children will sometimes do this. There are some whose estates are breaking up and who reach a point where poverty will

[1] See Appendix B.

not allow them to keep plough-cattle. They then give their fields to a share-cropper. Occasionally a man miscalculates the amount of seedlings which he will require for transplanting, and instead of buying more prefers to share-crop the field with someone who has planted too many seedlings. The work of bringing upland fields into cultivation after they have been fallow for several years sometimes proves too much for one man, and he calls in another to share the labour with him and plant the crop.

Only one rich man takes land as a share-cropper. He is a WARRIOR and an expert cultivator, and the land he takes is very good garden soil adjacent to the village street, belonging to a Christian recluse. Other share-croppers fall in the middle range of wealth. A rich man normally gets enough grain from his own land, and if he needs more can buy land or take it in pledge. A poor man cannot share-crop, since he has not the money to buy and maintain the plough-cattle. About half of those who share-crop have land of their own. The other half makes money in some other activity and uses some of this money to keep oxen and share-crop fields.

Many people share-crop one or two fields for a short time, but in the village there are only nine persons who take shares in other men's land sufficiently regularly and on a sufficient scale for them to be known as share-croppers (*bhagwali*). These are two Kond POTTERS, one a diviner and the other a carpenter, and both owning land of their own as well : two Boad OUTCASTES, who own land and whose family derive an income from trading and casual labour : two Konds, who both are farm-servants and cultivate share-cropped fields by borrowing their masters' oxen : two Ganjam OUTCASTES, who have no land of their own, but make a living as carters : and, finally, a FISHERMAN, who bought his first field in 1953 and who makes a fair living selling flaked rice.

Again, many people give one or two fields to share-croppers for short times, but those who regularly give out all their land are only six : a WARRIOR widow with three children ; two WARRIORS, one crippled by infantile paralysis and the other too poor to keep plough-cattle ; the Christian recluse ; a widow of the Boad DISTILLER caste ; and a HERDSMAN crippled by rheumatism. The crop from these lands is worth Rs.860 each year, of which the owners of the land will get Rs.430.

In the normal share-cropping agreement the owner of the land provides only the soil. He normally sends a representative to help with the harvest, mainly to see that he is not cheated. The man who takes the field must prepare it, provide the seed, do all the work of transplanting, weeding, harvesting, threshing and winnowing. All those who took land and those who gave it, with only one exception, declared that the cropper was entitled to deduct the amount of seed sown before the division of the harvest, and maintained that they did so. The other man claimed that he did not allow his share-croppers to deduct the seed, but made a straight division of the total harvest.

Whatever the details of the method, no-one gets rich by cropping another person's land. In the main it is a method for the cropper to fill a few more stomachs : for the giver of the land it is a means of getting something out of land that otherwise might have to be sold for want of means to work it. No-one has made a fortune by cropping. I could see no signs of competition among croppers, nor among owners to find croppers.

There is, however, strong competition to find plough-servants, and men, particularly local men, are reluctant to take on the work. A plough-servant (*holya*) is engaged before the first rains and dismissed eight or nine months later when agricultural work is finished (sometimes sooner, when the harvest is gathered and the rush of work is over). The plough-servant lives in the family. They clothe him and feed him. In the morning, before he begins to work he gets a drink of rice-water and a few handfuls of parched rice : at midday he is given a share of the family's meal of cooked rice : in the evening he takes home a glass [1] of rice to be cooked in his own house. In addition he normally is given a sum varying from Rs.5 to Rs.20, either in a lump at the end of the season, or by instalments on festival days which occur during the season ; and at two-monthly or three-monthly intervals he is given a cloth to wear.

In the 1953–4 season there were at first nineteen persons who kept plough-servants. Between them they employed thirty persons, of whom six were boys kept only to pasture cattle and two were women employed by a shopkeeper to clean his cowsheds and work in his compound and on his farm. The majority

[1] See Appendix A.

TABLE 20

CASTE OF EMPLOYERS AND PLOUGH-SERVANTS

Caste of employer	*Caste of servant*	*Number*
Ganjam DISTILLER A	Kond POTTER	4
	Muslim	1
Ganjam DISTILLER B	Kond	1
	Ganjam OUTCASTE	1
WEAVER	WEAVER	1
Kond POTTER A	Kond POTTER	1
Kond POTTER B	Ganjam OUTCASTE*	1
Kond POTTER C	Kond	1
WARRIOR A	Ganjam OUTCASTE*	1
WARRIOR B	Kond	1
	Boad OUTCASTE*	2
WARRIOR C	Kond	2
	Boad OUTCASTE*	1
WARRIOR D	Kond	1
	WARRIOR	1
	Boad OUTCASTE*	1
WARRIOR E	Kond POTTER	1
WARRIOR F	Kond POTTER	1
WARRIOR G	WARRIOR	1
WARRIOR H	Ganjam OUTCASTE*	1
BRAHMIN	Boad OUTCASTE	1
HERDSMAN	Boad OUTCASTE	1
Boad OUTCASTE	Boad OUTCASTE	1
Boad DISTILLER	Kond	1
Boad DISTILLER	Kond POTTER	1

* These are boys aged between ten and twelve, employed to pasture cattle.

of those employed in this way did only farm-work. But the shopkeepers kept men who worked sometimes on the farm and

---

PLATE V

(*a*) PLANTING A PADDY FIELD

This is the first field planted in the village. The *mutha* headman's son has performed the necessary ritual, and the women are beginning to plant, dancing round in a circle, and singing, as they put in the plants. After a short time they leave this planted circle and begin to plant systematically from one corner of the field. See page 233.

The houses in the background are the Kond hamlet mentioned on page 23.

(*b*) A FIELD HALF-PLANTED

This field belongs to the Postmaster. It is situated on the outer limits of cultivation to the north of the village, and the scrub jungle and mountainside can be seen beyond it. This is a stream-irrigated field (see page 286). Between it and the line of shrubs beyond are several rain-irrigated fields.

On the far bank of the field stooks of seedlings await planting. Other handfuls lie on the surface of the water, ready to hand. The labourers are working from left to right of the photograph and the left side of the field is planted.

In spite of the clouds the day is hot and the women wear cloths over their heads to keep off the sun. The women are casual labourers from the Boad OUTCASTES, the Kond POTTERS, and the WARRIORS. The Postmaster's wife and daughter are working among them.

(*a*)

(*b*)

PLATE V

sometimes went messages for the shop. One person, a woman, had been employed for ten years : three had worked for three successive seasons : two had worked for two seasons : the remainder were in their first season with that employer.

Any fit man who is reduced to offering himself as a plough-servant can get a job. The only restriction is that he will work only for his own or higher castes, since he could not eat from the hands of a lower caste. Men of higher caste will do casual labour for men of lower caste, providing they are above the line of pollution, since they can accept payment in uncooked food.

The demand for plough-servants exceeds the supply because a better, although more uncertain, living can be made doing casual labour and petty trading. Plough-servants are poor men, owning no land. In service they can do no more than support themselves.

In the history of the transfer of land within the village, these servants appear not as potential landowners, but as a means of enabling a rich man to enjoy leisure, or to cultivate an estate while fully occupied in other work.

Much the most common form of secondary income is casual labour. It also can be a primary source of income. Such a labourer, whether man or woman, is called *mulya*. Occasionally, for a big job like plastering the walls of a new house, or filling a gully made in a field by the monsoon rains, the labourer and his employer will agree upon a sum of money for the complete job, and may include in the contract the right of the labourer to be fed, so long as he is at work. But by far the most common method is to hire the labourer by the day and pay him or her two meals or the equivalent rice, and an amount of paddy adjusted according to the status of the worker and the difficulty of the work.

Labourers are most in demand at transplanting time and harvest time. For two or three weeks in August, after the main fields have been ploughed until they are nothing but a sea of level mud, seedlings are lifted from the nursery beds and replanted. There are about five hundred thousand such seedlings in a field forty yards wide by fifty yards along, and every one is planted singly by hand. The work is done mostly by women and the hand that carries the seedlings moves more quickly than the eye can follow. Yet the work cannot be spread, since the seedlings are not sufficiently mature to be moved from the nurseries before the middle of August, and if the work is left beyond the middle of September, then the harvest will be late. A man who has only enough land to provide food for himself and his wife cannot unaided complete the task of transplanting in time. He needs women to help and he needs them at a time when everyone is demanding labourers.

One way out of the dilemma is to sow fields instead of planting them, and everyone does this. But the aim is to plant as many as possible, since the yield is greater, both because the earth is systematically covered and every plant has room to burgeon, and because it is easier to weed fields when the rows of paddy are straight. Even in flooded fields the grass grows.

With such a heavy demand for labour at one time, it would need only a little organization among the labourers to drive up their wage. But this is checked in three ways. Firstly, the demand is slackened by pressing every available member of the family into service, including children of about eight years upwards. Secondly, the smaller landowners engage as labourers for one another and for the big landowners. Mutual aid is rare and takes place only between brothers and close friends, but there is often a tacit agreement by which A and his family help to plant B's fields for a day or two, and then B goes with his group to work for A. But they do not simply exchange labour: they pay one another wages. Thirdly, the village council decrees the wage of a labourer for agricultural tasks and has threatened penalties for any employer who bids above this level. If you hire a man and *his* yoke of oxen to work for four or five hours (from dawn until ten or eleven o'clock in the morning) then you must pay him R.1. If the oxen are yours, then he gets one meal or its equivalent in rice and two measures (see Appendix A) of paddy. The measure used for issuing wages or paying tithes is one-eighth smaller than the 'government' measure, which is used for honest transactions in the shop, and the village council's decree is aimed particularly at those who try to attract extra labour by paying wages with the larger measure. The same wage—one meal and two measures of paddy—is paid for all ordinary agricultural work, except that a man harvesting may be paid with two meals and two measures of paddy.

The crisis comes again at harvest-time, although not in so acute a form, since the cutting can be spread over five weeks or more. The danger of not keeping up with one's neighbours is not so much that the grain will spoil, but that when the surrounding fields are cut and cattle are put to graze in the stubble, much of the grain may be eaten. The herd-boys are proverbially careless.

Labourers are used for other tasks. Much, of course, depends on the wealth of the employer, but a moderately well-to-do man will need someone to fetch wood for his fire, to carry manure to his fields, to bring wood and build a fence around his garden, and to keep the banks of his fields in good repair, apart from the routine agricultural tasks of ploughing, sowing, weeding and harvesting the different crops. Women carry manure, plant and harvest paddy, harvest various other crops, husk paddy, and keep the mud walls of the house in good condition.

It was not possible to calculate the total wealth paid out annually to casual labourers. Out of 179 households, at least 120 have one or more members, who will be found doing casual labour on other men's farms at some time during the year. Of the remaining fifty, some are fully occupied, like the WEAVERS and the BARBERS ; a few never work for others ; but many will engage in the slack summer season for work that offers a change and some money. For example, a party of four WARRIORS built the wooden frame of a house for a HERDSMAN for Rs.40. Others will re-thatch a house. But this type of person is not usually to be found doing hack work on anyone's land but his own. On the other hand, there are only five houses which depend almost entirely on casual labour to make a living. Four of these are widows. The fifth is a household the men of which spend long periods in prison for selling liquor, leaving the women to support themselves and the children by casual labour.

There are no restrictions on offering oneself for casual labour, except where the labour involves handling goods which might be polluted. For example, a clean household could not employ an OUTCASTE woman to husk paddy.

Share-cropping, plough-service and casual labour, three methods by which the product of the village land is distributed beyond the owners of the soil, are indirectly relevant to a discussion of the transfer of the village land. When an estate is disintegrating, share-cropping can decelerate or even stop the process, since it frees the owner from his ultimate necessity to provide plough-cattle. But this has not often happened and is not a major factor in preventing land from coming into the market.

The institutions of plough-service and casual labour are relevant in another way, since they make it possible for one man to cultivate a large estate. If a man depended on his kin-group or his age-mates or on any group where the tie was predominantly social, then the size of the working-group under his management would be limited to some extent by his social role. In fact the relationship of employer and employee is a purely economic one and judging by the rapidity with which employer and plough-servant part company—the initiative comes from both sides—the persons concerned prefer to keep it so. Kinship, friendship and for the most part caste are irrelevant. With the single exception that a man of clean caste will not work for an OUTCASTE (the situation does not arise, since the OUTCASTE group are labour-exporters rather than labour-importers), any man will work for any other man, providing the economic conditions are appropriate. The employer looks for a good worker. The worker wants a man who pays up and does not bully. That is all which counts.

PLATE VI

(*a*) CARRYING HOME PADDY

The field is rain-irrigated and stands to the east of the village. The paddy has been cut and has lain for a day to dry. Now it is being taken home for threshing.

The owner of the field, who is the doctor mentioned at page 113, is a WARRIOR. He stands on the left. The casual labourer also is a WARRIOR.

The weight of paddy in the carrying-sling is between eight and ten stone, and I found that I could not lift a full sling from the ground. From this field to the owner's house is a distance of more than half a mile.

(*b*) USING THE PLANK

The field, the buffaloes, and the plank all belong to the *mutha* headman. The labourer is a Kond POTTER.

The instrument is used to assist in liquefying the mud, and to grind down minor irregularities in the surface, which might upset the even distribution of water.

This is a stream-irrigated field.

(*a*)

(*b*)

PLATE VI

Therefore, other things being equal, the size of the labour-force which a man can command is set by the amount of money or goods he can afford to pay. The technique of management is purely economic and no limit is set by social considerations to the size of the unit of management.

As a means of making a fortune and buying land, neither share-cropping nor plough-service nor casual labour are effective.

Small Trading

Women of almost all castes, except the Boad DISTILLER, go out trading for paddy in Kond villages. Other castes said that Boad DISTILLER women were useless and lazy. The men of that caste said that their women had no need to do anything except their proper work in the house and farm—an assertion in some cases obviously untrue.[1]

The women trade, buying paddy for cash from Konds in other villages and driving as hard a bargain as they can. They bring home the paddy, husk it, sell the rice in Bisipara and dispose of the husks for cattle-food. A few persons have money of their own. The majority borrow Rs.10 or Rs.20 from a shopkeeper or from other persons in the village at an interest rate of half an anna in the rupee for eight days. For the lender this represents an annual interest of over 150 per cent, but the borrower does not find such short-term loans, which are almost invariably repaid on time, very burdensome. The loan is productive. For example, Rs.10 at certain seasons of the year will buy about fifty measures of paddy, which with average luck is the amount got in two trips. The paddy then is husked and produces roughly half the quantity of rice, about twenty-five measures. Twenty of these are sold for Rs.10. Fifty measures of paddy produce about two kerosene tins full of husks, which can be sold at As.2 per tin. Therefore the sale of husks pay four out of the five annas interest required and the trader is left with five measures of rice as the profit of her week's work—enough to feed an adult for ten days. The price of paddy varies from month to month, the average for the year being six measures to the rupee. In this example I have taken a lower estimate of

[1] This is probably connected with the effort of the Boad DISTILLERS to improve their status. See Chapter IX.

five measures to the rupee, which was the price ruling at the time I made the investigation.

There are two periods in the year when this trade flourishes. One is from the middle of March to the middle of June. These periods correlate directly with the agricultural work. From October until December every peasant is busy getting in the harvest. Grain in the upland fields is harvested at the beginning of October and by the middle of that month the first crops of irrigated paddy are ready. There is a heavy demand for labour. The price of rice and of paddy falls abruptly and very few people, except the shops and those who have salaries, will buy at this time of the year. For these two reasons the woman does not go out trading. She is fully occupied elsewhere and her margin of profit would be small. Paddy-prices and rice-prices continue at a low level to the end of February, and although agricultural work has ceased almost entirely by the end of February, this is the season of marriages and festivities, when traders stay at home. From the middle of March onwards the price of paddy rises and continues upwards until October, getting higher and higher as more people exhaust their stocks and are forced to buy. The difficulty is most acute during the planting season when the cultivator has to provide food for a large number of labourers. In response to this demand women go trading around the Kond villages to find paddy, except during the weeks preceding and during the transplanting season—that is, from the third or fourth week in June until the third or fourth week in August, when they are either occupied on their own land or can make good wages labouring on other farms. After that, trading starts again and goes on until October when the harvest must be gathered and the price of paddy falls.

Sometimes the women keep the rice by which they profit for their own household. Sometimes they sell it to get cash for clothes or other needs. They never sell it to the shopkeepers, whose price is too low. It is passed on to the house of a friend or a relative, usually in the same street. There is here an obvious caste restriction in that OUTCASTE women can sell only to people of their own caste. Apart from this, participation in the trade and the sale of rice is unrestricted by social factors : the market is purely economic.

The usual trading-party consists of two or three women, at

least one of whom is married. As a rule they are from the same street and usually—although not necessarily—from the same caste. The work is normally restricted to women. A few old men will buy paddy, but they cannot complete the whole transaction by themselves, since men do not husk paddy.

Some women are more assiduous traders than others, usually because they have to be, but no-one can manage more than two trips in a week and twenty-five measures of paddy are about as much as a woman can carry on her head over the rough hill paths. Twenty-five measures weigh approximately fifty pounds. I have no information of actual profits made or of the frequency with which different women went out trading, but it seems unlikely that the reward could much exceed Rs.2/8 in a week, or enough to provide rice for one person for ten days. Nor did I ask how the profits of such transactions were distributed within the household. It seems likely that division of the profit would depend on the needs of the household and the indulgence of the husband. There was no sign that this was specifically woman's wealth to be kept apart from other household funds.

There is another class of traders who exploit the Kond hinterland. They differ from the paddy traders because for some this is their only source of income, because they deal in a variety of goods, and because they trade throughout the full twelve months. There are eleven traders of this type, all but one of whom are women. Three of them have no other source of income : three are fairly prosperous, having land and other sources of income : the remainder are poor, but not dependent on this trade alone for their living.

The traders take out with them small quantities of oil used for washing the body, salt, parched rice, parched paddy, black treacle and cash. In some seasons they take out dried fish, which is brought from the Chilka Lake on the Bay of Bengal, and traded throughout the Kondmals. These goods they exchange for paddy, other cereal and lentil crops, vegetables and root crops, and liquor-flowers (*bassia latifolia*), when these are in season.

These traders invariably go out by themselves and some have a fairly well-established round in two or three Kond villages, but the goods they carry are of very little value and the amount they can trade is limited both by the demand and by their ability to carry loads. I cannot estimate the total turnover, but since so few people take part in this trade, and since their individual turnover is so small, the total turnover cannot be large. During September 1953 one woman made nineteen expeditions, always to the same three villages. She sold salt and parched rice : she brought back mostly paddy and a little of two other cereal crops, which ripen at the same time. During this time she borrowed Rs.2 from one of her Kond customers. Apart from this she financed the trading out of her own profits. This profit amounted to about Rs.10 in the month, which, since she is old and living alone, would be enough to keep her.

Apart from those who live by such trading, there are many housewives who vary the normal paddy trading by occasional expeditions of this type, in which they take out goods as well as money. The caste and status of those who regularly take out goods for exchange is shown in Table 21.

TABLE 21

CASTE AND ECONOMIC STATUS OF SMALL FULL-TIME TRADERS

Trader	*Caste*	*Sex*	*Remarks*
1.	WARRIOR	F	Widow with grown unmarried son. Little land.
2.	WARRIOR	M	Widower living alone. No land.
3.	WARRIOR	F	Widow with grown son. No land.
4.	WARRIOR	F	Widow. No land.
5.	WARRIOR	F	Husband has land worth Rs.200 annually.
6.	Kond POTTER	F	Widow living with married son. Family lives by trading, farm labour and land worth Rs.15 annually.
7.	FISHERMAN	F	Prosperous trading household.
8.	Kond POTTER	F	Prosperous household.
9.	Kond POTTER	F	Her husband is a Government messenger earning Rs.40 per month.
10.	Kond POTTER	F	Land worth annually Rs.33.
11.	WARRIOR	F	Land worth Rs.66.

The reason that more people do not go in for this type of trading is that the market is limited and the profits are not attractive. Most of those who do go in for it are driven by necessity. A few seem to go trading because they like this way of earning extra money. No woman can trade regularly unless she can hand over the responsibility of the household to another woman or unless the household consists of no-one but herself. Most of the widows and wives who go trading either have a daughter over twelve years of age or a daughter-in-law living in the house. Young women with young children cannot go out. This type of trade, therefore, is limited by the size of the market and by requiring traders of a certain status—namely, those females freed from the normal domestic responsibilities of a wife.

It takes a long time to cook a meal of rice and dal, and the traveller or person who wants refreshment in the morning or at four in the afternoon or while he is working in the fields will prefer parched rice. The grains of rice are roasted with salt in a thick iron dish. Preparation of this foodstuff, which is eaten in vast amounts, particularly by children, takes time and trouble since only as much rice as will cover the bottom of the pan can be done at one time and the grains have to be agitated to prevent them burning.

Great quantities of this or parched paddy (which is made in the same way without first husking the grain) are needed at planting-time since it is customary to give the labourers a snack in the middle of the morning. But this also is the time when all hands are needed in the fields. Consequently there is a market for parched rice and there are two or three households who live mainly by selling the finished product. The market shows the highest demand at planting-time, but there is also a good demand at the time of weddings, since there is then much coming and going. Throughout the year travellers and persons coming to the shops in the village patronize the makers of parched rice, and small traders will sometimes buy it to take around Kond villages.

A similar, though more restricted, market exists for flaked rice. This is prepared by pounding the grains under a weight about three times as heavy as the pounder used normally for husking paddy. Two houses in the village keep these pounders and combine the sale of parched rice, flaked rice and parched paddy. Flaked rice is cooked and its value is not in handiness but in providing a change for the palate.

Preparation of any of these forms of rice entails a lot of work, and one factor governing the return is the amount of labour available in the family. Roughly, for each measure of paddy used in the preparation, the product is sold for cash or paddy equal to two measures. To estimate their income satisfactorily, one would have to know not only the return on the raw material but also the turnover, and although I kept records of one man's customers for about a fortnight, I concluded that there is too much variation between the different months of the year to allow even an approximate guess.

However, the status of the households concerned gives some indication of the profits of the work. One was a HERDSMAN, living alone with his ten-year-old son in a tumbledown house. He had land worth Rs.10 in a year, which he gave out to share-croppers. The man was crippled by rheumatism and unable to walk. Both were badly dressed and the boy was several times pointed out with pity and affection as a lad who had no time to play. They worked together the whole day and every day, and from the profits they fed themselves and met their modest needs. Another was a HERDSMAN widow who combined food preparation with itinerant trading and casual labour. She appeared to support herself without making a surplus, for when she wanted to go on a pilgrimage to Puri, she had to pawn a piece of jewellery to raise the Rs.30 required. Two others were FISHERMEN, one of whom enjoyed land worth annually about Rs.66 given by the Government to his father for operating a ferry over the Salki River. (The river now is bridged and the ferry closed.) The other's household consists of himself, his wife, his wife's mother, and his wife's stepfather. He takes some land as a share-cropper but his main income derives from making and trading parched rice and flaked rice. The two FISHERMAN households have the advantage of numbers in that production need not stop while one of them takes the goods to the various markets and fairs.

Demand is limited because the product can be and is produced by every housewife, although every woman does not have time to produce all that she needs. For the same reason—that no special skill is required in the production—the trade is open to a large number of people and in fact other households than those listed above do occasionally make parched rice either for sale to all-comers or to meet an order. On the other hand the number of suppliers who can take advantage of a full market is limited to the group of 'high' castes.[1] The 'low' castes

[1] See Chart I.

and the untouchables would find custom only in their own caste-groups.

There are weekly markets, each on a different day, in the following villages, which either are in the Kondmals or are within a day's walking distance over the southern boundary: Khejuripara, Phulbani, Phiringia, Tikaballi, Sankerakhol and Udaygiri. All these markets are within walking range of the village and all are commonly visited, except the last. The two markets at Phulbani and Phiringia are eight miles distant in opposite directions from Bisipara. They are the nearest markets and are most often visited.

These markets, in particular the two nearest, offer weekly or bi-weekly employment to about a dozen men from the village. These men act as the first rung in a ladder of middlemen. Perishables, like the rare cabbage or cauliflower or more commonly tomatoes and fruits, and semi-perishables, like potatoes and sweet potatoes, are usually sold directly to the consumer by the grower or his agent. But such things as rice, paddy, other cereal crops, lentils, oilseeds, ginger and turmeric are bought by merchants. Oilseeds, lentils, ginger and turmeric are exported to the plains and the other crops are sold in local shops, mainly to Government employees. The ordinary grower—in nine cases out of ten a Kond—brings small quantities to the market, too small for the merchant to handle at his own depot. There is savage competition among the merchants to buy these crops, combined with a very real co-operation to keep down prices. The merchant solves these two dilemmas by employing agents. The agents spend the day buying small quantities, and hand over the pile when the market closes. They are given an advance of money —a few use their own money—and they find out at the beginning of the day how much each merchant intends to pay that night for a measure of whatever is likely to come into the market at that season. They then compete physically to buy. As a grower comes to the market he is seized by a horde of shouting men, usually offering much the same price, but trying to steer the customer towards their own piece of ground. The ethics of the market-place say that victory goes to the trader who first lays hands on the customer, but except in the rare cases in which a customer knows his own mind, there is usually a scuffle. The grower who comes to the market has a good idea of what he should get and the trader's legitimate profit is very small: but he can often get more by sleight of hand with his scales. At least three of the dozen market-traders in Bisipara have been prosecuted in the last five years for owning weighted scales.

I kept records for three months of the market activities of such an agent, who was under an obligation to me. For each visit to the market he showed a profit between As.8 and As.12, but he was a very cautious man and other information leads me to suspect that a truer figure would be between R.1 and Rs.1/4.

The profits, then, of the middlemen's work at this level are not high, if they are considered as a sole source of income. Considered as a subsidiary source they are quite good, since Rs.2 is sufficient to provide rice for the meals of one adult for eight days, reckoning from the average price of rice through the year. The return at least is enough to justify two sixteen-mile walks on two successive days every week.

The vigour of the competition among traders in the market-place seems to show that there is not room for more of them. The trader needs to be a man, fairly active, and of a personality suited to the work. He needs no equipment except scales which costs about Rs.3 and lasts a lifetime, and some ability at mental arithmetic. Caste sets no limit on those who can engage in the work and OUTCASTES may handle even rice. The rice is transmitted through the merchant and a shop, and the customer, if he cares about such things, is concerned only that the man who weighs out and hands the food to him should be of clean caste. Those from the village who practise this trade are one WARRIOR, the WASHERMAN (since the time that his children have been big enough to do the washing), five Boad DISTILLERS and about five Boad OUTCASTES. I asked a WARRIOR why these castes should do the work and not others. He replied:

'WARRIORS? The rest of us don't need to do it. X started doing it when he was young and very hard up. DISTILLERS? It's the sort of work that suits them. The WASHERMAN? He's out for all he can get. Other castes, like the Kond POTTERS are not quick enough to do it. As for the OUTCASTES, they're good at any sort of cheating.'

The Konds grow two cash-crops, turmeric and oilseeds, and these with the liquor-flowers and hides are the area's exports.

Everyone with land, Kond or Oriya, will grow a small quantity of oilseeds of either of the common types, *sesamum indicum* or *brassica campestris*. Oriyas take theirs to the oil-presser and usually retain the oil for domestic use. The Konds produce sufficient to sell.

Turmeric is a root crop, which when dried and powdered is an ingredient of curry and is used for dye. In the village I have seen only two turmeric-gardens, and the Oriyas say that they can make more money trading in the crop than in growing it. They say that its cultivation involves too much hard labour. The Konds clear a field on the mountainside, where the slope is often 1 in 2 or 1 in 3. They cut down the secondary jungle and burn it and sow the crop in the ash and pockets of soil. The young plants have to be protected from the sun's rays, so that a fresh area of jungle must be felled to provide brushwood to shade the plants. This is why turmeric-growing is considered hard work. Then the root of the crop is dug up, cleaned, boiled, dried, lightly rubbed to clean it, rubbed more heavily a few days later, and then thoroughly dried. It is then ready for sale.

The liquor-flower grows on a tree, *bassia latifolia*, which requires no special cultivation. Trees which happen to be on a man's land are his property. Trees in the jungle near the village are owned by individuals who have established a customary right to them. The flowers of the tree can be dried and eaten, and many poor families—particularly Konds—live on them for a month or two in the year. They also can be made into liquor and it is for this purpose that they are exported to the distilleries on the plains. Distilling is illegal in the Kondmals, although many people have a home-still. The tree blooms in February. A month or so later a nut forms where the flower fell and this nut is gathered, boiled, shelled and the pith is used to make the cheapest form of oil available in the area. Poor people use this oil for washing and it can be used for cooking. It is not exported from the area, although the local shops sell it. Pressing the oil is a craft not confined to any particular caste. In the village a Kond POTTER and a Boad OUTCASTE own presses.

The trade in turmeric, which is much the most profitable and involves the largest sums of money, begins about the end of February and ends in April ; although small quantities continue to come into the market throughout the year. Here is a précis of an account of a season's trading in 1951, given to me by a reliable informant of the HERDSMAN caste:

(1) He began in March. He went with WARRIORS A, B and C to three Kond villages without success. On their way home, at a fourth village, they paid Rs.80 for a heap of turmeric, which they bought 'blind' (*khutu*), i.e. without weighing it. When they brought it back to Bisipara, the merchant-shopkeeper X weighed it at 246 pounds and gave them a commission on the money they had borrowed from him of Rs.2/13. Profit each As.14.

(2) They borrowed Rs.100 from the merchant X. The party consisted of the informant, and WARRIORS A, D, E and F. They failed to get any turmeric.

(3) (Sum of money borrowed for this expedition not known.) Informant, with WARRIORS A, D, E, F, G, Kond POTTERS A, B, C, D, and Kond A, went to one village and bought from one man 1,050 pounds of turmeric, which they weighed out in front of the grower and for which they paid him R.1 for every three pounds. The merchant's scales made it 1,200 pounds and he paid them Rs.1/1 per three pounds. Profit each Rs.6.

(4) Informant went out with WARRIOR A, having borrowed Rs.200 from the same merchant. The morning was a failure, but in the afternoon they found some turmeric, but when the growers discovered that they carried only five-rupee notes, they refused to sell. At that moment another party arrived, consisting of WARRIORS E, H, I, J, K and HERDSMEN B and C, and carrying coins worth Rs.400, Rs.300 of which had been advanced by merchant X and Rs.100 of which was their own. They weighed out 900 pounds from two growers and paid them Rs.200, i.e. R.1 for each 4½ pounds. They hired six carriers from the village and paid them R.1 each for two trips. On the merchant's scale the amount turned out to be 1,140 pounds and he paid them Rs.1/1 for every three pounds. Profit each Rs.20. (Later that week all the members of this party sacrificed a goat to Bagho dei, who in the circumstances might be called 'the bitch goddess'.)

(5) The informant, with Boad DISTILLER A, Kond A and Kond EHRDSMAN A, borrowed Rs.80 from merchant Y and visited three Kond villages. The turmeric was there but the growers would not bring it out.

(6) The same party went out next day and bought a heap 'blind' for Rs.40. The merchant bought it 'blind' giving them Rs.50. Profit each Rs.2/8.

(7) The same party borrowed Rs.80 from the same merchant and bought 90 pounds for Rs.20. The merchant gave them Rs.23 for it,

bringing down the price because the roots were wet. Profit each As.12.

(8) With WARRIOR L and Rs.80 of his money, he bought a heap 'blind'. They hired a cart to bring it home, dried it, and then sold it to merchant X for Rs.90, having retained 12 pounds for their own use, which is enough to last twelve months. Profit each Rs.4.

(9) With Kond A, Boad DISTILLER A and Kond HERDSMAN A, he borrowed Rs.200 from merchant X. They spent Rs.160 and sold the turmeric to a different merchant, Z, for Rs.185. They told merchant X that they had been unsuccessful and returned his money and profited each by Rs.6/4.

The informant then gave the details of four more expeditions, the profit from which was Rs.14/8. When April had come and the weather was warmer, he went out less frequently. But in all he made a further fifteen expeditions, the profit from which was Rs.28. His profit for a season of 28 expeditions, each of which lasted a day, was Rs.82/7.

Why do they go out in large parties, so cutting down the profit to individuals ? One reason is to save money on carriers, but a more important reason is that a large party is more able to intimidate and confuse the Konds. The turmeric is never out waiting to be bought. It takes hours of persuasion before a Kond will produce it, and things go easier when there are relays of persons to bully and joke with him. Again, as is obvious from expeditions 3 and 4, an important source of profit is under-weighing the roots. This can be done by shifting the string from which the scale is suspended : another way is to prop up the weighing pan with the big toe. When there are seven or eight men milling around the scales, shovelling in the roots, shouting at the grower, making jokes with his wife and daughters and causing havoc all round, cheating becomes easy.

The merchants too are cheated. During the season there is always one or more camping in the village and trying to intercept men who have borrowed money from other merchants and take their loads at a higher commission. This happened in expedition 9. Swindling, in fact, is the trader's art.

Although the men go out in parties, trading is highly individualistic. Parties, as is shown by the account above, are continually breaking up and reforming in different ways. There is a slight tendency for men of the same street to go out together, but no combination is impossible, except one which crosses the barrier of clean and unclean castes. The OUTCASTES do their own trading.

There are few restrictions of entry into this trade. Men only may go, and a man needs to find at least one other man who will go along with him. Apart from that, it is free for all, except for the one or two who have proved themselves incompetent or dishonest beyond the accepted level of dishonesty, and who no longer can get credit from the merchants.

Although the trade goes on year after year, very few people build up a goodwill contact with the growers. This is partly the result of the extreme suspicions of the Konds towards outsiders, even outsiders with whom they have been acquainted all their lives, and partly it is due to the cut-throat attitude of the trader to the grower. There are two exceptions to this. A party, the nucleus of which is two Boad DISTILLERS, neighbours, and Kond A, who appears in the trading story given above, has for the past three years monopolized the trade from three remote Kond villages, which formerly dealt with traders from Phulbani. This was represented as an unusual and temporary situation, for sooner or later the Konds were bound, so informants said, to realize that they were being cheated and want to change their traders. Villagers think that there is something odd about any economic relationship which endures for a long time and said that no master with his wits about him will keep the same servant for more than two years, and no sensible servant will tie himself to the same master for more than two years. The other exception is that the headman uses his influence to cause certain of the Kond growers to retain their crops until late in the season, when turmeric is getting scarce and the price is rising, and then sell it to him at the price ruling at the height of the season. They seem glad to do this, for he can oblige them in other ways.

No figures for the total profits of the village in trading in turmeric could be obtained, since the relationship which leads to the giving of such information can be built up with only a few persons. I would guess that most households whose men go out trading in turmeric will make about Rs.50 in the three months' season. All castes which are represented in the village by adult fit males went trading for turmeric except the BRAHMIN, the WRITER, the Ganjam DISTILLERS, the WEAVERS, the SWEEPERS, the

BARBER and the TEMPLEMAN. All these were occupied elsewhere. (From the middle of February to the middle of June is the slack season for cultivators.) The SWEEPER does not go, partly because he is a part-time goldsmith and can make money in this way, and partly because, being the lowest caste, he could join neither the 'clean' parties or the OUTCASTE parties.

The trade in liquor-flowers follows a different pattern. The crop from trees which belong to Oriyas in the village is normally sold directly by the owner to the merchant-shopkeepers. The traders deal with liquor-flowers brought to the village by Konds. They sit in ones or twos at the cross-tracks to the north and south of the village and intercept the Konds. The flowers are bought by volume. The trader gives R.1 for four kerosene tins of flowers and receives Rs.1/4 from the merchant. I asked how the trade was possible, when a further half-mile walk would take the Kond to the merchant's shop. Informants said that it is partly because the Konds are frightened of the shop and prefer to deal with persons they know and partly because the shopkeeper refuses to deal in small amounts. Since the goods are measured by volume, there is less opportunity for spectacular cheating, and for this reason Konds are not afraid to venture outside their village, particularly as the crop is so much less valuable than turmeric. One man can carry turmeric worth Rs.30 or more : but the liquor-flowers are bulky and baskets cannot accommodate more than the value of about Rs.2. I neglected to enquire how many people traded for liquor-flowers in 1953, but I think the potential traders are much the same as those who trade in turmeric. An account kept of seventeen days' trading by two young men in February 1953 showed that in that time—virtually the whole season—they made a joint profit of Rs.60.

I took no accounts of the trading in oilseeds and know only that it is done by men in February and March, that they go out to Kond villages, and that the profits are smaller for the time spent than are the profits of turmeric and liquor-flowers.

Seen from the State (Orissa) or the Indian economy as a whole, these cash-crops are of no great importance, although in the 1930's one official estimated that the Kond hills supplied 50 per cent of all the turmeric used in India. The District is poor and the State (Orissa) Government is reluctant to allot sufficient money even to improve the two roads which they maintain in the hills.

But from the point of view of the inhabitants the cash-crops are of primary importance, since they are the main source of cash for the Konds, and trading in them provides a considerable income for the indigenous Oriyas.

The trade, broadly speaking, is open to everyone. Furthermore, it is seasonal and takes place at a time when cultivators have no work on their lands. It does not draw labour from other productive activities, and the Oriya cultivator need sacrifice no time or resources that would otherwise be spent on his land. Nor does the trader need any capital of his own, since in the majority of transactions he acts as an agent for the merchant.

If, during those three trading-months, a man makes even as little as Rs.50, that is sufficient to provide five-sixths of the rice which an adult requires to feed himself, calculating at the average yearly price. If he can buy when rice is cheapest, he will get at least twice as much. Those who have no land can maintain themselves and their families by trading and casual labour. Those whose estates are small can make up the balance required for their needs or even make a surplus to be used in contingencies which otherwise might cause land to be sold. Those who are rich can acquire additional funds for productive investment.

No man can cultivate even the smallest paddy-estate unless he has plough-cattle. Even those who own no land except a small garden will borrow or hire a yoke of cattle rather than try to prepare the soil with a hoe. The single important exception is the hill-field of the Kond, in which turmeric and some cereals are grown. But in the Oriya villages no cultivation takes place without the use of plough-cattle.

Several people keep cows for breeding. But no-one's herd is big enough for him to be sure of being able to replace cattle which die or are taken by wild animals. Everyone, therefore, at some time or another, has to buy an ox.

The prices of cattle, the costs of their maintenance and their working life have been discussed in Chapter IV. The local cattle-market is at Tikaballi, about twenty miles from Bisipara. This is beyond the southern boundary of the Kondmals, but it is an area with which the villagers are quite familiar and where they have many affinal and uterine kinsmen. Another market, both cheaper and bigger, is sixty miles away, on the plains, three days' walk from the village. This is foreign country, and out of a sample of forty-six men questioned, not one could mention a relative or a friend in this area at whose house he could expect hospitality. The biggest and cheapest market is one hundred miles away, close to Berhampur. Most men who decide to buy cattle for themselves will go to Tikaballi or will search for the odd beast that finds its way to the nearer markets of Phulbani or, more rarely, Phiringia. A few will go in parties of two and three to the market sixty miles away. They go in the hot season, when they can camp out. They return in large parties and only disperse when they get into the hills. Other men buy from cattle-traders, either commissioning them or taking their chance when a trader comes back from an expedition.

These traders are always (in the village) Boad OUTCASTES, and they make the long journey either to the market sixty miles away or to the one near Berhampur. They go in parties of four or five by bus and return driving the cattle. They then hawk the beasts around their own village, around Kond villages or in the local markets at Phiringia and Phulbani.

Like most forms of trading which involve a heavy capital outlay, trading in cattle is financed not by the traders themselves, but by rich men, for whom the traders act as agents. There are two such men among the Boad OUTCASTES and their money provides at least the nucleus of the funds of most trading expeditions. I was not able to get a good account of the way in which profits are divided, or of the frequency of expeditions, and consequently I can make no estimate of the average annual income got by the traders, and by the men who financed them.

This trade is confined to the Boad OUTCASTES. It is not that they have any greater knowledge of cattle, for every cultivator can tell the age and condition and probable working powers of an ox or a buffalo. Nor are there any pollution concepts involved, while the beast remains alive. Other castes buy cattle for their own use and occasionally sell beasts to their fellow-villagers. But the Boad OUTCASTES alone follow this calling as a trade. The reason is possibly historical, since there is among the Boad OUTCASTES a long tradition of acting as agents for Konds and to a lesser extent for Oriyas, in economic transactions which involve contact with foreigners, that is, people from outside the hills. The victim for the rite of human sacrifice was usually kidnapped from the plains, and the work was done exclusively by the OUTCASTES. The ultimate reason for this remains obscure. The OUTCASTES may trade in cattle because until recently they had less land to keep them occupied than other castes, and because trading in food and cash-crops is less open to them owing to pollution concepts and perhaps to the fact that the Konds suspect their honesty even more than they suspect the honesty of Oriyas. But that does not explain why other castes should not trade in cattle. Possibly the profits are not sufficiently high.

Lorries travel from wholesalers in the plains to the shops at Phulbani and an occasional lorry gets through to the shop at Phiringia. The same vehicles take some of the cash crops down to the plains. Off the roads everything is carried by men, who use two baskets slung from a bamboo yoke, or by women who balance loads on their heads.

The other means of transport is the bullock cart. There are ten carts in the village, five of which are owned by shopkeeping families: two Ganjam DISTILLERS have one each; the WEAVER shopkeepers have two; the WRITER has one. Of the rest, two Kond POTTERS have one each, one Ganjam OUTCASTE has two, and another has one.

The cheapest cart costs about Rs.40. The best cart costs Rs.80. They are all built in the same pattern, but the cost varies with age and quality, and to some extent with size. The least one could pay for a pair of oxen, fit to draw a cart, is Rs.60. The price for really fine beasts, which are seldom seen in the hills, might go up to Rs.400 for the pair.

The capital outlay therefore is heavy and only those who can save a considerable amount are able to invest in a cart. An exception to this is a scheme promoted by the Leaf Company,[1] in which men can buy carts by hire-purchase over a two-year period. The only persons in the village who have taken advantage of this scheme are the two Ganjam OUTCASTE families.

A carter has three main sources of custom: the Leaf Company; merchants who want turmeric and liquor-flowers shifted to their depots; and casual custom from his fellow villagers. The Leaf

[1] The Leaf Company is described later in this chapter and in the following chapter.

Company offers most of its work from August to November. The leaves (*dyospyros menalexylon*), which are used for the outer wrapping of the Indian cigarette (*bidi*), are gathered from the jungle and packed into bundles about two feet square by five feet long, a load for four men. Carters are then employed to bring these bundles from outlying store-sheds to depots on the main road, where they can be collected by lorries for transport to the plains. The carters usually travel by night in convoys and there are always two men to a cart. Taking into account the expenses of feeding men and oxen, and of normal upkeep on the cart, the carter should clear between Rs.10 and Rs.15 in a week. The shifting of turmeric from the shops in the village to depots at Phulbani and Tikaballi begins in April and finishes around November. Liquor-flowers are shifted in the first part of this period. The rewards are about the same. Casual work consists of bringing a load of wood from the jungle at Rs.2, if the carter cuts the wood, and R.1 if the consumer has cut the wood.

No-one earns a steady Rs.15 throughout the season. Firstly, neither oxen nor men can continue the constant to and fro journeys through the night without a break. Carts have to be repaired. The turmeric movement does not get into its stride until August and it is not always possible for the carter to find an employer before that time. Those carters who are also shopkeepers need the cart for shifting stores. Those carters who have their own land find that their employers and the land are making the maximum demand on them at the same time.

Profits made from owning a cart have not been a significant factor in the transfer of land, although the presence of the Leaf Company may make a difference. It has been operating only five years. Formerly a man had to be fairly prosperous before he could afford a cart. Now he can get one through hire-purchase (or could—the scheme has been suspended for a year). But rich men, other than those who, like shopkeepers, needed a cart for their own work, saw no point in buying one, since carting clashes with cultivation.

I have described seven kinds of trade : in paddy ; itinerant small traders ; sellers of processed rice ; marketmen ; trading in cash-crops ; cattle traders ; and carters.

These activities fall into two groups : those which are (or

can be) supplementary to cultivation and those which exclude cultivation. Of the latter sort are the itinerant traders, most of whom are old women who either have no land or are freed by the presence of another woman from the responsibilities of the household and the farm ; sellers of processed rice, whose work tends to occupy them the whole time ; and carters, for whose services there is maximum demand at the height of the cultivating season.

Of the other trades which can be carried on by families owning land, two offer regular but not spectacular profit. One of these is trading in paddy, which is done by women and fitted into their household and farm duties, the latter taking precedence; the other is the work of the marketman. Activities of this sort are vital in providing for the wants of some households and in some they provide a useful small surplus. But they do not by themselves offer a return sufficient for investment in land. This is particularly so, since the profit comes in small regular sums and is likely to be spent as soon as it is earned, to provide for current needs.

On the other hand it is less difficult for a trader to save the profits of his trade in cash-crops, since they come all within three months and in relatively large sums. The same, possibly, is true of trading in cattle, but I have not sufficient information to be sure about this. Trade in cash-crops does not interfere with cultivation, requires no capital, and demands no particular skill or training. It is carried on by a much larger number of persons than is any other trade. It must be regarded, potentially, as an important source of income having an indirect effect on the movement of land, whether to provide sums for further investment in land or whether to prevent land being sold to meet contingent costs.

Services and Trading in the Economic History of the Village

Under the heading ‘ services and trading ’ I have grouped together four sets of activities : village service ; crafts ; agricultural work ; and small trading. I have tried to assess their significance for the transfer of land between individuals, and ultimately between one caste and another.

Of the village servants some can combine cultivation with their work and others are fully engaged and could not cultivate extensive estates. Some of them—in particular the ritual specialists—are well-off. But the village resents excessive riches in its servants and is able to discipline them and to some extent it can control their earnings. These servants are a part of the traditional village, and although some of them have been able to exploit the new economic situation in ways which will be described in following chapters, in no case has income from their service brought the main part of their wealth. As village servants, they are, so to speak, on the sideline of the economic conflict that has been fought out since 1855. In other capacities some of them have participated in the conflict.

Nor has the practice of a craft been made particularly profitable by changed economic conditions. A few craftsmen, particularly in the early years of this century, were paid in grants of land for Government service. On the other hand, such crafts as weaving have been adversely affected by competition from machine-made cloth.

I do not deny the usefulness of income from craft or village service to the small landowner, since on many occasions this additional revenue has enabled an estate to be kept intact. But the profits are low and the persons concerned are few in the total population of the village, so that in the general picture of land-transfer from one group to another, these activities are not an important feature.

Those who depend largely for a living on agricultural labour, whether as share-croppers, plough-servants or casual labourers, do not get rich. Before 1855 the person without land who had no special craft or service to offer, maintained himself largely by labour, as he does now. The difference, so far as the evidence goes, was in his relationship to his employer. Nowadays the great majority of such relationships are casual, short-lived, and rapidly changing. No bond other than the purely economic one of wage and labour given in exchange seems to develop, and both partners admit that they prefer it that way. But in the old days, to judge from statements made to-day and from the 'survival' of certain relationships of the master-client variety, the bond was much more personal and resembled the relationship to-day of the village servants to the village community. The labourer was in a position of quasi-kinship in his employer's household.

It is not the income of the labourers, but rather the exclusively economic character of the bond between landowner and his servant, that gives the institution of agricultural labour its significance for the problem of land-movements. The labourer never gets rich enough to acquire land for himself. But the fact that he has no ties with any particular landowner makes the labour-market free and has enabled those who acquired large estates to work them, although they are comparative newcomers to the village. The employers needed no qualifications based on social factors like kinship or caste or even political power in the village. The client has become the workman of anyone who will pay him a daily wage. Hence the virtual extinction of clientship.

Whether or not there were traders in paddy and itinerant small traders before 1855 is impossible to say. What evidence there is suggests that there probably were not. Such trading needs an environment in which it is safe for small parties to move around. In the early days there was hostility between the Konds and Oriyas and the country was more heavily infested with wild animals than at the present day. The trade is based on cash and I doubt whether Konds would have handled cash in those days. The only possibility was a trade in salt.

The same considerations apply to the sale of processed rice. But whatever is the truth, neither of these forms of trade have been an important factor in the transfer of land. As in the case of crafts and village service, the subsidiary income might be useful to landowners and might be a means of survival for those who have no land, but this form of trade has never provided a sufficient surplus for investment in land.

The first Britons to visit the hills stated that there were no markets, but they did observe a trade in the same products that are traded to-day—turmeric and oilseeds, though no mention is made of the liquor-flower. Some of this trade was carried on by merchants travelling in the hills (which indicates that the area was safer than one would imagine from other accounts) and at other times the Konds went down to markets in the plains. Unfortunately these first two observers (Campbell and Macpherson) frequently referred to everyone who lived in the hills as a Kond, although in some contexts it is clear that they were talking about Oriyas. Therefore we cannot be sure whether the visitors to the plains markets were Konds or Oriyas and we cannot guess how far developed was the trade in turmeric, and to what extent the Oriyas participated as middlemen, if they did so at all.

Even if this trade was as fully established as communications in those days would allow, and even if Oriyas were participating as middlemen, it seems unlikely that it could then have caused a re-distribution of wealth and a change in the pattern of village landowning, because it fails to do so now. The effect of wealth earned in trade on this scale is mainly negative, in that it prevents some land from being sold to meet contingent costs. Higher middlemen make bigger profits. But those who go out to Kond villages in search of turmeric cannot by this means alone amass sufficient money to make more than an occasional purchase of land. More often the money goes in everyday purchases.

Finally, since there are no caste restrictions on participation in these forms of trade, everyone can and does try to make money at them, and wealth derived from trade in the various cash-crops will not explain why land has moved away from one caste towards certain other castes.

CHAPTER VI

MERCANTILE WEALTH: SALARIES, INVESTMENT AND MANAGEMENT

JUST as cash-crops are a visible export, so service in the employ of the Government or of private individuals and companies is in effect an invisible export from the village. Whether or not they have to leave the village, the villagers export their labour and receive cash in return. Examples are the commission which the *mutha* headman draws on the revenue collected, the small salaries of village watchmen and the bungalow watchman, the larger salaries of schoolmasters, messengers and policemen, the wage paid to those who work for the Leaf Company and money which the Government pays to casual labourers engaged in public work. It is obvious that these sources of income have existed only since Government was established in the area in 1855, and many of the posts were not created until much after that date.

I will examine the main sources of this type of income, again asking how profitable they are and in what way they are restricted to certain groups or categories of persons, and whether they have been responsible for the particular pattern which land-distribution now exhibits.

The second part of this chapter concerns the use that is made of surplus income. The types of investment considered do not include investment in land or in such non-productive capital as gold and silver. I have arbitrarily extended the meaning of investment to include such activities as the lending of paddy, money-lending, the sale of surplus paddy or rice, and contracting. The same questions will be asked concerning the relevance of these sources of income to the transfer of land.

The third part of the chapter is concerned with commerce, not as in the previous chapter with the work of the small traders, but with a class higher up the ladder of middlemen—those who employ others to work for them or those who, even when they do most of the work themselves, are full-time merchants working on a large scale. The most important of these are the shopkeepers. The same questions will be asked, but in practice it was impossible to get accounts of the profits of running a shop, not only because the shopkeeper is much less frank about his profits than is the small trader, but also because one type of shop which has been a main factor in the redistribution of land in the village, no longer exists—the drink-shop.

Government Service

There are no members of the Civil Service resident in the village. Of junior departmental officials the only one stationed in the village within recent years was an assistant in the Veterinary Service—locally known as the 'Stockman'—whose office-building still stands. But the appointment was not filled between September 1952 and January 1954, when I lived in the village.

The village is the capital of Besringia *mutha*, and the *mutha* headman lives there. His position is hereditary, subject to confirmation by the Government. His principal task is to collect the revenue of which there are three types : a Watchman Tax, paid by every landowner ; a Plough Tax, also paid by every landowner ; and Land Tax, paid by Oriyas but not by Konds or untouchables, that is, not by Adibasis or Scheduled Castes. The headman is not responsible for the tax, providing he can show that he has made efforts to collect it, and prosecutions for arrears are undertaken by the Revenue Department. The headman is thus not a proprietor but an hereditary official. In addition to this, he must report deaths by violence and may hold court to try civil cases, but the litigants always have an appeal to the Government courts. He must also facilitate the work of visiting officials by ensuring that the appropriate persons are present when officers arrive.

The headman is paid 12½ per cent of all the Land Revenue which he collects and this amounts in most years to about Rs.35. But his actual income is much higher than this. From the earliest days the Oriya headmen have collected from their Kond subjects various dues (*mamul*). Apart from a few rupees, which they can levy as fees when they hear a case, they expect a gift when a rich Kond dies or gets married ; they expect and usually get free hospitality when they tour in their *mutha* to collect revenue ; and they can make all sorts of further exactions from the advantage of their position as Government representative. To-day these demands are much decreased through the constant efforts of the Government to protect the Konds, but they still represent a considerable source of income. How large this income is, I was naturally unable to discover, since the headman has an interest in concealing it, and since it comes from many different sources.

In the forty-nine villages under the control of the *mutha* headman, there are village headmen (*gram polis*). They are not paid, although they may get small fees for hearing cases as arbiters, and those with a strong personality and a following may be able to exact some dues. Their principal duty is to report deaths by violence and crimes in their village, and the *mutha* headman will expect their help when he tours to collect the taxes.

Only land in the vicinity of an Oriya village is surveyed and there are no village accountants. The only document which the *mutha* headman keeps is a list of taxpayers and the amount due from them. The list in current use was compiled in 1924 and the headman uses his personal knowledge to adjust the amounts according to the changes caused by sales and inheritance.

There are three village watchmen (*chaukidar*). They are paid Rs.6 a month and are *de facto* under the control of the *mutha* headman.[1] They assist the headman to collect revenue and they act as his messengers, carrying reports to the headquarters. All three are Boad OUTCASTES. These posts are in the appointment of the *mutha* headman, subject to Government confirmation.

Under the control of the headman are seven militiamen (*paik*). Their normal duty is to help the headman to collect the revenue, but in extraordinary circumstances they may be called to serve for a few days at a time at the Government headquarters. Their office is a survival of an hereditary landed militia, and each position carries with it a grant of land, sometimes large, sometimes small. With the exception of one Boad OUTCASTE and one HERDSMAN all are Kond POTTERS. Their appointment is on the recommendation of the *mutha* headman.

[1] Bisipara has a village headman (*gram polis*), who is related as father's younger brother's son to the *mutha* headman. In fact the latter controls village affairs.

All these men—*mutha* headman, village headman, watchmen and militiamen—are found in any village which is the capital of its *mutha*. It so happens that the headman of the *mutha* to the east, called Bhetimendi, also has his house and most of his land in Bisipara. A further difference is the presence of two more salaried servants, the bungalow watchman and the Postmaster. The bungalow was built in the days before motor-cars, but now that it is less than half-an-hour's journey by car from the District Headquarters, it seldom is used by senior officers. The watchman, a SWEEPER, is paid Rs.7 a month and has a grant of land. The Post Office has been opened five years and the man in charge, a WARRIOR, gets Rs.25 a month.

There are three types of Government appointments outside the village—police, schoolmastering and menial work in Government departments. One Boad OUTCASTE is a policeman at Rs.60 a month : two Kond POTTERS and one Boad OUTCASTE are messengers (*peons*) at the headquarters for Rs.40 a month : two WARRIORS, one Boad DISTILLER, one HERDSMAN and five Boad OUTCASTES are schoolmasters, receiving Rs.31 a month.

There are about 190 males aged twenty and over in Bisipara. (Ages are not easily estimated.) Of these, 28, or about 14 per cent, receive wages from Government either for such full-time tasks as schoolmastering or being a policeman, or for part-time work as a village official. The field is restricted by the number of appointments available.

But the field is restricted in other ways as well. In this part of the Kondmals the *mutha* headmen are all WARRIORS, and since the position is hereditary, it is not open to competition. Again, by tradition the village watchmen are always OUTCASTES. This policy was rationalized by an early British official on the grounds that the touch of an OUTCASTE pollutes and therefore he can discipline people simply by threatening to touch them. As part of the same tradition many of the lower ranks of the police are OUTCASTES. Bungalow watchmen are invariably SWEEPERS, since part of their duties is to clean the lavatories after officials, a task which no other caste will perform. One of the militiamen must always be a HERDSMAN, since water has to be supplied for the bungalow and HERDSMEN are the traditional water-carriers, from whose hands all castes may drink.

Apart from these restrictions which arise from pollution and tradition, there is discriminating legislation in favour of Konds and untouchables. A certain proportion of all minor Government appointments must be reserved for them and this explains the high proportion of Adibasis (who in the village are Konds, Kond POTTERS and Kond HERDSMEN) and Scheduled Castes among the militiamen and schoolmasters and messengers of Bisipara. In these three categories Adibasis and Scheduled Castes are 84 per cent.

Are the holders of these jobs able at the same time to cultivate an estate, or is their time fully occupied? All the appointments in the village are part-time and offer no obstruction to cultivation. Of the jobs outside, the policeman and the messengers work throughout the year, and if they have estates, they must find someone else to manage them. The policeman is in fact one of the five richest men in the village and the farm was managed first by his wife and then by his eldest son. To manage an estate of this size while doing another job is not difficult, since the estate can support farm-servants and casual labourers. Schoolmasters are in a better position, since all schools close for two months during the planting season. Furthermore none of the schools in which they teach are more than half-a-day's walk away from Bisipara. A schoolmaster can both manage the farm and himself do much of the work, if he chooses to do so.

The rewards vary. In theory only the policeman, the messengers and the schoolmasters receive what is meant to be a living wage. In fact one or two of the militiamen's estates are almost large enough to support a small family, and the SWEEPER receives a substantial part of his income, when the cash wage and the land allotment are added together. The two *mutha* headmen receive considerable sums, not so much through payment but through perquisites.

Are these rewards such as to explain the present distribution of land, on the theory that money gained in this way has been invested in land, or has prevented land from coming into the market? The latter certainly is true and income from all types of Government service in the village takes its place beside income from small trading, village service and crafts as a means by which the small landowner is able to meet contingent costs without selling land. From his salary alone the schoolmaster nowadays can barely live—a frequent lament at the meeting of the Schoolmasters' Federation—and he has no surplus for investment. If he already has other sources of income (such as an estate), then his position is very different and in some cases the entire salary is available for investment. There is some evidence that formerly the salary of schoolmasters was much higher, relatively to the cost of living, and in at least one case a man has built up a moderate estate out of his salary alone. The same remarks apply to the messengers' salaries, although on the whole they tend to think themselves lucky to have the job and are less vocal than the schoolmasters. The only appointments which in themselves might offer a surplus to be used in acquiring land are those of the two *mutha* headmen and of the policeman, and they have in fact been so used.

Has this affected the distribution of land between castes? One would expect perhaps to find that the privileged classes of Adibasi and Scheduled Caste had improved their position. The latter have; the former, on the whole, have not. How and why this has happened will be discussed in a following chapter.

The Leaf Company

The Leaf Company buys the right to exploit the District from the Government. The company is owned by Gujeratis and most of the overseers are from Gujerat. For the rest of the work—pickers, packers, and carters—local people are employed. The leaves (*dyospyros menalexylon*) are used for the outer wrapping of the *bidi* cigarette.

The leaves are picked from the jungle during the hot season, when they are fresh and strong. The pickers are mostly women and boys. There is a store-shed in the village and the leaves are taken there, set out to dry, and the pickers are paid according to the amount they have brought in. I kept accounts for some days in May and the money paid to pickers varied from A.1 to As.8 with an average about As.4.

From about May until November a team of about twenty men are out for varying periods pressing and packing the leaves. They travel from one store-shed to another and come home for a rest or to help with the farm after a period at work. The wage is Rs.1/6 a day. I kept records for a period of fifty days ending

July 6th 1953 for nineteen men and found that they had by then worked times varying from 50 to 9 days, earning a maximum of Rs.70 and a minimum of Rs.12. On the other hand the young men feed themselves while they are away, and are apt to be more reckless with their money than they would be at home. The least a man could spend would be As.8 a day, and some spent As.13. The net profit, then, for a period of fifty days is around Rs.40.

Packing work clashes with agriculture, but most of those who went belonged either to families with little land or to households where there were several males of working age. Again the worker does not contract for any definite time, but may come home when he is needed or when he wants a change. In fact, more people went at times when there is little to do on the farm —at the beginning of the packing season and after the transplanting season.

One man, a WARRIOR and a relative of the *mutha* headman (father's younger brother's son), is employed by the Leaf Company for nine months of the year as an assistant overseer. He acts as liaison officer between the villagers and the local manager. He is paid a wage and at the end of the year he gets a commission, with all the other regular employees, on the total amount exported under the contract. I was not able to discover how much this was.

At the end of the season the accounts for the local store-shed, which serves several villages, were as follows :

	Rs.
Buying leaves	2,856/7
Packing leaves	1,035/8
Transport	375
Wages	300
Total	4,566/15

I should estimate that at least three-quarters of this went to the village, but it is impossible to be sure.

Gathering leaves is work for women and boys, although not formally restricted to them. The binding is done by men, usually young unmarried men, and the work can only be done by the fit and strong. Officially there is no caste restriction in either of these activities, although since the local WARRIOR employee picks most of the workers for binding, they all are of clean caste.

The company has been working in the District for only five years and it is too soon to say whether wealth gained from this source is going to affect the economic and political structure of the village. The money given to the pickers is too little and spread among too many people to be anything more than cash for a few extras. The binders can earn substantial sums in a season and several of them are working for direct ends—for example, one HERDSMAN is working to get money to pay an exorbitant brideprice demanded by his prospective father-in-law. None of the binders are particularly rich and none are acquiring land. The WARRIOR overseer has been buying land.

Selling Rice and Lending Paddy

After the harvest is in, many people sell paddy or rice, if they have no other means of getting cash, and even if they know that they will have to borrow paddy before the next harvest. Apart from them, there are the small traders, who husk the paddy they get by trading and sell it with greater profit as rice.

But there are, as well, certain estates which bring in a sufficient harvest to allow sale of paddy or rice all the year round. The caste of the owners is shown in Table 22. There are, of course, others who sell rice or paddy from time to time, but these are

Table 22

Caste of Sellers of Rice and Paddy

Caste	*Number*	*Remarks*
Ganjam DISTILLER	2	In both cases paddy derived from own lands and the takings of their shops
Christian	2	Derived from own land
Boad DISTILLER	2	Derived from own land
WARRIOR	4	Derived from own land. In one case a joint-estate
Boad OUTCASTE	7	Derived from own land. One joint-estate
WEAVER	1	Takings of a shop
WRITER	1	Takings of a shop and controlled-price paddy supplied by Government
Miscellaneous	1	The village temple

the only houses at which one can be sure of being able to buy paddy all the year round. They tend also to be the wealthiest houses, but this is not necessarily so. In one case, a WARRIOR widow, who has only herself to support, is left with a surplus for sale, while larger estates have none for sale since they have more mouths to feed.

In most cases the surplus sold comes from the land of the seller. There are two exceptions to this. One shop in the village has the right to sell Government-controlled goods, among which are paddy, rice and cloth. His stock is got from the Civil Supplies Office at the headquarters and the price, at which he is supposed to sell it, is laid down. The other source (this time of paddy only) is the takings from those who buy goods using paddy instead of cash.

Who buys paddy? When the harvest is in, the cultivator who needs cash has three main customers. The first is the shop, which buys at a very low rate. Nominally the rate is approximately the same everywhere after the harvest—about R.1 for ten measures of paddy. In fact the shop-servants use a large-size measure and heap it very high each time and the seller is confronted by a 'take it or leave it' attitude which many find disconcerting. Some prefer to take their rice to market and try their luck with the marketmen, but again there is the chance of being cheated and the trouble of carrying the goods to market. The best customer is a fellow-villager, a man who 'gets rice to eat by buying it' (*kinikhia loko*), or a man who needs paddy to carry on his business, like the sellers of parched rice and flaked rice. The rates are usually the same as the rates which the shops give, but the deal is between equals and such bullying as goes on is reciprocal. These people will also buy rice for immediate consumption, giving about R.1 for three measures. Husked paddy (that is, rice) will not remain in good condition for more than two or three months (so I was told in Bisipara) and the shops will not buy it at this time of the year. The buyers are typically those with a salary or a fairly regular mercantile source of income (like a carter), who have not sufficient land of their own to feed their families. A few people buy paddy to start a paddy-lending business or to continue it when stocks have run low. One man buys as a speculation—a speculation with little risk—at the harvest-time rate of R.1 for ten measures of paddy and sells again in the three months preceding the next harvest at the scarcity rate of R.1 for about three measures.

Five months after the harvest paddy is expensive and many of those who sold grain to get cash after the harvest are buying it again. Paddy and rice are dearest at the time of transplanting, since cultivators need the grain not only for their own family but also to feed their labourers and to pay the daily wage. In September, when the harvest festival is held and the hill paddy is cut, the price begins to fall, but does not reach its nadir until December or January, when the main crop of irrigated paddy is brought home.

There is one important point about selling rice and paddy, which, although obvious, needs to be stated. There is a cash-market for surplus paddy and rice. The man with a large estate can use his wealth in a purely economic way as an investment to increase his capital. If there were not such a market, wealth could be used only to win prestige, either by feasts and other forms of conspicuous consumption, or by feeding and maintaining followers. In fact there are some people in the village who use their wealth purely for economic ends : there are others who are mainly concerned with keeping a following (the *mutha* headman is a good example) : and there are some who follow both ends (the leader of the faction of WARRIORS which is opposed to the *mutha* headman's faction does this).

Those who lend paddy are mostly those whose estates produce more than they need, but the number includes a few who have no land at all and who have built up a prosperous business from small beginnings.

From April and May until the end of September many households are running out of the stock of paddy which came from their own land. Those who have a cash income usually will buy grain, either as rice, or, with greater difficulty at this time of the year, as paddy. Those who have no cash must borrow paddy to eat, and a few cultivators need to borrow seed paddy, having already consumed their seed.

Paddy, which is rice in the husk, can be kept in good condition for eating for two to three years, and if it is stored with care in a dry place—in the cooking room—it might last for four years. Seed paddy is good for two years.

The rate of interest from the time the grain is borrowed to the next harvest (on which the lender has first call) is 50 per cent.

If seed paddy is borrowed the rate is 100 per cent. These high rates are the means by which those who have no land or little land are able to build up a paddy-lending business. A typical beginning, which with luck might end as a prosperous business after a few years, occurred in 1953. The mother's brother of a twelve-year old HERDSMAN boy gave him a goat. The boy and his mother, who is a widow, butchered the goat and sold the meat and with the money they bought paddy at the cheap rate immediately after the harvest of 1952. They bought ten units of paddy. They managed to get through the year without making inroads on this stock, and they lent it out and got back in January 1954 more than fifteen units of paddy.

The caste of those who lend paddy is shown in Table 23. The statement that the paddy lent is 'derived from own land' means merely that the lenders also are landowners. Whether the paddy came out of last year's interest on loans or out of last

TABLE 23

CASTE OF LENDERS OF PADDY

Caste	*Number*	*Remarks*
Christian	2	Derived from own land
Boad BRAHMIN	1	Derived from own land
Ganjam BRAHMIN	1	Derived from own land
WARRIOR	3	Derived from own land. One joint-estate
HERDSMAN	2	No land. Lent paddy first in 1953
Ganjam DISTILLER	2	Takings in shops and in one case from land
WEAVER	3	One has a little land, the others none
Kond POTTER	4	Three have a little, and one has much land
Boad DISTILLER	2	Derived from own land
Boad OUTCASTE	7	Derived from own land
Miscellaneous	1	The village temple

year's harvest, I had no means of knowing. Lending does not necessarily mean that the land is producing more than the family needs, since these wants may be met out of mercantile activities. Again, where it is stated that the lender has no land, this usually means that the business has been built up in ways like that described above. Except in one case, a WEAVER woman, the lenders are not dependent on income from this source alone.

The business of selling rice and lending paddy has grown out of the situation I described at the end of the last chapter. Estates have become smaller and now are held by individuals instead of joint-families. These cultivators cannot grow enough paddy for themselves. They make money in other ways, and use this money to buy paddy. At the same time many of those who formerly had no land were in a relationship of quasi-kinship with the groups which owned large estates and received their food through these ties. Now the tie is purely economic, and the former clients have become customers.

I doubt whether men become rich in this way. But there is always the possibility, given the luck to make a start. The existence of large lending businesses in the possession of those who are without land shows this. However, the main significance of transactions with rice and paddy is that the rich have a simple productive investment, which requires no particular skill or knowledge of markets. Through these means estates get bigger, without any great effort on the part of the owner, providing they are producing a reasonable surplus. Other things being equal, the estate continues to build up, until it is divided between several heirs.

Contracts

Some craft-work is done by contract—not to imply by that word any written document or formal procedure, but simply an agreement to do a particular piece of work for a given payment. A man might contract with the carpenter to have all the wooden parts of a new house made and erected for a settled sum. The owner of a cart might approach the carpenter and ask him to re-set a wheel for an agreed price. One carpenter agreed to solder sealing discs on kerosene tins for so much a tin. The same carpenter repaired four wooden leaf-presses belonging to the Leaf Company. When the road was washed away during the rains, the Leaf Company contracted with a group of Boad OUTCASTES to build a temporary causeway for Rs.80, rather than wait for the Government to do the work.

More formal contracts are offered by the Government for the upkeep of their property. One man, a Boad DISTILLER, is a full-time contractor. At one time and another he has contracted to feed the prisoners in gaol and to collect market tolls from those who sell in the market-place ; and he is now concentrating on building-contracts. He keeps a house and owns land in Bisipara, but he has built himself another house in the headquarters village, Phulbani. Apart from him, four people have taken one Government contract and one has taken two contracts between the beginning of 1952 and the end of 1953. About the beginning of that time the Overseer, a Government official concerned with the upkeep of public buildings, came to the village and canvassed for persons willing to take a contract to repair a school in a nearby Kond village. A man of the FISHERMAN caste rushed to his house and brought out a gold necklace which he offered as security for good work. He got the contract, did the work well and has since then been able to take other contracts. Another man, a schoolmaster of the Boad DISTILLER caste, took a contract to repair three schools, squandered the money on high living, and ended up with a third of the work done, and a debt of Rs.2,000. Action is still being taken against him. The WRITER took a contract to repair and redecorate the village bungalow, work which was done to the satisfaction of the authorities. Later the *mutha* headman took a contract to repair other parts of the same building. Finally both *mutha* headmen who reside in the village had contracts to repair wooden bridges in their respective *muthas*.

The field of those who compete for contracts is very limited, since normally they are given only to men of substance. The profits are said to be very high, although it is quite impossible to estimate what they are. There are frequent accusations of bribery and default, and astronomical figures are quoted in support of these accusations.

Money earned in this way has had no effect on the pattern of landholding (except that it looks as though the lands of the Boad DISTILLER who defaulted in so spectacular a way will be distrained to meet his default), since until 1947 most of the tasks which now are given to small contractors were carried out by forced labour.

The Trade in Hides

The trade in hides is one of the few sources of substantial wealth in the present-day economy, which is restricted by ideas of pollution.

When a beast dies it belongs to the SWEEPERS and the Ganjam

OUTCASTES. They cart it away and sometimes they eat the meat. If the owner is of clean caste, he will have nothing more to do with the dead animal and he demands no payment for it. The hide will be worth anything from three to six rupees, depending on whether it is in good or bad condition, how big it is, and whether or not the animal had been branded.

The hide is bought by a man who is agent for a leather-factor, a Muslim who lives sixty miles away in Russelkonda in the plains. The agent is a Ganjam OUTCASTE who lives in Bisipara. He maintains a system of sub-agents over large areas of the Kondmals. Most hides pass through the hands of local untouchable caste-groups, then to the sub-agents, and then to the agent in the village. He and his son sit in the two markets at Phulbani and Phiringia, and buy skins which are brought there. Once or twice a month the factor from the plains sends up a lorry to take away the store of skins.

The annual or monthly profits of this trade are impossible to estimate, especially as the trader was a secretive man. But that the trade is lucrative is shown by the man's history. He is between fifty and sixty years old. When he was young, he owned nothing. Now he has land worth more than the land of the rest of his caste-group put together. He gets from it an annual income of about Rs.400.

This man's history, although it forms a small part of the total economic history of the village, is interesting in several ways. First it demonstrates clearly how wealth gained from other sources is turned into land. Secondly it is one of the only two examples (the drink-trade is the other) in which occupations restricted to certain castes have remained restricted, after they became part of a modern mercantile economy, and in spite of the fact that they offered considerable profits. The reason was that they involved handling polluting materials.

SHOPKEEPING

Already in the 1840s Macpherson mentioned 'resident Hindu merchants', who supplied the Konds with 'salt, cloth, brass vessels, ornaments and other necessities'.[1] Again we know no details.

[1] W. Macpherson, 1865, p. 63.

Those who now have shops in Bisipara have all come to the village since 1855. Three are Ganjam DISTILLERS: one is a WEAVER: one is the TEMPLEMAN: and one is a WRITER. The first four were established by the fathers (or relatives in the parental generation) of those who now hold them. The WRITER came five years ago and has been keeping a shop for three years. The TEMPLEMAN came as a boy and has opened a shop only in 1953.

All the shops sell rice, paddy, spices, lentils and oils. In addition the following goods can be purchased at one or other of them: sugar, tea, tobacco, matches, kerosene, soap, medicinal herbs, lanterns and wick-lanterns and spare parts, local cloth, machine cloth, turmeric, liquor-flowers and ropes. Some of the shops sell such fancy goods as religious pictures, mirrors, combs and various trinkets.

Formerly there was a flourishing trade in alcoholic drink. In the beginning, when the country first was annexed in 1855 and for some years afterwards, the Konds were free to manufacture their own liquor. In 1870 the liquor-shops of Ganjam were closed and the Ganjam DISTILLERS migrated in large numbers into the Kondmals. At the same time the Konds were forbidden to make their own drink and an enormous trade sprang up to the profit both of the Ganjam DISTILLERS and the Boad DISTILLERS. By 1887 there were 470 stills in an area of 800 square miles. From about 1890 onwards there began an agitation to have the shops closed, since the Konds were rapidly becoming paupers. But the Government was reluctant to lose the Excise Revenue and the shops continued to flourish until a letter by a Baptist Missionary to a Calcutta newspaper in 1910 caused an outcry, and the Government of Bengal ordered all liquor-shops in the Kondmals to be closed. This was done.

The sellers of drink in Bisipara built up large estates. Some of the fields were acquired from Konds in other villages. Others belonged to Konds who lived in hamlets nearby and whose fields adjoined the lands of Bisipara. Others have been acquired indirectly from castes who did not drink, such as the WARRIORS, through the process described in Chapter IV.

Forty years have gone by since the drink-shops were closed, and it now is impossible to recover the details of their transactions. We can judge by the result that is apparent in the distribution of land to-day. The Boad DISTILLERS own as much as the WARRIORS, judging income per head from land : the Ganjam DISTILLERS, who have continued in commerce as shopkeepers, own four times as much per head as the WARRIORS (see Table 9).

Among Hindus these opportunities were restricted to the DISTILLER castes for several reasons. Firstly higher castes, and even the other 'low' Hindus, would have been polluted by handling drink, and untouchables would have defiled the liquor so that none but themselves could drink it. Secondly those who would most have liked to make their own drink—the Kond customers—were forbidden by law from keeping stills.

The social consequences of this sudden enrichment will be discussed later.

SALARIES, INVESTMENT AND MANAGEMENT IN THE ECONOMIC HISTORY OF THE VILLAGE

In this chapter I have considered such sources of income as service of the Government, work for the Leaf Company, the sale of rice and the lending of paddy, contracts, the trade in hides, and keeping a shop. Some of these activities like minor service of Government, occasional work for the Leaf Company, and small loans of paddy, have the same effects on the re-distribution of land as do those services and forms of trade described in Chapter V. In themselves they do not provide spectacular wealth, but they may be a means of meeting contingent expenditure and so preventing the sale of land. Other activities, like that of the *mutha* headmen, the trader in hides and the shopkeepers (particularly, in the past, a drink-shop) provide in themselves considerable wealth. The higher range of salaries, such as those of the schoolmaster, the postmaster and the policeman, are in a middle position, in that, if the incumbent already has another source of income, the wage is free for investment : but if he must try to live on his wages alone, then this in itself is unlikely to give a surplus.

There were a few schools before 1870, but the majority have been founded since that date, at first out of the Excise Revenue and later out of other funds. The Leaf Company began to exploit these hills five years ago. The small contractors have come into existence only since the abolition of forced labour in 1947. There were headmen ('Hill Chiefs' they are called by Campbell and Macpherson) before 1855, and there were probably militiamen and watchmen. But their position then would be different from what it is to-day. Every WARRIOR landowner is likely to have been a militiaman in the service of the Raja of Boad and the headman in theory depended for his position on his allegiance to the Raja. In fact the Raja seems to have had no control over the hills, and the 'Hill Chiefs' were in effect kings in their own domain, acknowledging the ritual supremacy of their Raja and obeying his secular commands when it suited their purpose. The power which the headman wielded would depend not on his being the representative of an all-powerful outside authority, but on the resources he could himself command—on such things as his wealth, the size of his kin-group, and his personal prowess in war and intrigue. To-day the powers that the *mutha* headman exerts still depend to some extent on his wealth, on the size of his following and on his prowess in intrigue, but they rest ultimately on the fact that he represents the Government in his *mutha*, and he represents the people of his *mutha* before the Government. He is still in a position to do favours, and consequently receives favours. During the first years of the Administration it seems there was little limit to the dues which the headmen extracted in the name of the Government. Before that time, when the Kondmals were still not annexed, the powers of the headman would be restricted by the threat of rebellion or transfer of allegiance to a rival headman. Their riches in the last hundred years have come from the removal of these two sanctions, from the ferocious discipline imposed upon the Konds by the first Tahsildar, and by the fact that for many years these headmen were the sole interpreters of Konds to the Government and of the Government to Konds.

The militiamen, who to-day receive a grant of land and are drawn from OUTCASTES and the Kond POTTER caste, before the annexation would be WARRIORS, and the group of militiamen would in fact consist of the entire group of landowners, instead of, as to-day, being a privileged section within the landholding category. The watchmen, I conjecture, were village servants paid by a tithe like the other servants, or else they were the personal henchmen of the headman. Now they are paid by the Government.

I have argued also that the sale of paddy and the lending of paddy have developed only or mainly since 1855. Those who now buy or borrow paddy would formerly have been either full members of large self-sufficient joint-families or would have had with those joint-families a relationship of quasi-kinship as clients, which entitled them to be fed from their masters' fields. The demand for paddy and rice, either as a loan or sale, enables a man whose estate produces a surplus to invest it in a way that makes no demands upon skill or time. Further, this is a purely economic investment designed to increase capital (either in land or paddy) and is not necessarily for use in acquiring political power in the village. The mere possession of wealth, and the possibility of appeal to Government courts, makes a following politically irrelevant.

Hides were probably exported from the hills before 1855, but we do not know who were the middlemen concerned. It seems unlikely that commerce after the fashion of the present agent could then have been carried on. It is more probable that there was either direct exchange in the markets on the plains at the edge of the hills, or else hides from the interior were given to itinerant traders. Good communications are essential to the centralized structure of present-day trading in hides.

Finally we know that the liquor-shops boomed only after the Konds were forbidden to make their own liquor : and although resident merchants are said to have lived in the hills before 1855, demand for manufactures and the services of shopkeepers on the present scale has certainly developed within the last hundred years.

Some of the most lucrative sources of income considered in this chapter are restricted wholly or partially to certain castes. The Administration supported the existing political structure among the Oriyas, and chose its headmen from the politically dominant WARRIOR caste.[1] The position is hereditary so that although *de jure* anyone can be chosen for headman, *de facto* most headmen continue to be WARRIORS.

[1] In the eastern part of the Kondmals most Konds speak Oriya, and in this area the majority of the headmen are Konds. See Chapter II.

Because they handle polluting goods the DISTILLERS and the OUTCASTE were able to exploit new economic opportunities denied to the others. Since the demand for drink was high and the trade actively encouraged by the Government, who were interested in Excise Revenue, a large part of the two DISTILLER caste-groups became wealthy, and it is this wealth which explains why these caste-groups to-day own a high proportion of the village land.

With prohibition these opportunities ceased. Until that time the struggle lay between the WARRIORS and the two DISTILLER caste-groups, with the latter gaining land at the expense of the former. For the Boad DISTILLER group, this process has come to an end. They now are ranged beside the WARRIORS in a struggle partly with the Ganjam DISTILLERS, who still have large commercial interests, but mostly with the Boad OUTCASTES.

The present prosperity (relative to their former poverty) of the Boad OUTCASTES results ultimately from the advantage they have taken of opportunities offered them by the Government and legislation discriminating in favour of Adibasis and Scheduled Castes. Why almost alone among untouchables and Adibasis in the village the Boad OUTCASTES have profited, and why some men more than others within their group have benefited, are questions which will be considered later. A sign of their new prosperity is their increased share in the ownership of lands around the village.

CHAPTER VII

MERCANTILE WEALTH AND THE OWNERSHIP OF LAND

WHEN a villager presents a petition, especially if he is applying for a job, he always begins by saying that his is a poor and backward country and he is a poor man. He knows the political value of poverty. But beyond this there is a systematic understatement of wealth, whatever the context, since to proclaim prosperity, whether in oneself or another, is to invite the attention of the evil eye. A rich man will admit that long ago he was fairly wealthy, but things now are changed and he is as poor as anyone else.

In fact there are relatively large differences in wealth. Some have no land : others have large estates. Some live by casual labour and petty trade : others have land, and a salaried appointment and several commercial sources of wealth. The differences of wealth on the whole are not sharply marked by differences in the style of living. All wear the same type of clothes, although a rich man will have more clothes and his wives and daughters will have more jewellery. The rich man's house is often bigger and in better repair than that of the poor man, but it is built after the same fashion and contains the same amenities. Rich and poor eat the same type of food, although the rich man may eat more meat. The very rich may have a gun or a bicycle—there are four guns and two bicycles in the village. But rich and poor of appropriate caste frequent the same places, enjoy their leisure in the same way, and associate quite freely together. Grouping depends not on wealth, but on caste.

Riches beget riches. Salaries and wealth got from trading are invested in land. Surplus from the land is easily invested to bring in 50 per cent interest in a year. Rich families get richer, in the normal course of things, until a man is survived by several heirs. Then the process begins again. There is great mobility between the different income categories. Multiple inheritance brings down the rich. A single heir and the opportunities for mercantile wealth elevate the poor. With certain exceptions, there is a constant up and down movement, and it is common to find an old man on the margin of penury who in middle-age was counted wealthy.

In this chapter I shall show how wealth is distributed at the moment, and try by case histories to illustrate the dynamics of wealth and the validity of—and exceptions to—the generalization that the present distribution of landed wealth can be explained in terms of the system of inheritance and the opportunities for getting wealth from mercantile sources.

The Distribution of Landed Wealth

Table 24 summarizes the way in which wealth is spread between individuals and castes. This is landed wealth and does not represent total income. Income gained from share-cropping is included, as well as income got from land owned, or taken in pledge.

The five wealthiest men all have a lucrative occupation as well as their estates. Two of the WARRIORS are *mutha* headmen. The third is the village postmaster. The Ganjam DISTILLER keeps a shop. The Boad OUTCASTE is a policeman.

Four out of the five were sole heir. The exception is the *mutha* headman, who so manipulated things that he was in effect the only heir.

All five inherited a large part of their wealth, and it seems that estates of this size cannot be accumulated in one generation, possibly because sufficient land does not come into the market during one man's lifetime. It is possible that men have acquired as much wealth as these five men in their own lifetime, but I think that it would not be possible to transfer it into land. However, this is conjecture.

In four of the five cases the father of the present holder had a second source of income: two, like their sons, were *mutha* headmen; another was a shopkeeper; the father of the postmaster was a telegraph linesman and the malicious gossip of the village says that the family's fortune is founded on false expense accounts. I have no information about the father of the Boad OUTCASTE.

What will happen in the next generation? How the Ganjam

TABLE 24

DISTRIBUTION OF LANDED WEALTH BETWEEN HOUSEHOLDS BY CASTE

Caste	*Annual income in units of paddy per household*					*Total households*
	nil	1–49	50–99	100–150	*Over* 150	
WARRIOR	3	16	9	3	3	34
Boad DISTILLER	2	7	2	4	—	15
Ganjam DISTILLER	—	2	—	1	1	4
Boad BRAHMIN	—	1	—	1	—	2
Ganjam BRAHMIN	—	3	—	—	—	3
HERDSMAN	6	2	1	—	—	9
BARBER	2	—	—	—	—	2
WASHERMAN	—	1	—	—	—	1
WEAVER	4	4	—	—	—	8
TEMPLEMAN	1	—	1	—	—	2
FISHERMAN	—	2	—	—	—	2
ORIYA	—	—	1	—	—	1
Christian	—	2	—	1	—	3
SWEEPER	2	3	—	—	—	5
BASKETMAKER	—	2	—	—	—	2
Boad OUTCASTE	5	13	1	9	1	29
Ganjam OUTCASTE	4	6	—	1	—	11
Kond	3	4	—	—	—	7
Kond HERDSMAN	4	1	—	—	—	5
Kond POTTER	9	15	7	1	—	32
WRITER	1	—	—	—	—	1
Muslim	1	—	—	—	—	1
Total households	47	84	22	21	5	179

DISTILLER will arrange the succession I neglected to enquire. He is a man of about thirty and presumably his family will yet increase. One *mutha* headman has two sons, the elder of whom told me that the younger brother would get only sufficient of the estate to live from—that they would make the same arrangement as that under which their father had benefited. The other *mutha* headman has no sons and he is selling his land and giving the money to his daughters and their sons. The postmaster plans to educate three sons so that they may find jobs and he may leave the estate intact to the remaining son. If he succeeds, there will be four wealthy men. If the three fail, there will be four poor men. The Boad OUTCASTE also has four sons, none of whom are at the High School. Unless they too find work as police or messengers, they will not be rich men.

There are twenty-one men in the second category of wealth. The sources of their income, apart from land, are shown in Table 25.

TABLE 25

SOURCES OF INCOME OF HOUSEHOLDS IN CATEGORY 100–150 OF TABLE 24

Caste and number of persons	*Shop*	*School-master*	*Hide-trader*	*Govt. service*	*Village service*	*Father rich*	*Father poor*	*Sole heir*
WARRIOR (3) . . .	—	1	—	—	—	3	—	3
Ganjam DISTILLER (1) . .	1	—	—	—	—	1	—	—
Boad DISTILLER (4) . . .	—	1	—	—	—	4	—	1
Kond POTTER (1) .	—	—	—	—	1*	1	—	1
Christian (1) . . .	—	—	—	—	—	1	—	—
Boad BRAHMIN (1) .	—	—	—	—	1	1	—	—
Boad OUTCASTE (9) .	—	3	—	3†	—	6	3	2
Ganjam OUTCASTE (1)	—	—	1	—	—	—	1	—
Totals (21) . . .	1	5	1	3	2	17	4	7

* This man is the priest of the earth and receives two fields for the work.
† Two of these are watchmen. The third, until recently sacked, was a messenger in the Roads Department.

Thirteen of the twenty-one in this category have a regular outside source of income. In addition to this all the households except three carry on business lending and selling paddy and rice. The exceptions are one OUTCASTE household, which has many members and very little surplus, one WARRIOR and a Kond POTTER. I was not able to discover what the last two did with their surplus. Both have the reputation of being bad managers and slovenly cultivators. All households in this category profit from one form or another of small trading, except the Christian and the BRAHMIN. The members of some families go labouring.

In the parental generation of seventeen of the rich men in the second category, I know that nine had a regular outside source of income. Two WARRIORS and two Boad OUTCASTES were 'good cultivators and used to lend paddy'. About the other four Boad OUTCASTES I neglected to enquire. We may presume that all enjoyed an income from trade.

What of multiple inheritance? The fact that some men, although one of several heirs, are yet in the next highest income category partly reflects the size of the father's income. This is particularly true of the two DISTILLER castes and the Christian and it indicates that before prohibition the rich were richer than they are now. In other words, these estates were so large that it will take two generations of multiple inheritance to bring their heirs near to poverty.

A high proportion of those in the two wealthiest land-categories are either sole heirs, or have a secondary source of income, or both, or are the sons of those who had a secondary source of income. This is a pattern which the analysis of the preceding chapters would lead us to expect.

How do the secondary sources of income appear from the other direction? Are all those who have a secondary source of income rich? The answer to this should show not only how many big landowners have a secondary income, but also how many of those who make a substantial income outside agriculture choose to invest it in land. I confine attention to those who have a regular (i.e. salaried) source of income or who are conspicuously successful in commerce. The result is shown in Table 26.

TABLE 26

SIZE OF ESTATES BELONGING TO PERSONS WITH A MERCANTILE INCOME

Source of income	*Annual income in units of paddy per household from land owned, share-cropped or taken in pledge*				
	Nil	1–49	50–99	100–150	over 150
Government . .	2	5	8	9	4
Hide trade . . .	—	—	—	1	—
Shops	1	2	1	1	1
Paddy-lending . .	4	2	4	5	5

The upper end of the table repeats what already has been discussed concerning Table 25, namely that those who own a large estate have also other sources of wealth. But the first three columns at first sight seem to cast doubt on the assertion that money is made outside agriculture and then invested in land. There are seven people with no land and nine with land that gives them less than 50 units of paddy each year, although they possess a secondary source of income. Of those who have no land, two of the paddy-lenders have begun this year to lend for the first time and have but a small capital; another is a WEAVER who is not a regular lender. The Government servants are two schoolmasters, one a boy of nineteen in training and the other a man about fifty, who has been a teacher for many years. In the second category (1–49) are a young schoolmaster, two messengers both young, a middle-aged village watchman, and the middle-aged bungalow watchman, the WEAVER shopkeeper, a Ganjam DISTILLER shopkeeper, and two men who lend small amounts of paddy.

We can give two reasons which suffice to explain the comparatively small estates or lack of any estate, in all cases except three. The reasons are, firstly, lack of opportunity and, secondly, lack of ability. In several cases the persons concerned are young men who have had no time to amass capital. Others have had time, but their income is small and they have not had the luck or the ability to profit by it. The village watchman is an example of this.

Others, like the bungalow watchman and one of the schoolmasters, are conspicuously lacking in managerial ability. I did not see much of the schoolmaster, but the other man drank heavily, was invariably behindhand with his cultivation, and every year had to borrow paddy. These two factors, luck and ability, defy this sort of sociological analysis, but they cannot be ignored in surveying the dynamics of wealth, when attention is directed on particular cases. For instance, it is possible to say with truth that the size of an estate depends to some extent on the amount of mercantile income which supplements the income from land. It also depends on the number of heirs at each act of inheritance. In terms of these two variables we can account for the distribution of land between individuals and between groups. But this does not mean that bad luck or bad management cannot reduce the size of an estate, even when there is a long line of single inheritance and even when each incumbent has a lucrative secondary source of income.

A few examples will illustrate this. The father of a young Boad DISTILLER made large profits from a drink-shop. After the shop was closed he became involved in a law-suit, which cost him at least Rs.600. When he died, his son, in spite of being an only son, had but a small estate. Again, it seems as though the Boad DISTILLER who defaulted on a contract will leave no land to his sons, although he inherited a large estate and has been a schoolmaster for many years.

There remain three persons who are wealthy and yet possess little or no land. One of these is the WRITER shopkeeper, who arrived five years ago. One reason why he does not acquire an estate in Bisipara is that in his native village on the plains he has land. His wife and family live down there. Another factor is that being an Oriya he would need permission from the magistrate to buy land in the locality. This in itself is no serious deterrent since land can be taken in pledge. The reason probably is that he is fully occupied managing his shop and does not choose to acquire land in the village. He may be investing his profits on the plains. In the same way the two other persons are unwilling to acquire land, although they could do so. One of these is a Ganjam DISTILLER, born in the village, the son of a shopkeeper and the brother of another man who keeps a shop and who has bought land. He is wealthy. Undoubtedly he could have acquired much more land had he chosen to do so. Instead he supplements the income of his shop by the usual methods of lending paddy and small sums of money, and by importing gold and silver and selling it to be made into ornaments. The third person is a woman, who has built up a prosperous business lending paddy. She is alone in the village, and the reason she has not bought land might be that she mistrusted her ability to manage it. But again there are examples of women who control estates—nothing is easier than to give them out to share-croppers—and the reason might simply be that she prefers not to be a landowner. A further possibility is that she is not so rich as the village says she is, and could not have bought land even if she wished to do so. I was never able to get a reliable estimate of her income.

So far as I know, these are the only three persons of considerable wealth who have made little or no investment in land.

In short, the biggest estates belong to those who have mercantile sources of wealth and the majority of those who have mercantile wealth have invested in land. With average luck and ability it takes two generations to reach the highest category of landed wealth, and there were some estates large enough to survive multiple inheritance and yet leave the heirs with an estate in the second highest category. Even to reach the second highest category of wealth seems to take more than one generation, with the opportunities available to-day, since only four of those in this category of wealth were born poor.

Acquisition of Wealth and the Transfer of Land

Before 1855 the village consisted of a group of joint-families of WARRIOR caste, who owned the land, and their attendant service castes. Relations between these groups were organized either on a tithe system or on such quasi-kinship arrangements as that between a master and his client. In this way a share of the product of the village lands was distributed among those who were not the proprietors.

After 1855 the village came under the Administration and became increasingly integrated into the larger economy of India. There were new opportunities for making wealth outside the traditional agricultural system. Disparate incomes and divergent interests broke up joint-families. This meant that every time a man was succeeded by more than one heir, estates were reduced in size, until some of them reached a point where they could no longer meet contingent costs (as at a marriage) without selling land.

Those original settlers who profited from the new economic opportunities and the immigrants who had come to exploit these opportunities bought land which came into the market, using money got from mercantile sources. Some of them acquired very large estates which they were able to manage, because the old system of master-client was replaced by a casual, temporary and purely economic wage-relationship. Over the years, the institution of clientship has all but disappeared.

From some of the new economic opportunities almost everyone benefited. But the reward was not such that it enabled them to invest in land, although it might provide money to meet contingent costs and so prevent dis-investment. Other opportunities were restricted to certain castes or categories of people, and it was largely these which were the most profitable.

Some men of the WARRIOR caste-group (especially the *mutha* headmen) have profited from the new economic opportunities and consolidated and improved their position as landed proprietors. Men of many other castes have acquired small estates. But the biggest gains went to the DISTILLER caste-groups, who profited from a monopoly arising out of caste-beliefs and Government support. The trend was stopped about 1910, when prohibition was introduced. Since that date land in increasing quantities has been going to the Boad OUTCASTES, who are encouraged by discriminating legislation.

This redistribution of the land has modified the political structure of the village. At the same time the village was inducted into the larger political system represented by the Administration.

These changes will be discussed in Part III.

PART THREE

POLITICAL ADJUSTMENTS

CHAPTER VIII

AN OUTLINE OF THE CHANGE IN POLITICAL ORGANIZATION

THE existence of the Konds and their country was discovered by the British, when in 1836 their armies went into the hills in pursuit of the Raja of Gumsur. There followed more than ten years of campaigning to put down the rite of human sacrifice, and the men who were responsible for this campaign wrote reports and subsequently two of them published books, which to-day are the only accounts of the region at that time. The books are not systematically compiled. Neither man spoke Kui and their knowledge of Oriya does not seem to have been extensive. Their acquaintance with the hills was confined to military expeditions in the winter season. One of them, General Campbell, is bombastic, unreliable and fiercely determined to blacken the character and achievements of the other man, who was dead when Campbell wrote his book. The second book (Macpherson) is an *apologia* written by the brother of the dead man, using letters and official reports. In these circumstances it is not surprising that no coherent picture of the political organization of the hills can be obtained from these sources.

In 1908 O'Malley published the *Angul Gazetteer*, which includes an account of the Kondmals. This bears the stamp of having been written at second hand from the information of local officials, and is quite inaccurate in its account of the history of the region, in so far as it concerns the role of the Oriya chieftains and the history of Oriya settlements in the hills.

In this chapter I shall discuss the political role of the Oriyas and their Hill Chiefs, as the early authorities call them, and the political organization of the village before 1855. Inevitably some of this must be reconstruction, and I have used written sources and tales told to me in the village and fitted them together in the light of what is known from similar societies elsewhere. As a literal, historical and factual account, this probably is inaccurate. We have no means of knowing. But it offers certain principles of political organization, which give a basis of comparison with political organization to-day, and permit the construction of a coherent account of the development of political organization under the pressure of economic change.

The Hill Chiefs become *mutha* Headmen

On the north, the east and the south the Kondmals were surrounded by feudal states. The Rajas of these states and the lords under them lived in fortified villages (*garh*) to protect themselves from each other and from rebellious subjects. There were periodical wars between the states and there was constant guerilla warfare on the borders. These Rajas claimed overlordship in the hills adjoining their territories.

The Kondmals were counted part of Boad, but at no time did the Raja of that state exercise effective control over his hill subjects. He seems to have had to protect his frontiers against Kond raiders, and he did so by establishing a series of fortified villages in the hills. This was the form which the Oriya invasion took, but it is not possible to say how far this represents conscious planning by the Raja of Boad, and how far the emigration arose from overpopulation and faction-fighting within the state.

These fortified villages in the hills were controlled, like similar villages on the plains, by chieftains. Macpherson, Campbell and other servants of the East India Company, who first came into the hills, had many dealings with these men and attempted to use them to control the Konds. Indeed they were largely compelled to do so, if only because the Hill Chiefs spoke both the Oriya and the Kui languages. They were called 'Bissye', an obvious corruption of the Oriya title 'Bisoi', which now is the name of certain WARRIOR lineages.[1]

Right through the literature there is uncertainty about the role and status of these Oriya chiefs among the Konds. The *Angul Gazetteer* says that the village Bisipara was founded and settled by the Administration and implies that the chief was no more than an appointed and imported servant of the Government. Elsewhere it says that the Oriyas were there on sufferance, and in fact made token obeisance to the resident Konds, giving them, for instance, free entertainment every time they visited the

[1] See also page 243.

village. The older authorities, Campbell and Macpherson, on a misreading of whose work this part of the gazetteer seems to be based, make it clear that in their opinion the Oriya chieftains were an important part of the political organization of the hills, and that no control could be won over the Konds without first enlisting the goodwill and active support of these men. Their importance to the East India Company was based on more than just the fact that they were bilingual. They had come originally, says Macpherson, to provide a deep protection for the frontiers of Boad. In another place he claims that they were in fact invited by the Konds, so that they might mediate in quarrels between different Kond groups and so that they might lead in warfare.

It is, however, possible to build a moderately coherent picture of the role and status of the Oriya Hill Chiefs, by extracting sensible passages from the literature and by combining these extracts with the accounts which Oriyas to-day give of their history. This picture may then be tested against the logic of the situation.

Firstly, it is clear that when the Oriyas first came into the hills, the Konds were in active opposition. There are different accounts of the founding of Bisipara, and each caste attributes a major role to its own heroes, but these accounts are unanimous in speaking of the hostility of the Konds. Here is one account given by a man of the WARRIOR caste:

> After settling at Bolscoopa, their numbers multiplied exceedingly and they came to Bisipara. They saw that the Konds were doing many wrong things. The Konds tried to drive them out. At that time the WARRIORS were great heroes and very skilled in magic. The most wicked of the Konds were the Koinjabari group. After a long war the WARRIORS burnt their houses and drove them out. The well which now is in Market Street is a memorial to those Koinjabari Konds. Then the Domosinghi Konds were attacking over the Dolopori mountain and they killed Poholo Bisoi's son, Bhagirodhi Bisoi. At another time Drono Bisoi fell surrounded by Konds. The Konds were victorious and they drove back the WARRIORS. Our great hero then was Ongo Bisoi. When his own brother Drono fell amid the Konds, Ongo Bisoi went to save his brother with powder, shot, gun and battle-axe. He crept under cover right close to the Konds and let off his gun. The Konds were frightened and many of them fled far away. Ongo got close to his brother and the two of them chased

the Konds, killing them. Large numbers of Konds fled. This was the war of Dolopori. In this fashion time passed until the Kondmals came under British rule. It must be added that Ongo and Drono, having eaten a certain substance, were invulnerable. Shot, sword and axe could not hurt their bodies.

Another account, given by a Boad OUTCASTE, is this :

[The Oriyas had colonized Gonjagura, on the east bank of the Salki river across from the present site of Bisipara. The Kond village there was protected by two Kond heroes, Biniki and Saniki Kohoro.] No Oriyas were able to settle in Bisipara. Those who came were murdered. From Bolscoopa a Biswalo family and a Behera family [WARRIOR lineage names] had come to settle in Gonjagura, but they were not able to take Bisipara.

The progeny of Mondano and Gopalo Sahani were Bonia Sahani, Gobindo Sahani, Chetu Sahani and Kartiko Sahani.[1] Their courage was renowned. A message was sent to Bolscoopa to fetch them. They were met on the way at Barikumpa and asked to come. 'You can mingle with Konds and you can be their advisers. Therefore come. In Bisipara (which then was called Talopara) Biniki and Saniki Kohoro are murdering Oriyas. Feed them on liquor and then win their faith and murder them. Then we can settle there together.' At this those four men settled in Gonjagura and with liquor they tamed the two Konds. When Biniki and Saniki were drunk they killed them with battle-axes and brought their heads to the Boralo God at Bolscoopa. Afterwards the Biswalo and Behera families and Gotikrisno Bisoi's ancestor Budho Bisoi settled at Bisipara.

These accounts obviously have been adjusted to provide a glorious history for the teller's ancestors and are not to be taken for historical fact. But I think it would be safe to conclude that Oriyas established themselves, at least in this village, by forceful conquest and intrigue.

This conquest gave the Oriya chief control over the fortified village, which he established, and over its immediate surroundings. In time his domain was extended to include Kond villages in the neighbourhood. The exact size of these realms and their histories and their internal organization are not known, but certain assumptions are possible. Firstly, the extent of the domain would depend on the power, whether in war or intrigue, of the chieftain. This is not simply that the chief ruled only where he could exact obedience by force. The chief had

[1] 'Sahani' is the name of a lineage of Boad OUTCASTES.

something to offer his subjects. He could mediate in quarrels between groups under his influence. He could also offer them some protection against outsiders. This, I think, is what lies behind Macpherson's statement that the Oriya chieftains were invited into the hills by Konds, so that they might be arbiters and put an end to internal warfare. At first this was not their role. But later, as their domains extended, so they took on a limited judicial function. As for their second function, it is to be noticed in the story of the WARRIOR given above, that after the founding of the village the enemy is not the local Konds, but the Domosinghi Konds who lived across the Dolopori mountains.

The force at the disposal of the Oriya chieftain was not very great. He could not rely on the help of the Raja of Boad in disciplining his Kond subjects. He was not the representative, as later he became, of an overwhelming outside force. His domain was in a country which had no traditions of subservience or centralized government. His family and his village would fight on his behalf. By intrigue he might enlist some of his Kond subjects to join in disciplining others. It is possible that he had superior military techniques (e.g. guns) and it is probable that he had greater administrative and political experience than any of his subjects. But on the side of the Konds lay the important sanction of being able to transfer their allegiance, especially when their village lay some distance from that of the chieftain. Just as the Oriya chieftains themselves sometimes changed their allegiance from the Boad to the Gumsur Raja,[1] so their subject villages, if pressed too hard, might rebel and invoke the protection of a rival leader.

This is, of course, conjecture, but I think it will explain the equivocation of the Oriya chieftains during the wars with the East India Company, and the confused notion of their role, which their very equivocation instilled in the minds of the Company's servants. On the one hand there are explicit statements that the Oriya chieftains were the key to the political organization of the hills and without their co-operation the rite of human sacrifice could never be suppressed. The Oriyas are viewed as detached from the Konds and exercising some control over them. On the other hand, at least two of the revolts against the East India

[1] W. Macpherson, 1865, p. 41.

Company were led by Oriya men,[1] and to-day Oriyas insist that everyone, including themselves, upheld the rite of human sacrifice. In Bisipara they can point to the place where these sacrifices were held and one man knew the descendants of a person who had been sacrificed by one of his ancestors. The Oriyas here are clearly linked closely to the Konds by political ties and by their common participation in the rite of human sacrifice. Hence the equivocation : on the one hand they were the champions and protectors of the Konds ; on the other hand they were being invited to suppress a rite which they and their subjects thought vital to their welfare, and the invitation came from a power which they probably recognized to be invincible. If they failed the Konds, then at first sight they lost their allegiance ; if they defied the East India Company, they came into conflict with a greatly superior force. A few of them came out openly on the side of the Konds. Some quite early joined forces with the Company. The majority kept an uneasy balance between the two, until it was clear that the East India Company was going to win.

Oriya was the language of the newcomers, the servants of the East India Company, and has continued to be the language of administration up to the present day. This also was the language of those who already exercised some sort of political control over the hills, so that it is not surprising to find the first administrators recognizing and confirming the power of the Hill Chiefs. The Kondmals were divided into fifty *muthas* and over each was placed a headman (*sirdar* or *muthadar*). In the central and western parts of the Kondmals these men all are Oriyas. In the eastern part they are Konds, whose language now is Oriya.

The *mutha* headmen are the successors of the Hill Chiefs, but their role is very different. They are the representatives of an effective outside force and they have exploited this position to gain great personal wealth and influence.

The first administrator, Dinobandu Patnaik, ruled with great ferocity and seems to have stamped on the minds of the Konds a lasting fear of outsiders in general and the Administration in

[1] C. von Fürer-Haimendorf (1945 (2), p. 168) describes the prolonged resistance of Reddi Hill Chiefs during the Rampa rebellion, and comes to a similar conclusion about their status.

particular. It is this fear, more than any delegated power, which put the *mutha* headmen in such a strong position, for they could play upon it in two ways. On the one hand they were still the only protector and champion of the Konds against outside authority. They alone could speak for the Konds to the new authority. On the other hand, they could now back their demands by the threat of irresistible force and there was now no question of the Konds being able to rebel or to transfer their allegiance.[1]

The *mutha* headmen have two main functions, fiscal and jural. Their annual excursions to collect the Watchman Tax and the Plough Tax are a constant reminder to the Konds of their power. Their jural role puts them in a position of being able to exact favours from their subjects. Crimes such as murder must go before the Government courts. But land disputes and marital disputes are often brought before the *mutha* headman, although the case can always be taken on to the Government courts, if either party to the dispute desires.

Over the years the *mutha* headmen built up a formidable list of perquisites attaching to their position. This varied from *mutha* to *mutha* but it would almost always include such items as the following : a contribution of paddy from the harvest ; a gift on the occasion of a wedding or a funeral feast (often a gift as substantial as an ox or a cow) ; contributions to funerals and weddings in the headman's family ; free entertainment when the headman was touring the Kond villages ; and so forth.

The more recent years have seen a gradual curtailment of the powers of the Oriya *mutha* headmen. This has partly been brought about by a policy of protecting Adibasis and partly by the increasing sophistication of the Adibasis themselves. The power of the *mutha* headman—at least in the *mutha* in which I lived—is still considerable, but, as he laments, it is nothing to the power exercised by his father. Most recently, the fact that the Konds of this area now have a man of their own race as Member of the Legislative Assembly of Orissa, and that he is active on their behalf, promises their gradual emancipation from the control of the descendants of the old Hill Chiefs.

[1] The threat of desertion provides a similar check to-day on the authority of the Hill Chiefs of the Rampa Agency of East Godaveri District in Madras. See C. von Fürer-Haimendorf, 1945 (2), p. 173.

The Political Organization of the Village

The Oriya Hill Chiefs were of the WARRIOR caste and this caste appears to have been dominant in all the Oriya villages of the Kondmals. It was by virtue of his position as head of this caste-group that the headman controlled the village and ultimately the surrounding district.

In theory succession passed from the father to his eldest son, unless the latter were conspicuously unfitted for the post. Then it might go to a younger son, or, in the absence of male issue, would go to collateral lines in the lineage. How this system worked in practice is not known, but one may conjecture that faction-fights, which informants mention as a feature in the life of their ancestors, were sometimes occasioned by disputes over succession. It also is clear that these faction-fights sometimes took place between as well as within lineages. For instance, I was told by several different people that the lineage which at present rules in Bisipara and its *mutha*, Besringia, had supplanted another lineage of a different name many years ago. The present holders of the headmanship are called Bisoi. Those whom they supplanted were called Naik, and that particular family of Naiks is said now to be extinct.

Whoever succeeded, and whatever his method of achieving succession, he was always a WARRIOR, a member of the caste-group which dominated other caste-groups in the village. It will be remembered that the castes originally in the village were BRAHMIN, WARRIOR, HERDSMAN, BARBER, WASHERMAN, DISTILLER, OUTCASTE, and perhaps SWEEPER. Villagers at the present day see castes as a hierarchy with high castes at the top, low castes in the middle, and untouchables at the bottom. The BRAHMIN, the WARRIOR and the HERDSMAN were high castes and that was their order of ritual precedence. Each would accept cooked food from the caste above it, but not from the one below it. Then followed a group of low castes, the internal order of which is not clear, but probably was BARBER, DISTILLER and WASHERMAN. Below them again came the untouchable group.

But the relationship of castes was not simply one of ritual practice. The division of wealth and of political power followed the same lines as caste division, and the hierarchy in these fields approximated to the ritual hierarchy. Except for the single family of BRAHMINS, the WARRIORS were ritually superior : they were the wealthy class : they had the political power. The political relation of any other person to a WARRIOR depended on his position in a caste hierarchy. Caste, in other words, had a political function. Caste, viewed as a ritual system, was congruent with the political system.

The systems no longer are congruent. There are now many wealthy men of castes other than WARRIOR and their political relations with the WARRIOR group has in some cases ceased to depend on their relative position in a ritual hierarchy. The relationship is worked out in Government courts, which take no heed of caste.

In the following chapters I shall show how a shift in the distribution of wealth has been followed by an adjustment of the political relations between WARRIORS and the newly rich. In some cases this adjustment has taken place within the system existing in the village polity. In other cases groups or individuals, resident within the village boundary and in some respects members of the village community, either prefer to work within the new political framework provided by the Administration, because it pays them to do so, or are compelled by ideas of pollution to remain outside the jurisdiction of the village council and seek justice in the Government courts. In what follows I shall examine these different adjustments to the new order, and relate them to what I think was the political role of caste within the village.

CHAPTER IX

THE BOAD DISTILLERS

The Liquor Trade

FROM the distant past the Konds have made their own alcoholic drink, which I will call 'liquor'. It is distilled by a simple technique from the flowers of the *mohua* tree (*bassia latifolia*), which abounds in the Kondmals. Until about 1870 the Konds and everyone else were free to make their own liquor, and it may be assumed that distilling was not a particularly profitable trade.

In 1870 the drink-shops in the region to the south of the Kondmals were closed and the sellers of drink migrated in large numbers across the border from Ganjam into the Kondmals. Shortly after this the Government made it illegal for the Konds to distil their own liquor. Home-stills were closed and the Konds were compelled to patronize out-stills,[1] which were run by men of the DISTILLER castes, both those who had recently come in from Ganjam, and those from Boad, who had long been resident in the village.

By 1887 there were 470 out-stills in an area of eight hundred square miles. In their thirst for liquor, many Konds lost all their land and became labourers in the service of the new land-owners. This situation was not viewed with equanimity, particularly by local officials, and several enquiries were held. But while one held in 1894, after a report had been made to the Superintendent of the Tributary Mahals, that the Konds were in need of protection caused some of the out-stills to be closed, it did nothing to alleviate the distress of the Konds. Power to distil simply was concentrated in fewer hands. In 1887 the Konds themselves are said to have held a meeting and taken an oath of temperance. The enquiry begun in 1894 dragged on until 1908, when the opponents of prohibition succeeded in obscuring the issue by bringing charges of immorality against

[1] A similar Excise policy, with similar results, is mentioned in W. Grigson's book on the aboriginals of Bastar State. See W. Grigson, 1949, p. 15.

the Sub-Divisional Officer, who then was the champion of prohibition. The officer was vindicated, but the enquiry closed without taking any action against the out-still system. The difficulty of those in favour of prohibition was that they faced two enemies : the DISTILLERS, perhaps the most vocal part of the population, and the Government itself which was interested in the Excise Revenue. Finally, in 1910, a letter from a Baptist Missionary to the Calcutta *Englishman* put the issue before a wider audience, and the Government of Bengal, of which Orissa was then a part, decreed and carried out the closure of all drink-shops in the Kondmals.

The drink-shops were closed forty years ago and there is now no-one alive who managed one; therefore I was unable to get any detailed account of the economics of an out-still. In any case, persons who make such spectacular and semi-illicit profits do not talk about their work. But from the fact that many of the sons of those who had drink-shops, even when there were two or three heirs, are yet in the second-wealthiest category of land-holding, we may judge that these profits were considerable.

The profits from drink were invested mainly in land. This was a frontier society and still somewhat beyond the boundary of commerce, so that there was very little else for productive investment. Good rice-lands were limited. In addition, in an agricultural community land offers prestige, and finally the drink-sellers were compelled to accept land since this was the main wealth which their customers possessed. I heard one account, when I was discussing this topic with an old man of the HERDSMAN caste, of how land could be transferred directly. A drunken customer would be asked to put his mark to a document transferring a field for Rs.5, and be given Rs.5 credit for liquor in exchange. The DISTILLERS encroached also on the land of castes who did not patronize their shops, by buying land which was brought into the market by the economic forces which I have described in preceding chapters.

This history is reflected in the share which the Boad DISTILLERS have of the village land to-day. From owning land, the average income per head of their caste is 21·5 units of paddy per year. The same figure for the WARRIOR caste is 21·7 units of paddy per year. The Boad DISTILLERS form 6·7 per cent of the population and they own 10 per cent of the income from the village land.[1]

It is not possible now to find out how much land this caste-group owned before 1870, when Governmental intervention made the drink-trade profitable. But I shall assume that they had little or none, and that these years offered them a sudden and spectacular increase in landed wealth. Further, I shall argue that this economic change goes some way towards explaining the history of their activities between prohibition in 1910 and the present day.

The Hindu Rules

Sellers of drink are necessarily low in the caste ritual hierarchy, since alcoholic drink is polluting. The higher castes are not allowed to touch it. I assume, therefore, that before 1855 and during the period from 1870 to 1910, when the drink-trade was flourishing, the Boad DISTILLER caste occupied a lowly position in the caste hierarchy—among the low (*nicho*) Hindus but above the line of being themselves polluting (see Chart 1).

Since prohibition the Boad DISTILLERS, who, as owners of the village land, are now on a level with the WARRIOR caste-group, have followed a way of life very similar to that of the WARRIORS. Their main income comes from the land they own. They go in for trading, as the WARRIORS do, but they are not, like the Ganjam DISTILLERS, engaged in large-scale full-time commercial activities. The Boad DISTILLERS, in the last forty years, have made active, conscious, and on the whole successful efforts to raise their ritual status and their political status within the village. Indeed, the caste as a whole in the Kondmals has tried to better itself according to the Hindu rules.

According to the Hindu rules (which is a translation of a phrase frequently on the lips of informants) there is only one way of improving oneself, and that is to approximate one's behaviour to a stereotype of the behaviour of a BRAHMIN, in particular with regard to what is eaten. This the Boad DISTILLERS have done. They no longer deal in drink, being forbidden by the law to do so. Nor, unlike some of the other castes, do they keep illicit stills for their own use. What is

[1] See Table 9.

more, their caste-council has laid down rules forbidding members to touch alcoholic drink. These rules, promulgated and reiterated every three or four years at the meetings of the caste-council, have also put a ban on eating flesh in any form—that is, on eggs, meat, and fish. These are the rules. The practice is another matter. I know they eat meat, for goat-meat is bought and sold by them quite openly. They also eat fish. However, they do not eat eggs and no chickens are kept in their street. Nor do they drink, at least openly. But the behaviour of individuals, particularly if it is discreet, is unimportant. The point is that the new stereotype of the good Boad DISTILLER, who observes all the rules laid down by his caste-council, like the stereotype BRAHMIN, is a vegetarian. In fact they are not. Neither, in Bisipara, are the BRAHMINS.

Approximation to the behaviour of an ideal BRAHMIN is, however, only the first step in improving one's ritual status. For the new status must be asserted, made public, and reinforced by separating oneself from others with whom one formerly was associated, usually on the grounds that they are not observing the new restrictions. This is the familiar process of the emergence of sub-castes and the split becomes overt in the refusal of the aspiring group to dine or to marry with the rest. Such divisions do in fact exist in the Boad DISTILLER caste. Those in Bisipara call themselves the 'Great DISTILLERS' (*Boro Sundi*) and neither inter-marry nor inter-dine with the other two sub-castes. But whether this division has arisen since 1910 and as a direct result of the efforts of the former sellers of drink to better themselves, or whether it is the result of some earlier conflict, I am unfortunately unable to say, since I had no contact with members of the other two sub-castes.

But the new status needs to be publicized not only by overt action against supposed backsliders within one's own caste, but also by asserting superiority over other castes, and directly by demonstrating the inferiority of caste-groups within one's own village, whom formerly one acknowledged to have been ritually superior. The normal way of doing this is not by direct statement, but by refusing to accept cooked food from the others. Of course, the other caste-groups will normally reject the pretensions of the aspirant group and mock at them, but nevertheless the aspiring group is half-way to its goal. By refusing cooked food it is asserting its own superiority, although it is unable to demonstrate the inferiority of other groups by persuading them to accept cooked food.

The Boad DISTILLERS do all this, and, as one would expect from *parvenus*, they exaggerate. BRAHMINS accept water from the hands of men of the HERDSMAN caste. But the Boad DISTILLERS refuse it. BRAHMINS accept butchered meat from the hands of any of the high castes, including Adibasi castes such as Kond and Kond POTTER. But the Boad DISTILLERS get their share of the meat—for instance at a big wedding—on the hoof. They are given a goat which they take away and butcher for themselves. Through actions like these they have become accepted as a respectable caste. They themselves claim to be second only to the BRAHMIN in the caste hierarchy and they will not accept cooked food from the WARRIORS. Everyone else agrees that WARRIORS come after BRAHMINS, then the WRITER, then ORIYA.[1] Some would accord the next place to the Boad DISTILLERS, but others say that next must be the HERDSMAN caste, since everyone except the DISTILLERS will accept water from them, while no-one among the higher castes will take water from a DISTILLER.

CHART 2

RISE IN RITUAL STATUS OF THE BOAD DISTILLERS

	Order of some caste-groups in Bisipara	
	19th century	*To-day*
A High Hindus	BRAHMIN WARRIOR HERDSMAN Adibasi castes	BRAHMIN WARRIOR *or* DISTILLER HERDSMAN *or* DISTILLER Adibasi castes
B Low Hindus	BARBER DISTILLER WASHERMAN	BARBER WASHERMAN
	Line of pollution	
C Untouchables	Boad OUTCASTE BASKETMAKER SWEEPER	Boad OUTCASTE *or* Ganjam OUTCASTE BASKETMAKER SWEEPER

Note: The word "*or*" indicates that these caste-groups dispute for precedence.

[1] 'ORIYA' is the name of a particular caste as well as of the inhabitants of Orissa. Here, in capitals, the word refers to the caste.

By these three inter-connected methods—approximating their behaviour to the ideal of Hinduism, asserting their superiority over other groups within their caste, and claiming precedence over other caste-groups within the village—the Boad DISTILLERS undoubtedly have bettered themselves. Their ritual status and the respect they command is higher than formerly it was. This is illustrated in Chart 2. A number of smaller caste-groups, mostly from the low-caste category, have been omitted for the sake of simplicity, and because their rating is not directly relevant to the problem. The DISTILLERS have risen from a position in the category of 'Low Hindus' to a place near the top of the category of 'High Hindus', and they themselves claim to be second only to the BRAHMIN.

The Boad Distillers in the Village Political Organization

An increase in the wealth of their caste, coupled with the accident of prohibition, has enabled the Boad DISTILLERS to enhance the ritual status which their caste-group enjoys in the village. But they have also improved their political status. I think they now have a greater say in the management of the village and they are able to combine effectively for political action, when they think it necessary. But ritual and political status are not necessarily connected, if we mean that those who are high in the ritual hierarchy are therefore politically effective. This is not so: the BRAHMINS of Bisipara are politically negligible. The reverse, however, seems to be true. Augmented political effectiveness leads to efforts to improve ritual status and in certain circumstances this goal can be achieved. This is simply a variation of the common-sense sociological principle that the newly-rich adjust their patterns of behaviour to existing wealthy classes. The situation here is complicated by the fact that the ideal behaviour is that enjoined by Hinduism, and not simply the pattern followed by a wealthy class.

Formal political management of the village lies in the hands of the village council (*panchayat*). This council has juridical, legislative and executive functions. A random survey through the proceedings of the council during 1953–4 shows it engaged in the following activities: formulating a new set of rules for the periodical cleaning of public places in the village; allocating responsibility for the upkeep of a temple which lies beside the village; organizing the repair of the village dam; deciding which villages shall be invited to the annual drumming festival; listening to a complaint that the water-buffaloes of the WASHERMAN have damaged the garden of his neighbour, a HERDSMAN; fining a young man of the WARRIOR caste who had abused an old WARRIOR widow who lived in the next house; decreeing that certain perquisites which formerly attached to the WASHERMAN and the BARBER should be abolished; tactfully refusing, not openly but by procrastination, to intervene in a dispute between a BRAHMIN youth and his mother's brother; and so forth.

There is a rule that the heads of all households—'all men of importance', as the villagers themselves say—should attend the council meetings. Fines are imposed on those who do not attend and on those who come late, and the money is used to provide kerosene for the pressure-lamp which lights the meetings. In fact attendance is restricted to the heads of all households of castes above the line of pollution, since the meetings are held in a building which houses sacred objects. Even when meetings are held outside, no part is taken by the members of untouchable castes, unless one is directly concerned, for example, as party to a dispute. No woman is allowed to attend a meeting.

The council imposes fines and may allot tasks in punishment, but its ultimate sanction is the power to decree ostracism. Anyone dissatisfied with the decisions of the council may appeal to the Government courts, providing they will take cognizance. But this is a dangerous expedient since these courts are unable in practice to prevent the village from making life unbearable for those whom it does not like. Apart from such open measures against a man whom the village decides no longer 'to make its brother', as the refusal of the BARBER, the WASHERMAN, the BRAHMIN, and the village cowherd to offer their services, he also would have difficulty in raising labour to work his land, he would have no-one to help at the times of death and marriage, and he would suffer from the innumerable subtle discomforts which could be inflicted on him with impunity as a result of the loss of status.

Formal political control of the village and its affairs rests with the council. But the members of the council are not simply the heads of households, each speaking in his own interest or in the interest of an abstract justice. They belong to different castes. Some are wealthy and some are poor. There are different factions. Some are more educated than others. Some are vocal and articulate. Others are mere passengers, who listen but seldom speak. These different characteristics and divergent loyalties affect the working of the council.

Firstly, the division into wealthy and poor has little immediate relevance, for it is overridden by the division into factions and partly by the division into castes. In no sense is there any overt class-grouping within the council into rich and poor.

Secondly, although these different loyalties very often affect the parts which the different individuals play in the debates of the council, they do not invariably do so. There are some occasions when the council speaks with the unanimous voice of one village, particularly when they are involved with Government officials or with other outsiders. For instance, during the past five years there has been an Experimental Post Office in the village. This service is not extensively patronized since the literacy rate is not high and even those who are literate have little occasion to use the postal services. But the institution is appreciated, since it saves an eight-mile walk to Phulbani and since it adds to the prestige of the village. However, since the village is a mile off the main road in the dry season, and three miles off in the wet season, it was necessary to employ both a runner and a postmaster, and the Postal Department made a loss. At the end of 1953 they decided to close the Experimental Post Office in Bisipara. The village petitioned against the decision. The Post Office naïvely replied that if the village cared to make good the loss over the past five years and to guarantee no loss in the future, the service could be continued. The council met and no hint of faction or caste divided them over this issue. They replied by asking this question : If the Post Office had made a profit over the past five years, would it have given the money to the village ?

Again there are some issues which come before the council and are debated in the light of an abstract justice, and not according to the factional loyalties of the persons concerned. This might be when the issue is so clear-cut that there can be little debate about who is in the right and who is wrong. For instance, in October 1953 an old WARRIOR widow complained that she had been wrongfully abused by her young WARRIOR neighbour. The council listened and then decided without a voice of dissent to fine the young man. He admitted his guilt and paid the fine. These persons belonged to the rival factions of WARRIORS, but the issue was sufficiently clear, and sufficiently unimportant, to allow the matter to be considered without reference to factional loyalties. Again, there are sometimes cases brought by Konds from the villages of the *mutha*, and although these primarily are placed before the *mutha* headman, he normally will be attended by some members of the council, who assist in giving judgement. In those cases which I witnessed I could see no tendency for him to draw upon members of his own faction only, or for the members of the panel to line up according to their factional loyalties.

Division into factions starts within the WARRIOR caste-group. Here the division is complete and extends into the field of ritual. A faction allows a much more restricted course of mourning at the death of a man of the opposite faction than for a death within its own faction. In the same way it modifies assistance given at weddings according to factional loyalties. Every WARRIOR lineage belongs to one or the other faction and the loyalty of every household is known. (There are a few examples where a disgruntled household has parted from the rest of its lineage and changed faction.)

This division into two factions is extended into the other castes, mainly through the attachment of individuals to the heads of the two WARRIOR factions, in particular to the *mutha* headman. In these castes the division is not complete and while one can say, for instance, that certain Kond POTTER households will always be found alongside the *mutha* headman and his faction, there are other households who side sometimes with one faction and sometimes with the other, going either along the line of their own interest or according to their idea of what is just.

Much more could be said about factions, but I have given this outline because I want to avoid creating the impression that the members of the village council invariably or even usually divide along the lines of caste loyalty. The statement that the Boad DISTILLERS have raised their status not only in the ritual hierarchy, but also as a political group, does not mean that the Boad

DISTILLERS are a united party within the village council, following the party line. They are not: in the majority of disputes DISTILLERS are to be found arguing on both sides, either in support of factions or in the interests of justice.[1]

Indeed, apart from the ban on OUTCASTES and the other untouchables, caste has little relevance in most of the business that the council conducts. It is true that the caste-groups often sit together in the council. But that is only because they have come along together from their street. There is no rule to this effect and late-comers sit down anywhere they can find room. Again, there is no fixed order of speaking and the talk passes from one person to another without reference to caste.

It is only when an issue patently involves the rights, status, or prestige of a particular caste that the council tends to divide along the lines of caste. It is not often that such a clear-cut issue comes up, and there is a reason for this. The reason is that many such cases do not come before the village council, but are dealt with by the caste-group, or, if sufficiently serious, by a meeting of the caste-council, which serves all the Kondmals. Thus, if a man has an indiscreet liaison with a woman of lower caste, then his caste will act against him, and the woman's caste either may ignore her or may punish her. But the woman's caste will not bring the affair before the village council, unless she had been taken by violence and against her will. Nor will the man's caste try to turn the affair into a dispute with the whole of the other caste. Each is concerned to discipline its own members. The same, obviously, is true when the dispute arises entirely within the caste, as when a party to a marriage defaults on the payment or if disputes were to arise over the ownership of the dowry of a deceased bride.

From late in 1952 to early in 1954 there was only one dispute in the village council which brought a caste-group to act together as a political group (speaking here only of clean castes), and that concerned the Boad DISTILLERS. Many years ago the father of one of these Boad DISTILLERS had allowed a Kond farm-servant to build a small one-roomed house in a garden in

[1] The role of factions in the judicial, legislative and administrative activities of the village council could be illustrated by case material. But the question is not directly relevent to the present analysis. I hope to present the material elsewhere.

the street of the Boad DISTILLERS. This hut is at the extreme end of the street and detached from the other houses, most of which are built to form one continuous line. There is a garden in the street of the DISTILLERS, which many years ago fell by escheat to the Government. It is fairly clear that there were in fact heirs, but the situation was manipulated between the *mutha* headman and one of the Government clerks, and the land was made to appear without heirs. The present-day heirs have given up hope of recovering the title to the land, although they have in fact been able to enjoy its produce. This strange situation arose, because the holder of title was a Government servant who had never been to the village. Now he has died and the land has been allotted to the Kond. This garden is in the middle of the south side of the street of the DISTILLERS, and the Kond sought permission from the village council to build a house on the land. He had already been refused permission by the Boad DISTILLERS.

There are, in fact, two disputes here, and the reaction of the Boad DISTILLERS differed significantly in each. The Boad DISTILLER who claims to be the true heir to the land (more is involved than just this garden) and who asserts that it was wrongfully taken by the Government, has no support from the fellow-members of his caste-group. No doubt they are sorry for him. But they have taken no action to support him—even if any action were possible—and they are not very interested, since the thing happened many years ago and they lost nothing by it. Moreover some of them are active henchmen of the *mutha* headman, whose father was partly—and consciously—responsible for the land passing to the Government. But now events have taken this unforeseen turn and the Kond proposes, like everyone else, to have a house beside his garden-land. This has provoked the united opposition of the Boad DISTILLER caste. For they have chosen to regard it as an infringement of their caste rights, if a man of lower caste were to live not at the end of their street, but in their midst, and to live not in a house built for him as a servant with the permission of his Boad DISTILLER master, but in a house built by himself in his own right as a landholder. The dispute was still unresolved when I left the village.

When the village council is listening to a dispute, or trying to reach agreement over administration, the individuals who together form the council must strike a balance between many claims on them, which sometimes are in conflict. There is the abstract claim of justice. They must keep in mind their own interests. They are pulled by loyalties to the faction to which they belong. They might be influenced by ties of kinship or friendship with one of the disputants, or they might dislike one of them. Finally they owe a loyalty to their caste in certain situations, and if they are convinced that its status and prestige are at stake, then the members of one caste will act together in its defence. It is in this way that caste-groups sometimes function as political groups.

Conclusion

The point which I wish to emphasize is that the Boad DISTILLERS have continued throughout this period of change to act mainly within the political framework provided by the village council. They attend its meetings. They back its decisions and participate in its debates no less than, for instance, the WARRIOR and the HERDSMAN caste-groups. Implicitly they acknowledge themselves to be within its jurisdiction.

I do not know how the village council functioned when the Boad DISTILLERS had their drink-shops nor, before that time, when they still were poor men. Until very recently no records of the proceedings of the village council were kept. But it seems probable that they now play a greater part and exert more influence in the council than they did in the nineteenth century. They are now men of property and substance.

At the same time they have come to command greater respect within the ritual system of caste. This is not fortuitous. A high ritual status does not necessarily lead to political power. But the reverse tends to be true. Increased wealth leads to a desire for a greater say in the management of the community. At the same time the aspirants wish to assume the guise of respectability, and they do this by improving their placing within the ritual ranking of the Hindu caste system. Their increased wealth makes them politically more effective, and this enables them to enhance their ritual standing as against other caste-groups in the village.

The point which distinguishes the Boad DISTILLERS from the other two groups, whom I am going to consider, is that they have achieved their new status within the existing ritual and political framework of the village. Positions within the structure were altered. The structure itself was left intact.

CHAPTER X

THE GANJAM DISTILLERS

Shopkeepers

THE Boad DISTILLERS came from the north, about the time the village first was colonized. The Ganjam DISTILLERS came from Ganjam in the south after prohibition was introduced in that District in 1870. The difference in Excise policy arose from the fact that then Ganjam was part of the Northern Circars of the Madras Presidency, while the Kondmals and the Tributary States to the north were subjects of the Administration of Orissa, which itself was part of Bengal. These two groups of DISTILLERS, although they bear the same Oriya name (*Sundi*) and have the same traditional occupation, are nevertheless considered to be, and consider themselves to be, separate castes. They do not inter-dine and they do not intermarry.

Up to the time of prohibition in 1910, the economic history of the two groups is very similar and both derived spectacular profits from the sale of drink. However, in Bisipara at least, if not elsewhere in the Kondmals, the shops run by Ganjam DISTILLERS sold not only drink, but also general merchandise, while the Boad DISTILLERS tended to concentrate on the sale of liquor.

At prohibition the Boad DISTILLERS retired from commerce and lived like the rest of the peasants in the village on the produce of their land and the profits of small seasonal trading. Agriculture became their main source of income. But the Ganjam DISTILLERS continued in commerce as general shopkeepers and merchants. They retail manufactures and primary products to the people of the district. They buy primary crops such as turmeric and liquor-flowers and transmit these to the large middlemen in the plains. They are called *sahukar*, a word which I would translate as 'merchant'. (The word often is translated as 'money-lender', but in the village it was applied to anyone who had large-scale commercial dealings, and was not specifically limited to lending money.)

There were five households of Ganjam DISTILLERS when I first arrived in the village. P has a large well-established shop and owns the biggest estate in the village, as well as an estate in his ancestral village. He spends most of his time in Bisipara, although his wife and children live on the plains. Q and R are brothers each having their own shop. Q has invested in land and owns an estate which falls into the second-largest category (see Table 24). His wife and family live in the village with him. R, who as well as dealing in general merchandise, is a gold and silver merchant, has little land in the village. His wife and children live on the plains of Ganjam, where, presumably, they own land. Although his business and his kin connections take him on frequent visits to the plains, he spends most of his time in the village and would be counted in the Census list, and is inscribed on the recent Voting list, as a resident of Bisipara. S has no shop of his own and works as an agent, formerly for P, but recently for a shopkeeper in the village of WRITER caste. His wife and his brother and a sister's son, adopted by him, live in Bisipara. They own some land, the remnant of a considerable estate which was frittered away by the youthful improvidence of S. The last Ganjam DISTILLER household consisted of one young man, a nephew of Q and R, who had come to the village about six years ago. He made a scanty living assisting his uncles and doing a little business on his own account. In 1953 he gave up the struggle and got a job as a schoolmaster in a village about sixty miles away.

It is not difficult to account for the fact that the Ganjam DISTILLERS have continued in commerce while the Boad DISTILLERS abandoned it and took to farming. Their work demands considerable powers of managerial organization. They sell a wide range of products and need to know the right prices to pay and the appropriate sources from which to seek them. In addition they handle large amounts of money as middlemen in the trade that carries primary products out of the district. They were already engaged in this trade—to what extent we do not know—before prohibition came, and it was natural that they should continue afterwards. The experience of the Boad DISTILLERS was confined to running drink-shops, and this, compared with the management of a merchant's business, is a simple matter. Furthermore, there was room for an infinitely greater number of drink-shops than there is for general stores, and one would expect that in the ensuing competition, those who were without experience would have been squeezed out. I do not know whether or not the Boad DISTILLERS made any attempt to continue in commerce as general merchants. If they did, none of them was successful, for at the present day none of them owns a shop in Bisipara. A further point in the favour of the Ganjam DISTILLERS is that there is a commercial horizon only to the south. The routes which connect the Kondmals with the larger economy of commercial India run all to the south to the point on the Madras-Calcutta railway at Berhampur, which is just one hundred miles away from the centre of the Kondmals. All manufactures come from this side and all the primary products of the region are despatched in this direction. This is the homeland of the Ganjam DISTILLERS and they have here the contacts which a general merchant requires. To all men of other castes in the village, including the Boad DISTILLERS, the land below the hills to the south is a foreign land. They move freely about the hills, but they are apprehensive of a journey which might take them to the plains of Ganjam. They do not feel the same way about the plains of Boad. If they go to the southern plains, for instance to buy cattle at one of the markets there, they go in parties which stick together until they have climbed the long hill to the plateau. Then they disperse. These are the reasons why I think the Ganjam DISTILLERS have been able to continue in commerce after prohibition, while the Boad DISTILLERS have not.

By village standards, all four Ganjam DISTILLER households which remain in the village, even the household of the agent who has no business of his own, are well off. The three shopkeepers are very rich and one of them is far and away the richest man in the village, both in landed property and other forms of capital. As a caste they are the richest landowners in the village. They form 2 per cent of the population of the village. They take 12·5 per cent of the income from the village lands. While the average income per head from owning land among the WARRIORS is 21·7 units, and among the Boad DISTILLERS is 21·5 units, that of the Ganjam DISTILLERS is 96 units, almost five times that of the other two (see Table 9).

The Relationship of the Ganjam Distillers and the Village

The part played by the men of the Ganjam DISTILLER caste in the everyday affairs of the village is not at first sight distinguishable from the part played by householders of any other caste. They are to be seen watching the festivals and the ceremonies, which take place during the year. Like the other landowners in the village they wait until the *mutha* headman has made a ceremonial opening to the planting season before they begin to transplant their rice seedlings. Like everyone else they do not harvest their upland rice until the *Nua Khia* ('new eating' or first fruit) ceremonies have marked the beginning of a new agricultural year. When the old wooden village temple was demolished and work was begun to erect a new stone building, like other men of substance they sent along a labourer to take their share of the work burning lime or carrying stones for the foundation. When the old village dam was rebuilt, after the collapse of a larger dam built by the authorities, the Ganjam DISTILLERS took their share of the labour. Their houses are sited within the village boundaries in Market Street (see Map 3). They benefit from ritual measures taken to protect the village from disease or malignant spirits. Their fields are intermingled with the fields of other landowners who live in the village. They are in no sense geographically separated from the rest of the village community. Furthermore, all but one were born and grew up here in Bisipara. The exception is the richest man, who was born in the plains and subsequently took over the shop and the land from his father's younger brother.

However, one gets the impression on closer observation that these men are not part of the village to the same degree as men of other castes. Just before midday, and again in the evening, the men sit around in the street gossiping or just watching people go to and fro. In the evening the work is done. In the morning they have come back from ploughing or cutting wood, and they are resting before they go down to the river for a bath, in preparation for the midday meal. Men of other castes who live in Market Street sit around like this: but not the Ganjam DISTILLERS. Again, they do not participate as fully as others in the informal leisure activities of the men. Every day, in the hot season, at the hottest part of the day, the men protect their heads with a towel and their feet with sandals and go out to hunt rabbits, which come above ground during the daytime in the hot months. They hunt in gangs and kill the rabbits by throwing sticks at them. It is a very popular sport and everyone except the Ganjam DISTILLERS indulges in it. Nor do they go out with the groups who at the beginning of the dry season dam the river and catch fish in the shallow water. Nor do they take part in the hunts for bigger game—deer and wild boar—which take out every able-bodied man in the village. No doubt there is a good reason for this. These activities of hunting and fishing belong to the life of a farmer, and the shopkeeper has no time. Time matters to the farm only at certain peak periods during the year. The shopkeeper's time is valuable all the year round. His work, in this way, separates him from the rest of the village community.

In the more formal activities of the village the same pattern of separation is apparent. Of the group of Ganjam DISTILLERS only Q regularly attends the meetings of the village council. This situation is accepted by the village council and they do not exact fines for non-attendance from the other Ganjam DISTILLERS, as they do from men of other castes. There is no question of an overt boycott of the council. On the whole they abide by legislative and executive decisions reached by the council. If the council decrees that every household shall contribute one rupee to pay for hiring an expert diviner from another place to come and clear the village of evil spirits, the Ganjam DISTILLERS pay up like the rest. They contribute the standard gift of a measure or half a measure of rice to be used in feeding the drumming parties who are invited from other villages to participate in the drumming competition. Occasionally, when there is an interesting case before the council, or when such a major issue as the rebuilding of the village temple is under discussion, they come along and listen to the council and sit among the rest and occasionally offer a contribution to the debate. There is no hint in their overt behaviour of contempt or pride and they behave as equals among other men of substance. They seemed to me to make no noticeable effort to associate themselves with, or dissociate themselves from the other men of the village.

Neither do they take any covert part in village politics. They have no henchmen and no-one in the village council speaks regularly on their behalf. They are associated neither with the heads nor the members of factions, and they do not try to form factions of their own. They remain aloof from the politics of the village council, and as a rule, insofar as their lives are touched by the decisions of the council, they obey it. Beyond that, they avoid entanglement.

This attitude of polite respectful detachment is reciprocated by the villagers. They make an effort to avoid getting themselves entangled with the shopkeepers in any but the economic sphere. There is not the same flood of trivial complaints brought before the council concerning the shopkeepers as there is between the other people in the village. At first sight this is surprising, for in the relations of shopkeeper and customer there are many potential points of friction. Many customers keep small running debts, which the shopkeeper is happy to allow since it binds in the custom. But he cannot let it get too big, while the customer on the other hand likes it to be as big as possible since it is free of interest. Concerning the general relationship of customer and shopkeeper the villagers themselves are perfectly cynical and say that it is a question of cheating or being cheated. Many years ago a rich Christian ran a shop in the village, and he is still spoken of with a mixture of respect and derision, since it was known that he never cheated. It was quite safe to send a small child to do the shopping since this man would never give short weight. The informant goes on to say that things are very different in the other shops. The customers have little chance to cheat over retail transactions, but they get their turn when they take advances of money from the same shopkeepers, in their capacity as merchants, to buy turmeric and liquor-flowers. The small traders take full advantage of these opportunities and will relate with relish the spectacular successes of their friends (they are more coy about their own dishonesties) in skimming away the merchant's profits.

Yet, in spite of this big field of potential conflict, there are very few cases either before the village council or in the Government courts of a dispute between a shopkeeper and his customers in the village, or between the same parties as merchant and small traders. Again there are good reasons for this moderation and for the willingness of both sides to be content with the usually temporary economic sanction of discontinuing business in that quarter. For their part the villagers know that to complain to the village council would be useless since the council is unwilling or unable to take action against the shopkeepers. Indeed the only action open to the council is the ultimate sanction of ostracism, and this, to my knowledge, has never been tried. The shopkeepers, on the other hand, do not press petty claims, partly because, with their greater sophistication and knowledge of the world, they realize that it would be bad for business and partly because a shopkeeper who tried to exact retribution for every bad debt or trivial loss, or who stood too much upon his pride, would be engaged in perpetual litigation. They have more important things on hand, and prefer not to squander their resources over small losses or slights, in the way that villagers will between themselves.

An instance of this happened in 1953. The servant of a shop, belonging as it happened to a man of the WRITER caste and not to a Ganjam DISTILLER, got drunk and then went off to the street of the Kond POTTERS and joined in a drunken fight that was already in progress when he arrived. They made so much noise that another man sounded the alarm and the householders from all the streets around came and broke up the fight. When the fighters were sober, they were called before the council. All submitted to the rebuke and the fine except the shop-servant, who had been brought temporarily to the village from the shopkeeper's own village on the plains. He abused the council and told them to do their worst. But that evening the shopkeeper himself prevailed upon the servant, who was related to him, and the next day when the council met, the man appeared and apologized for his behaviour and paid the fine. This undoubtedly is an example of the tact of the shopkeeper and his eye for expediency, for the village could have taken no direct action against the offender, since he was only temporarily resident in their community. Nor, very likely, would they have attempted to visit his guilt upon the shopkeeper, who himself had done nothing to offend them.

If trivial cases like this are rare, serious cases are much rarer. If, for some reason, the shopkeeper feels he cannot compromise, then he will go before the courts of the Government rather than before the village council. In cases of a bad debt he will not need to go to court, but only to threaten to do so. The ordinary villager is in awe of the courts and in any case is convinced that victory will go to the man who can hire a good lawyer, and he knows that the shopkeeper, with his greater wealth and wider contacts, will better be able to do this. Consequently, although shopkeepers nowadays often appear before the courts accused of sharp practice or evasion of tax, there seldom is a case between a man of this village and a shopkeeper. The one case which informants could quote arose out of an accusation by an unmarried Kond POTTER woman that one of the shopkeepers was the father of her child. Her kinsmen and caste-fellows attempted to interest the village council in the affair, but nothing came of it. Then they went to court and tried to get damages from the shopkeeper. He hired a lawyer and won his case.

The Ganjam Distillers and the World outside the Village

It is obvious that the Ganjam DISTILLERS have considerable ties with the world outside the village. Although they are resident in the village and count themselves members of that community rather than of any other village, yet in a sense they are much more citizens of the region or the State (Orissa) than are men of other castes in the village.

I have already explained how their ties of kinship and commercial connections bind them to the foreign land south of the hills. In addition they have to deal with all the agents of commerce and the other people who have business in the centres in the hills, in such market settlements as Phulbani, Tikaballi, Udaygiri and even Baliguda away in the south-west (see Map 1). The ordinary farmer has no contact with these distant businessmen and very little to do, except as an occasional customer, with those close at hand in Phulbani.

It is clear that the Ganjam DISTILLER shopkeeper can—indeed, must—organize his relations with the world of commerce without reference to the political organization of the village and the village council. The people who move in this world are beyond not only the jurisdiction and cognizance of the village council but even beyond the awareness of its members. Commerce, no doubt, has its own structure and probably its own system of morals, by which those engaged in it regulate their behaviour and settle disputes. Ultimately the only judicial authority in this system is the Government court and in the last resort it is in the courts that the relations of the Ganjam DISTILLERS and the people with whom business brings them into contact are organized.

But this statement has a wider application than is at first apparent. The Ganjam DISTILLER must use the Government courts to obtain redress not only against his fellow-merchants, who reside in the trading centres in the Kondmals or beyond the southern boundary of the Kondmals, but also against a large part of his customers. The shops serve not only the householders who live in Bisipara, but also those who live in the villages around. I was unable to get any information to show what proportion of the custom of the shops was in Bisipara and what was outside. Shopkeepers do not readily talk, however innocuous the enquiry, and other informants could offer nothing that was based on more than casual observation. There were always people from other villages at the shops and, judging by the siting of shops in other villages, the village is a commercial catchment area for at least fifty villages, of varying size. Some of these villages lie within the *mutha*, of which Bisipara is the capital, and the village council could, through the person of its headman, perhaps exert influence over them. But insofar as the shopkeeper does not choose to prosecute defaulters in his own village through the village council, and insofar as the council does not entertain complaints brought by its own members against the shop, so much the more are the relations of the shopkeeper and those only marginally within the jurisdiction of the village council unlikely to be organized within the framework of the village political system. Again, there are many customers of the shops who are *de jure* outside the jurisdiction of the *mutha* headman. In fact the shopkeeper is able to exert the same sanction over these people as he can over the people of his own village. He can threaten to take them to court, and since they are mostly Konds who are infinitely more ignorant of judicial procedures and their rights at law than are the Oriyas, the threat is doubly effective.

The fact that much of his custom comes from outside the village is one reason why the shopkeeper is immune to ostracism, the severest sanction at the disposal of the village council. This sanction could probably not be enforced beyond the village. I am not claiming that such action could not drive a shopkeeper out of business. The situation has never arisen and there are no figures of the comparative size of the categories of customers by which to predict the course of such a dispute. But this is an additional reason to make the council think twice about trying its strength against a shopkeeper, even if it could overcome the latent fear of retaliation through the Government courts, and decide to act. In fact the shopkeepers, on the whole, are too subtle to let such a situation arise.

The shopkeepers are brought into relation with three sets of people : the other merchants and the wholesalers ; their customers from other villages ; and the customers from the village in which the shop is situated. With the first two of these the shopkeeper's political relations must be organized without reference to the political organization of the village, through the Administration. Although theoretically it would be possible for him to work his relations with the third group within the framework of the village political organization (and so far as legislation and administration are concerned, he finds it expedient for the most part to do so), nevertheless in the last resort the shopkeeper is beyond the jurisdiction of the village council, and his jural relations with his fellow-villagers are worked out ultimately in the Government courts.

Conclusions

Wealth is the ultimate determinant. Because the shopkeepers are rich, the men of the village believe that they can make effective use of the Government courts. To hire a lawyer, they think, is to win a case. It is this belief that induces the villagers to avoid entanglement with the shopkeepers, and this is made easy by the tactful behaviour of the shopkeepers towards the village council and the legislative and judicial actions which it takes.

The political structure of the village, to use a metaphor, coped successfully with the disturbance set up by the redistribution of wealth in favour of the Boad DISTILLERS. There was an internal readjustment, but the structure itself remained the same.

But the wealth acquired by the Ganjam DISTILLERS has had different results. They have modified their behaviour to conform approximately with the BRAHMIN stereotype. But they have not tried to participate in the political management of the village : they do not seek a following or try to obtain leadership within the village. Nor have they made a direct assault upon the political system of the village. But they do ignore its judicial aspect and it is on its juridical powers that the strength of the council is ultimately founded. Partly they do this because, unlike the Boad DISTILLERS, they never were part of the village community. Partly they do so because their political and social horizon extends far beyond the village. They are able to do so, because they are wealthy enough to patronize the judicial services offered by the Government of India.

But, because the Ganjam DISTILLERS ignore the political system of the village, this does not mean that the structure is therefore unimpaired. To ignore a court—with impunity—is to attack it. To appeal from the council to the Magistrate is to transfer the case to a court which operates in a different juridical system. These two systems are in practice inimical. Such an action would be roughly analogous to appealing against the decision of an Ecclesiastical court to the secular authorities. It is not an appeal from one court to another which is higher but in the same juridical system. The village council knows this, and before a serious case they exact an oath from both parties that they will not appeal to the Government courts, and threaten ostracism on those who do appeal. The Government of India also knows it, and because, particularly after Gandhi's teaching, they value the village community, they are trying to set up statutory village councils in an attempt to revive village councils that are in other places defunct.[1]

The coming of the Administration has affected the political structure of the village in two ways—directly and indirectly. Directly the Administration asserts full political authority (legislative, administrative and judicial) over the village, and in particular it claims the right to hear appeals from decisions of the village council. Indirectly, the coming of the Administration set up a chain of economic events which led to the redistribution

[1] The opposition of the village and the Administration is discussed at length in Chapter XII.

of wealth within the village. One class of beneficiaries, who reside within the village boundaries, prefers to order its relationships with other men in the village in the larger all-India political system (in particular the courts) rather than within the political structure of the village.

CHAPTER XI

THE BOAD OUTCASTES

THE UNTOUCHABLES

IN the village there are four castes whose touch is polluting. These are the Boad OUTCASTES, the Ganjam OUTCASTES, the BASKETMAKERS and the SWEEPERS. Their proportions of the village population are given in Table 9 and are: Boad OUTCASTE 21·7 per cent; Ganjam OUTCASTE 6 per cent; BASKETMAKER 1 per cent; and SWEEPER 2·6 per cent. The Boad OUTCASTE group is thus more than twice as numerous as the rest put together and forms approximately one-fifth of the population of the village, larger than any other caste-group in the village. The WARRIORS come next with 19·5 per cent and then the Kond POTTERS with 16·5 per cent.

The SWEEPERS are the lowest in this hierarchy, and consequently the lowest caste in the village. No other caste will accept food and water from their hands, and they themselves accept cooked food from anyone, both in practice and in theory. The BASKETMAKERS come next above them. The division between the two highest caste-groups among the untouchables is not rigidly observed. Both have the same name in the vernacular (*Pano*), although the Ganjam people are usually distinguished by the addition of the place-name Ganjam, or its ancient equivalent Gumsur. However, the mere possession of a common caste-name is not evidence of being one caste. It is not so in the case of the DISTILLERS (*Sundi*), nor in the case of the WARRIORS (*Sudo*), for to the south of the Kondmals there is another distinct group of WARRIORS, ruled by a council different from that which rules the WARRIORS of the Kondmals. But between the group of Boad OUTCASTES and Ganjam OUTCASTES in Bisipara there have been at least two intermarriages in the present generation of later middle-age, and these two family-groups dine together on occasions of family-ritual. Nor, so far as I know, is there any ban on interdining in other contexts. But in spite of this the two groups consider themselves separate.

They do not, as castes, assist at one another's funerals or weddings. A death in the street of the Boad OUTCASTES will mobilize the whole of that street, but will be attended by no-one from the street of the Ganjam OUTCASTES unless the death occurred in one of those families linked to the other street by affinal and uterine ties. The same applies, *mutatis mutandis*, when a death or a marriage ritual is observed in the street of the Ganjam OUTCASTES. Again, the two groups live in separate streets, one to the east and the other to the west of the main part of the village. Finally, the distinction is at present sharpened by conditions of acute hostility.

In this chapter I shall describe the history and present condition of the Boad OUTCASTES. They are by far the more numerous. Further, I think that their present relationship with the rest of the village shows well the way in which the combined effect of economic change and administrative intervention is altering the traditional political functions of the caste system. But it must be remembered that there are other groups beside the Boad OUTCASTE who labour under the disabilities of being untouchable.

The Boad OUTCASTES came from the north and belong to that group of Oriyas who first colonized the village in the hills. Their myth claims that the village could be founded only by the valour and cunning of OUTCASTE heroes (see Chapter VIII). Needless to say, men of other castes dispute and ridicule this account, but they agree that Boad OUTCASTES came in the beginning.

There is ample evidence that the position of the Boad OUTCASTES has always been a lowly one, whether this position is measured in terms of the ritual structure of caste or by their role in the economic system of the original village. This evidence comes from both sides. The WARRIORS claim that Boad OUTCASTES were their farm-servants. The latter admit this. The myth goes on :

Boad OUTCASTES were not educated. They did not know how to cultivate by themselves. They always got their food from others. They said 'We killed the foes of the Oriyas. Give us a potful of rice'. And so they survived. They called the Bisoi their great lord and became his clients. They ate from his house. The Boad OUTCASTES came with the Oriyas in the beginning, but they did not cultivate fields and gardens like the Oriyas. They were very uneducated and senseless. If they had made fields and gardens, they would have had a share of the land with the Oriyas.

This position of economic subservience is parallel to ritual disability. As I will describe later, the Boad OUTCASTES have improved considerably their economic standing, but they still labour under extensive ritual disqualifications.

The touch of an OUTCASTE pollutes certain objects and persons. If by accident a man of clean caste comes into physical contact with an OUTCASTE then he must bathe and change his clothes as soon as he can. This ban extends to the houses and the street of the OUTCASTES, which is in fact a ghetto segregated from the rest of the village. No man of clean caste will ordinarily venture into that street. For some of these men, particularly the older generation of WARRIORS, the miasma seems to extend for some distance around the street of the Boad OUTCASTES. Ordinarily the village paths are so adjusted that a man can leave the centre of the village in any direction without having to come too close to OUTCASTE street. But sometimes, as when returning from a hunt, the nearest route is obviously close along the end of the gardens of the street of the OUTCASTES. When this happens, the party make a wide detour through the scrub jungle and the fields to reach a path coming in from the north and avoiding OUTCASTE street.

The persons of the Boad OUTCASTES do not carry this miasma. They move freely about the streets of the other castes. If they have business there, they may go also into the courtyards behind the houses, but not, of course, into the house itself. When they meet important men of clean castes they normally will stand aside. Good manners also dictate that if they are sitting in conversation in the street, for instance, of the WARRIORS, then the latter squat on the verandahs of the house, while the OUTCASTE men squat on the ground. There is, however, no question of the person of the OUTCASTE spreading pollution within a certain range. Physical contact alone is what matters. If money or other small things are passing between persons in clean and unclean categories, then one party cups his hands and the other drops the object into them. In other cases the object is laid on the ground to be picked up by the other party.

In some respects this behaviour is stereotyped and not pushed to its logical conclusion. The rules, for instance, are suspended on a bus. Contact is not, of course, sought, but if it occurs accidentally, then there is no outcry. In the school, where formerly pupils were segregated, they now by Government ordinance sit side by side: and since there is a Government ordinance and the building belongs to the Government anyway, the rules of caste concerning physical contact are tacitly suspended.

There is a marked difference in the behaviour of the old and the young towards untouchables. The *mutha* headman, for example, led a wide detour around the street of the OUTCASTES, when returning at the head of a hunting party. But his son, who is twenty-one years old, readily accompanied me not only on the short cut that led beside the street, but also into the street itself, when I had occasion to go there. This difference in the behaviour of the generations is sufficiently marked to be noticed and to excite comment from the older villagers themselves. An old schoolmaster of the HERDSMAN caste remarked on it, and with a surprising indifference. He compared the behaviour of X, the young man, with that of his father. He did not condemn X. He took it as evidence that caste was breaking down. 'It's not the same now as when I was young. Education does it. X has been to the High School. That's why he behaves the way he does. It's ignorance that makes the village behave in this way.' However, this development is not to be exaggerated. In a sense X was excused the rules of caste since he was working for me, when he went into the street of the OUTCASTES. Like everyone else, in his normal life he avoids physical contact with untouchables. Although the system may be less rigid than it was a generation ago, it would be a mistake to think that the pollution concepts which regulate the contacts of men of clean and unclean castes were falling into complete disuse. They are not.

Informants of clean castes would often rationalize their ritual abhorrence of untouchables by saying that they were dirty in their habits and persons and dwellings. 'They eat beef,' an informant said, and then, remembering to whom he was talking,

'And not just beef, like a Sahib or a Christian, but carrion. They eat cattle which have been dead five or six days and are stinking. That is why we feel dirty when they touch us.' He then went on to say that they were dirty in their persons and their street was a slum. As a broad characterization, this is true. OUTCASTE Street had its dandies, but on the whole the people were dirtier than, for instance, the WARRIORS. This statement is not based on immediate quantitative data, but on observation. I lived astride the paths that led from the village to the river and a much smaller proportion of the OUTCASTE street took a daily bath than did WARRIORS. Skin infections, which are propagated by dirt, were much commoner among the OUTCASTES than among the rest of the village. Again, their street was very much overcrowded and consequently difficult to keep clean, especially as there was no regular system of sweeping. In other words, the accusations of the men of clean caste were not without substance. OUTCASTE street is, in some respects, a slum, and the way of life of its inhabitants, compared to that of dwellers in the clean streets, approximates to a commonly-held stereotype of the behaviour of slum-dwellers, that is, of an economically depressed class.

Apart from this restriction on contact between persons, the untouchables are disqualified as well from entering the village temples. Of these there are three, one just outside the village and built to serve all the Kondmals, a second one in the street of the WARRIORS, which is the village temple proper, and a third one built a generation ago in Market Street by a rich trader, but now more or less deconsecrated. Untouchables also are forbidden the village meeting-house, part of which is a shrine. Being forbidden to enter does not necessarily mean that the untouchables may not worship at these temples. Their offerings, in such non-polluting media as coconuts and cash, are welcomed. They may make vows or pray for the divine assistance at any of these shrines and in fact they do so, mainly at the Kondmals temple. At all the rites which take place at these temples, and at other festivals which occur throughout the year, the only active role which is the prerogative of the untouchables, is providing certain kinds of music. At present this task is confined to the Ganjam OUTCASTES and the SWEEPERS.

Except for the temples and the meeting-house, no public place in the village is closed to untouchables.

It might seem that the rules of personal contact, segregated residence, different standards of hygiene and the prejudices which it permits, economic disparity and restriction of access to places of worship, would long since have separated the group of Boad OUTCASTES and the untouchables in general from the rest of the village. But this is a mistake. The formidable corpus of rules, formal and informal, arises out of the frequency of contact of the persons of the two groups, for the two groups were interlocked in the economic organization of the traditional village, and to some extent they still are. Each WARRIOR joint-family had its Boad OUTCASTE client family. The client came every day to the house of his master. He took his meals there. He took home rice or cooked food to feed his family, when they were not working at the master's house. At harvest time he took a share of the grain from his master's fields, or he might have one or two fields to till for himself. In times of sickness or distress the client was at hand to help by carrying messages and when sickness fell in his house, he could rely on the master to provide what help he could. The relationship was close and partook as much of kinship as of economics. This institution of master and client is now all but dead. The relationship most like it at the present day is that between a master and his farm-servant, who works for him throughout one season. In the 1953–4 season six farm-servants in the houses of WARRIORS and other clean castes came from Boad OUTCASTE Street. In addition to this a large proportion of the casual labour employed at the time of transplanting and harvesting comes from that street. The economic link between the landowners of the village and the men of Boad OUTCASTE street is still there, but it now is devoid of its quasi-kinship aspect.

Economic subservience, ritual disqualification, physical segregation—these are the features of the relationship of the Boad OUTCASTES (and other untouchables) to the rest of the village. This system of group relationships functioned so as to allow a multiplicity of person-to-person ties, mainly economic in character, between households on different sides of the barrier of pollution. This is the background against which the conflict described later in this chapter is taking place.

New Opportunities

The legend of the Boad OUTCASTES goes on:

In 1901, when the British official A. J. Ollenbach came, he saw that the Boad OUTCASTES were foolish, uneducated and poor. He slowly established schools and taught them and educated them in cultivation and gave them unsettled land. They were given loans for agriculture and to buy plough cattle. They were taught. Before this Boad OUTCASTES out of hunger used to steal and then have to go to sleep in the gaolhouse. A. J. Ollenbach who now is dead put a stop to this. Now they observed the law of the powerful Sahibs. They cultivated their land and those who were landless traded or worked as coolies and labourers and so supported themselves. Nowadays among the Bisipara Boad OUTCASTES some cultivate their own land, some share-crop and some have land on service-tenure; and some live by trading and some pass their days as labourers.

Ollenbach, was Sub-Divisional Officer of the Kondmals from 1901 until 1924, at a time when the region was administered as part of Angul District. I could find no records in Phulbani of the system of agricultural loans which is mentioned in the text, and know nothing about it if it existed, beyond what is said here. Ollenbach certainly was responsible for the many village schools which exist in the area, but these schools were not supplied, as the text hints, solely for the benefit of the Boad OUTCASTES. Attendance was compulsory, and men who did not send their children were fined, whatever their caste. The Settlement mentioned took place about three years before Ollenbach died, so that, technically, 'unsettled' land did not exist before that date. However, although the text may be inaccurate as to historical particulars (hence I have called it a legend), yet it gives a good impression of the improvement in the economic status of the Boad OUTCASTES over the last thirty to forty years.

The Boad OUTCASTES and others have been favoured against Oriyas by discriminating legislation. Scheduled Castes (which includes the Boad OUTCASTES) and Adibasis pay no Land Tax. This concession is of no great importance, since that tax is very low compared, for instance, to that paid by cultivators on the plains of Boad. Furthermore these two categories do have to pay the Watchman Tax and the Plough Tax. More important is a statute which reserves for these two categories a proportion of all minor Government posts, such as schoolmaster, policeman, messenger in the Revenue, Forest, and Agricultural departments, and so forth. The Boad OUTCASTES have taken advantage of this rule and the Government posts filled by them are shown in Table 27. For purposes of comparison the same figures for the WARRIOR and the Kond POTTER caste are given.

TABLE 27

GOVERNMENT-EMPLOYED PERSONS IN THREE CASTE-GROUPS

Caste	*Percentage of population*	*Number of household*	*Salaried Government posts*						
			A	B	C	D	E	F	*Total*
Boad OUTCASTE	21·7	29	5	1	2	—	3	—	11
Kond POTTER .	16·5	32	—	—	2	—	—	—	2
WARRIOR . .	19·3	34	2	—	—	1	—	2	5

A . . . Schoolmaster
B . . . Policeman
C . . . Messenger
D . . . Postmaster
E . . . Watchman
F . . . Headman

The Boad OUTCASTES are a Scheduled Caste and the Kond POTTERS rank as Adibasis, so that they both have the same benefit from discriminating legislation. The WARRIORS are classified as Oriyas and are without this benefit.

In the first column I have given the proportion which each of these caste-groups forms of the population of the village. However, this figure (see Appendix A) is designed to show the total consuming population and does not give a good idea of the number of adult males who are or who have been potential candidates for Government employment. The second column gives the number of households and this is a better index of the employable male population, although since it includes the houses of widows it is not perfect. But it shows at once that although the Kond POTTERS are a smaller proportion of the population, nevertheless their employable male population is slightly larger and thus it becomes legitimate to compare the numbers of men in each group employed by the Government without making adjustments for the size of the group. The posts considered are given in the remaining columns. They are schoolmaster, police, messenger, postmaster, watchman, and headman.

In trying to assess the part which discriminating legislation has played in the economic improvement of the Boad OUTCASTES, only those posts which are open to competition need be considered. This means that the last three jobs considered—postmaster, watchman, and headman—can be ignored, since the latter two are open by tradition only to the castes concerned, and competition for the first is restricted by the fact that a bond for Rs.500 is required. It is only in the field of service as a schoolmaster or policeman or messenger that the discriminating legislation becomes relevant, for, other things being equal or nearly so, a candidate from the Scheduled Castes or the Adibasis will be preferred to an Oriya candidate.

If we compare the WARRIORS with the Boad OUTCASTES, there is a *prima facie* case for saying that discriminating legislation has worked in favour of the latter. They have eight posts while the WARRIORS have only two. However, exactly the same applies to the Kond POTTERS. With about the same number of potentially employable males as the Boad OUTCASTES and with the same discriminating legislation working in their favour, they yet have only two men employed in Government jobs.

I have found it impossible to account satisfactorily for this in sociological terms. There are some possible and partial reasons which might account for the different degree to which the two groups have taken advantage of the legislation in their favour, but ultimately the question seems to come down to intelligence, adaptability, initiative and so on, and these things were beyond the terms of my systematic enquiries. One factor obviously connected is that the Boad OUTCASTES are reproducing themselves much more rapidly than the Kond POTTERS. The comparative figures are given in Table 28. To that vague complex

TABLE 28

AGE-GROUPING IN KOND POTTER AND BOAD OUTCASTE CASTE-GROUPS

Age-group	*Kond Potters* %	*Boad Outcastes* %
0–14	29 or 28	62 or 39
15–29	31 or 31	52 or 33
30–44	28 or 28	28 or 18
45–59	11 or 11	13 or 8
60 plus	2 or 2	3 or 2
Total	101 or 100	158 or 100

of characteristics attributed to the Boad OUTCASTES—intelligence, adaptability, initiative, and so forth—must be added vigour. I have no means of accounting for the presence of this complex of characteristics in one group and not the other. But it is obvious, since the mortality of children is not different to any great extent between the two groups, that because the Boad OUTCASTES have more mouths to feed, they have a greater incentive to seek new economic opportunities. Why they should have more mouths to feed must, in this enquiry at least, be taken as a demographic datum. The fact that they have is of cardinal importance in discussing their economic behaviour.[1]

As one would expect, the Boad OUTCASTES have invested in land. With 21·7 per cent of the consuming population, they get 20·5 per cent of the income from owning village land. While the income per head of the WARRIORS in units of paddy is 21·7, and of the Boad DISTILLERS is 21·5, and of the Ganjam DISTILLERS is 96, and of the Kond POTTERS is 11, that of the Boad OUTCASTES is 13 (see Table 9). The balance of their requirements is found in trading and labouring.

Recent Conflicts

When news of agitation about Temple Entry reached the village in 1948, the Boad OUTCASTES came in a body to the Kondmals temple and demanded admittance. They were not

[1] I was told that Boad OUTCASTE children attended school more regularly than children of other castes—at least in the junior grades. But I collected no figures to prove this.

PLATE VII

(*a*) THE KONDMALS TEMPLE

The photograph was taken on the day of a festival. The procession of persons of clean caste has just arrived, and they are playing music and singing songs in front of the temple.

(*b*) BOAD OUTCASTES IN PROCESSION

This photograph was taken later the same day. The procession is on its way to the Kondmals temple.

The musician and the man to his left in the photograph are younger brothers of the schoolmaster who heads one faction in their group and who is portrayed in Plate II (*b*).

(*a*)

(*b*)

PLATE VII

content to place their offerings outside, as they had always done before, but insisted on going into the shrine. The rest of the village, led by the WARRIORS and the headman, objected. They did more than that. They stationed guards, armed with battle-axes, the traditional weapon of these hills, at all the entrances to the temple and threatened to kill any Boad OUTCASTE who tried to go inside.

The Boad OUTCASTES sent to Phulbani for the police. They claimed that this now was their right under law, and they asked that the police should see that this right was enforced. The Sub-Inspector sent to investigate suggested that the Boad OUTCASTES should be allowed to go inside. But the WARRIORS still refused. They renewed their threat to kill any untouchable who tried to enter the temple. But, diplomatically, they accompanied this threat with an offer of conciliation. They said that this temple was not theirs alone, but belonged also to every Hindu in the Kondmals. They, the WARRIORS of Bisipara and the men of other clean castes in the village, were not the owners of the temple. They were merely the trustees. But if the police or the Boad OUTCASTES first consulted the Hindu people of the Kondmals, and the latter agreed to untouchables being admitted, then they too would stand down. As guardians they could not betray the trust put in them by their fellow-Hindus.

The Boad OUTCASTES then dispersed and the police, satisfied that civil disorder was averted, went away. So far as I know the other Hindu people in the Kondmals never were consulted. The Boad OUTCASTES, since that day, have never renewed their demand to be admitted. They still worshipped and made their oaths at the Kondmals temple, remaining always outside and handing their offerings to the BRAHMIN priest, but they never again attempted to win admittance.

Instead they have built their own temple to the same deity in a garden in their own street. Of course, no BRAHMIN will officiate on their behalf and the temple is ignored by the men of clean caste. Rites parallel to those carried on in the main temple are performed in the OUTCASTE temple by one of their own men, a schoolmaster. This has not excited the derision that one might have expected from persons of clean caste. Discussion of this incident never aroused much comment on the propriety or impropriety of building the new temple. The attitude seemed to me to be that on the whole this was a reasonable course to have taken and infinitely preferable to have gone on raising trouble about the Kondmals temple. The oad OUTCASTE schoolmaster who officiates is regarded by the WARRIORS as a modest, learned and decent man.

At this time the Boad OUTCASTES were the official music-makers of the village. At festivals and at the rites performed at the different temples they provided music. They also would be invited by a well-to-do householder to play when there was a wedding in his house. In return for this they received a share of whatever food was going, and their performance entitled the musicians at the end of the day to go around the houses of the wealthy and beg for a small gift in cash or kind. In addition, at certain times of the year, they were licensed to beg a little food or money from every clean house in the village. This privilege was shared with the BRAHMIN and certain other village servants.

Shortly after the incident of the Kondmals temple, the village council suddenly deprived the Boad OUTCASTES of the privilege of providing music and gave it to the Ganjam OUTCASTES and the SWEEPERS. They decreed at the same time that the privilege of begging was withdrawn from the Boad OUTCASTES and sanctioned this pronouncement by saying that anyone who gave to a Boad OUTCASTE at the time of privileged begging would be fined the very large sum of Rs.25, on pain of ostracism. The reasons which then they gave—and informants still give—is that the Boad OUTCASTES had become too importunate. It was not the musicians only who came begging. It was the entire street—one-fifth of the population of the village—which paraded around the houses demanding to be fed. The villagers said that they abolished the system because it had become too expensive.

If this were the whole story one would expect them rather to have decreed that musicians only should receive the gifts or that the Boad OUTCASTES should depute a section of their people to collect on behalf of all. There is more behind the action of the village council than a simple loss of patience because the Boad OUTCASTES were immoderate in their demands. In part this lack of moderation occasioned the decree. But also it was punitive and arose out of the temple incident and the general feeling that

Boad OUTCASTES were getting above themselves. The decree has been completely effective and the ritual tie, which united the Boad OUTCASTES through common participation in ceremonials with the rest of the village, has been severed.

The last incident happened about two months before I left the village. An elderly Boad OUTCASTE was returning from the market. He had passed through the village and was going along a narrow pathway which leads from the street of the Boad DISTILLERS in a north-easterly direction towards a suburb of the street of the Boad OUTCASTES, where his home lay. It was late in the evening. From the other direction a WARRIOR youth, about fifteen years old, was coming back from fishing in the paddy-fields. They met on a narrow section of pathway, which runs four feet above the level of the fields, which at that time were under water. What happened then is not clear. They each have their story of a polite offer to withdraw in favour of the other answered by a coarse insult. But, whatever happened, the youth ended up head first in the mud of the paddy-field. The Boad OUTCASTE fled. The youth came wailing until he met a man of the Boad DISTILLER caste, who, on hearing what had happened, sounded the alarm. (This is an empty kerosene tin used to summon the men of the village when a disturbance breaks out.) Men came running from all the clean streets and there was great indignation. They went out to the scene of the incident, but when they reached there the Boad OUTCASTE was already safely in his own street. They then returned to the village and the council assembled in the meeting-house.

First they sent the village watchman to fetch the Boad OUTCASTE to hear what he had to say for himself. It already was nightfall and the message came back from the street of the Boad OUTCASTES that the man and his caste-brothers would attend in the morning so that they could discuss the matter. The council broke up and the men went to bed.

During the night the Boad OUTCASTES sent a deputation to Phulbani asking for police protection, for, they said, the WARRIORS had come to attack their street with sticks, axes and guns. Before the village council could assemble in the morning, the police were in the village. They took statements from each side.

That same day it happened that there was a Minister from the State (Orissa) Government touring in the area. His party was intercepted by a deputation from the Boad OUTCASTES, who told him the same tale that they had told to the police, and prayed that he would intervene on their behalf.

This resulted in a second police investigation by a higher official. After both sets of evidence had been scrutinized and there had been consultations in the headquarters, it was judged that the Boad OUTCASTES had not proved their case, and it was dismissed with the right of appeal to the Deputy Commissioner. The Boad OUTCASTES took up this right and appealed, and the case was awaiting hearing when I left the village.

Outstanding in these incidents are the separatist tendencies of the Boad OUTCASTES. Understandably they refused to defer to the judgement of the village council. Implicitly they denied its political right to regulate relations between them and the village and preferred to call in outside authority. On two occasions they did this. When denied the right to enter the shrine, they built a temple of their own. Their position of formal dependency as village musicians is ended. They are moving out of the social structure of the village.

The Leaders of the Boad Outcastes

Shortly after the incident of the temple, the Boad OUTCASTES held a meeting and passed the following rules: they would no longer deal in dead cattle and hides (in fact the village council had already handed over scavenging to the SWEEPERS and the Ganjam OUTCASTES); they would no longer eat meat, fish or eggs, nor would they drink liquor; from that time on they would no longer be called *Pano* (their Oriya name) but *Harijan*, the children of God, the name by which Gandhi dignified untouchables.

The meeting was organized, and the whole attempt to improve their standing according to the Hindu rules is led by one faction among the Boad OUTCASTES, the nucleus of which is the family of a schoolmaster and the policeman. These are easily the two richest men in the caste-group. Opposed to these, in long-standing enmity, which extends at least to the days of their fathers who now are dead, is another faction led by a schoolmaster and a village watchman. These two factions comprise about a quarter each of the population of the caste-group and the remainder belong to no faction.

Everyone, irrespective of their factional loyalty, attended the meeting and subscribe, at least verbally, to the new rules. In fact they are observed in all their rigour only by the family of the policeman and his ally the schoolmaster. Drunkenness, in spite of prohibition, is still common in the street of the Boad OUTCASTES. They still eat eggs and keep chickens and most people eat goat's meat and fish. But, so far as I know, they no longer deal in hides nor eat carrion.

This abstemiousness achieves them a certain grudging respect. The WARRIOR informants spoke of the schoolmaster-policeman faction, particularly the schoolmaster himself, as good and modest men. But immediately they go on to say that the schoolmaster will never persuade the rest of the caste-group to behave as well as he does.

It seems to me that the men of the schoolmaster-policeman faction accept the traditional structure of the Hindu village and the hierarchy laid down by the rules of caste. Although they never said so explicitly, they gave the impression of thinking that providing their behaviour approximated to that of the BRAHMIN stereotype, then their social position would be improved and they would achieve the respect to which they felt, no doubt, their wealth and education entitled them. They aspired to follow a course similar to that of the Boad DISTILLERS. They would rise within the traditional caste structure of the village. Indeed, such an ambition is implicit in their attempt to reform their behaviour and the behaviour of their caste-fellows. They try to avoid violence and in no sense are they revolutionaries. Hence the respect in which the WARRIORS hold them.

The opposite of this is implicit in the behaviour of the other faction. They stiffened the resistance in the dispute over the boy who fell into the paddy field. They sent for the police. They petitioned the Minister. They are appealing to the Deputy Commissioner. Of course, they are backed by the members of the other faction and by all those who belong to no faction, for the caste-group is united by its common opposition to the rest of the village. But the leadership in these tactics comes from the schoolmaster-watchman faction. Implicitly they demonstrate their belief in aggression. They are the revolutionaries.

It seems to me that this aggressive faction has grasped something which escapes the other faction. It may only be that the leaders of this faction are by nature more violent than those in the schoolmaster-policeman group. But implicit in their behaviour is the realization that they can never better themselves according to the Hindu rules, because they are on the wrong side of the barrier of pollution. They cannot rise within the existing ritual and political structure of the village. Even if, by some miracle of coercion, the whole caste throughout the Kondmals could be made to behave after the BRAHMIN stereotype, yet they would still be disqualified from going into a temple and they could never in the foreseeable future command the same degree of respect that rich men of clean caste can achieve. This may or may not be in their minds, but it is implicit in their behaviour. The course into which their political and social aspirations are leading them is inevitably made different from the course of the Boad DISTILLERS, in roughly the same situation, by this single irreducible fact. The barrier of pollution stands between them and their goal. The traditional political system of the village, incorporating a barrier of untouchability, is not sufficiently elastic to let the Boad OUTCASTES adjust themselves politically and socially to their new economic status, as the Boad DISTILLERS were able to do. They inevitably are driven to act not in terms of the village polity, but as subjects of the Administration. In fact, they are showing the first signs of becoming a separate village community.

CONCLUSIONS

In the original village the Boad OUTCASTES were economically subservient, physically segregated, and they laboured under numerous ritual disqualifications. They were, however, bound closely into the structure of the village in part by having a role in village ritual, but more by the quasi-kinship economic tie between masters and clients.

After the change in the economic environment which followed on the coming of the Administration, the master-client relationship broke down and was replaced by a more casual system of daily labour, which produces no lasting or close ties between the employer and the worker. At the same time new economic opportunities arose and the Boad OUTCASTES made striking use of them, partly through legislative favours and partly under the stimulus of an increasing population.

An increase in wealth has led to the heightening of their political aspirations. They no longer are content with the position of ritual and political subservience, which formerly the village offered them. The route which another caste in the same situation followed—namely approximating their behaviour to the ideal of Hinduism, and so making their political status appropriate to their economic status—is closed by the barrier of pollution. Since there are no prospects within the social structure of the village, the Boad OUTCASTES are tending to separate themselves from the rest of the village and to try to order their relationship with other caste-groups in the village not in terms of village structure, but within the framework of the Administration.

It might be argued that this attempt of the Boad OUTCASTES to improve their status is common to the whole of India and arises here not from local economic conditions, but from propaganda and directly from legislative encouragement. This is undoubtedly a valid argument. But it would be more accurate to say that legislation and the urgings of propagandists have moved the Boad OUTCASTES to act in this way only because economic conditions are appropriate. The campaign to help untouchables, with the great inspiring figure of Gandhi in the background, has dignified the struggle of the Boad OUTCASTES and obscured the fact that this fundamentally is an attempt by men economically qualified for power to achieve social recognition of that power and an environment in which they can exercise it. Supporting this hypothesis is the fact that in the village the Ganjam OUTCASTES and the SWEEPERS side with the group of clean castes in the struggle against the Boad OUTCASTES. It pays them to do so.

CHAPTER XII

THE CHANGING VILLAGE

IN the course of this essay I have described the economic life of Bisipara, and I have directed attention to the detailed working of certain economic mechanisms, which are causing a redistribution of the village land. Later I discussed modifications to the political structure of the village, which are the result of changes in the economy.

In this final chapter I shall summarize my argument by discussing not the detail of economic processes, but the more remote and more general principles which lie behind them. In the second and third part of the essay I asked how these processes worked. Here I shall ask why these processes rather than any other have characterized the economic and political development of Bisipara during the last hundred years.

This development is not something unique, nor is it a problem of local interest only. It is one example of a situation that is found in all parts of the world, one of an almost infinite series of variations which result when a relatively simple peasant economy or tribal economy is brought into contact with the modern world.

The common element in all these different situations is the interaction of two systems, and the emergence of a third complex system. The nature of this third system is demonstrated, when the elements which compose it are conceptually made discrete, both historically and in their present function.

Agriculture and Commerce

Before 1855 agriculture was the basis of the economy of Bisipara. This economy was near to the line of subsistence and was relatively self-contained. Agriculture to-day is still the basis of the economy, and almost all the crops which are grown in the village are consumed there. In this sense, agriculture is still for subsistence. But the village is no longer self-contained. Part of its income is derived from commerce with the world outside.

Although as cultivators the men of the village do not produce for an outside market, nevertheless agriculture to-day differs from that of a century ago. This difference arises from contact with the world of commerce. The role of individuals as traders has had a profound effect on their role as landowners.

It is important to make clear what is meant by saying that one hundred years ago Bisipara was relatively self-contained. In his prefatory article to a series of brief studies of Indian villages, Professor Srinivas [1] stressed the unity of the traditional village and its opposition to, and independence of, other villages. Since then other writers [2] have emphasized that the village is not 'a fully self-sufficient unit'. The 'Indian Village' is inevitably a vague conception. In talking of Bisipara I can be more precise.

To-day the cloth that men and women wear in Bisipara might be woven in Bombay or Calcutta. Some of the hoes they use are made by the Tata enterprises. The shops sell paper which is manufactured in Bengal mills. Kerosene is distributed from the rail depot at Berhampur. Locks come from Aligarh. A few men have sandals made by a Czechoslovak firm manufacturing in India. The bicycles are British. Of the two pressure-lamps that light the village meetings, one was made in England and the other came from Germany. Of the four guns in the village, two were made in Britain, one in America, and one in Spain. Purchases of this sort, and the export trade which makes them possible, are activities which bind the village into the larger economy of India. A hundred years ago goods which fulfilled the same needs as these manufactures could be produced locally.

It is not necessary to assume that all the goods and services which Bisipara required in the past could be provided within its own boundaries. There was probably trade between villages in the Kondmals, and between those villages and others on the plains of Boad, and to a lesser extent on the plains of Ganjam. Boad has a tradition of fine weaving. There are

[1] M. N. Srinivas, 1951, *passim*.

[2] M. W. Smith (1952, p. 53) is here speaking of villages in the Punjab.

records of salt being transported through the area from the coast of Orissa. Iron ore is found in the east of the Kondmals and must have been traded either raw or as manufactures to other districts to meet the needs for axes and plough-shares. The red earth, which is used for colouring the walls of houses and for washing hair, is found only in a limited number of places. The functional castes probably served several villages. There is, for instance, no record of a potter ever having lived in Bisipara, and it may be assumed that the men of Bisipara have always gone elsewhere to buy their pots, as they do to-day.

But contacts of this kind are not an example of the interaction of two different systems. The goods were made or carried by persons in close contact with cultivators and all these activities—pot-making, ironwork, and so forth—were part of the complex of activities of the traditional Indian agricultural village. The trade was carried on either by the tithe system or by barter of goods, and not through money. Nor could it have had the characteristics which mark modern commerce and help to disrupt the traditional village economy.

Bisipara, then, was self-contained in the sense that all the goods and services it required could be supplied from the locality, by barter and not by money, and through contact not with businessmen but with craftsmen, whose economic status was not radically different from that of their peasant customers.

Finally it must be remembered that this discussion refers to the economy of Bisipara. It is obvious that in the field of kinship the village was not a ' little republic ', since the network of affinal and uterine ties spread over different villages. The same, to a lesser extent, is true of the village as a ritual unit, and, minimally, as a political unit, since in both these fields allegiance was owed to the Raja of Boad.

I found it convenient to regard the interaction of agriculture and commerce as the progressive extension of an economic frontier. Hancock [1] distinguishes several kinds of frontier, all of which can be economic in their implications. The Kondmals, for instance, offered an example of a settlers' frontier, when

[1] W. K. Hancock, 1940, Chapter I. I have derived the concept of ' frontier ' from this book.

the Oriyas came and took over the best land.[1] This, obviously, radically altered the economic life of the indigenous Konds and may be the reason why to-day they grow the cash-crop, turmeric, and the Oriyas do not. If the Konds had sufficient rice-land, they might not have the incentive to grow turmeric, the cultivation of which is said both by Konds and Oriyas to be very hard work. But this is speculation, and the regional implications of the Oriya settlers' frontier are not discussed in this essay.

The economy of the modern world reached Bisipara first in the form of a traders' frontier and this is still the most important link between the village and the world outside. Indeed, at first sight Bisipara is only marginally integrated into the national economy, if we compare it with villages in other parts of India and in Central and South Africa. There are no towns in the Kondmals. There are no factories. By its remoteness the village is insulated completely from the immediate effects of urbanization and industrialization. The tea-estates of Assam used to draw labour from the Kondmals, mostly from Scheduled Castes and Adibasis, but the numbers involved, relative to the total population, were small. Furthermore, the plantations preferred to take whole families and did not, like enterprises in Africa, create the problem of villages-without-men. Bisipara, then, is protected not only from the direct effects of proximity to modern towns and industries, but also from remote contact through labour migration.

One of the characteristics of a traders' frontier is that the people who advance it are not natives of the country in which they are working. At a later stage gifted persons among the indigenous population begin to share in the work, but the pioneering and management are almost always confined to outsiders. There are numerous examples: Syrians in West Africa; Indians in East and Central Africa; and Europeans everywhere. At a different level of management there are great trading houses such as the United Africa Company. Indeed, in its origins the East India Company belongs with such concerns,

[1] Similar, though more recent and less warlike, colonizing is described by C. von Fürer-Haimendorf in the Adilabad District of Hyderabad (1945 (1), pp. 66–82) and in the Rampa Agency, East Godaveri District, of Northern Madras (1945 (2), p. 246).

but by the time its domains extended to the Kondmals it was an organ of government rather than of trade.

The same is true to some extent of the advance of the traders' frontier into Bisipara. The combined inducement of trade and Government-employ attracted the ancestors of at least 25 per cent of the present population of the village. Not all of these have achieved striking success in trade, but the larger commercial enterprises (the shops) are entirely in the hands of families who came after 1855 from outside the Kondmals.

But when the view is narrowed from the Kondmals as a whole to Bisipara and other Oriya villages in particular, then the remarkable fact is the degree to which the indigenous population was able to participate in the new economy. Bisipara became, in effect, a village of traders.

The reasons for this are obvious. The Oriya villages lay along the lines of communication. The Oriyas were the instruments of the Government and trade followed the flag. Bisipara, in particular, was fortunate in being for a time the capital of the area and the seat of the Administration. The Oriyas spoke the language of the larger middlemen from the plains of Ganjam, through whom trade goods came from the manufacturing centres of India and from the rest of the world.

This combination of circumstances has had equally obvious effects on the development of the village.

By a paradox, it is responsible for certain elements of conservation in the traditional system of agriculture. The men of Bisipara do not need to grow a cash-crop in order to get money for trade-goods. As cultivators, they can devote themselves entirely to the subsistence crop of rice, while Konds must divide their labour between rice-fields and turmeric-plots. Furthermore, the trade in turmeric and liquor-flowers happens to take place at a time of the year when there is no work in the fields, so that it does not make demands which conflict with the demands of cultivation.

The integrity of the system of rice-cultivation, in spite of changes in the distribution of land, its antiquity, and its separation from modern elements in the economy, are demonstrated by a high degree of ritualization, and by the strict control of the village council over men in their role as cultivators. There is no rite or festival in the village which is without agricultural implications. There are innumerable personal and private acts of worship performed by each cultivator to ensure the fertility of his fields. There are several rites to avert blight and insects from the growing crop. No-one may plant a field until the headman has ritually placed his first seedlings. No-one may cut paddy until the day appointed for the first-fruit ceremony, when everyone must eat at least a token amount of the new crop. All these restrictions and observances are enforced not only by supernatural penalties, but also by sanctions exercised by the village council. The council is active also in secular matters. It controls all agricultural projects, which demand collective action. It maintains the irrigation channels. It prevents the depredations of cattle and goats.

These two elements, ritual and control by the community, are absent almost entirely from commercial activities. I recorded one instance of a rite arising from a trading expedition (see page 134). There were no collective rites performed by the community in the interests of trade, nor was the community in the habit of positive direction in matters of trade as in cultivation.

The crop which India demands from the region is turmeric and not rice. Inside the village, and to a lesser extent within the Kondmals, rice is a cash-crop, in that some is bought and sold. But these are internal transactions. The reasons why rice did not become an export crop are obvious enough. Rice-land is limited on the plateau. The yield above the ghats, so local officers told me, is much inferior to the yield on the plains. All the rice grown in the hills is required to feed the population, and to-day the Kondmals import rice from the Orissa plains.[1] Finally those plains are themselves one of the major exporting areas of rice in India, so that there could be no demand for Kondmals rice within the province.

As a factor of social conservation the continued existence of

[1] This assertion is based on the existence of a Civil Supplies Office in Phulbani, and information from a member of the staff that they found it very difficult to procure supplies of paddy locally. I have also heard villagers discussing whether to buy local rice or to wait and see what would be the price of 'control' or 'lorry' rice. Unfortunately I did not seek figures from the Civil Supplies Officer.

subsistence cultivation of rice cannot be overestimated. The point may be more forcefully made by considering what might have happened had there been an abundance of land suitable for rice-cultivation, and a good market for the product. The population of Orissa has increased from 1,296,365 in 1822 to 14,654,946 in 1951.[1] This produced considerable pressure on land and even as early as 1870 Hunter could describe internal colonization and increasing fragmentation of estates.[2] Scarcity of land would have driven increasing numbers of colonists into the hills, and the indigenous population of villages like Bisipara might have been submerged. Had there also been a good export market for rice, then conditions like those described by Furnivall in Burma would have arisen. In lower Burma cultivation depended heavily on outside finance and title to the land rested with absentee financiers. Land changed hands with great rapidity. In newly-settled areas, in such conditions of flux, communities with a corporate sense did not develop. Even in areas on the fringe of 'industrial agriculture' communal institutions broke down.[3]

Sometimes it is idle to speculate on what might have been. But here the significance of the ecological and environmental features is put into proper perspective by comparison with another area. Because there was no export trade for rice, and because rice-lands were limited, the opening of the Kondmals was delayed until the middle of the nineteenth century. Even after they were opened, the modern economy intruded as a traders' frontier, bringing comparatively few newcomers, and not as the inundation of a settlers' frontier.[4]

The export trade in turmeric and the relative abundance of land on which turmeric can be grown did not have the same

[1] The figure for 1822 is taken from W. W. Hunter (1872, vol. 2, p. 129). The second figure comes from the 1951 Census of India. Since these figures were compiled by different methods and do not apply to the same area, the comparison is a very approximate one, but sufficient to demonstrate a great increase in population.

[2] W. W. Hunter, 1872, Chapter 9.

[3] J. S. Furnivall, 1948, pp. 77–98, 108–9, 298 *et passim.*

[4] 'Inundation' is not too strong a word. The extraordinary rapidity with which colonist-farmers overran parts of Adilabad District in Hyderabad, once communications had been opened, is described by C. von Fürer-Hamendorf (1945 (1), pp. 65–6, 155–6 *et passim*).

effects in the Kondmals and the rest of the Kond hills as did rice exports and abundance of rice-land in Burma. Enquiry into this will give further reasons for the coming of a traders' frontier rather than a settlers' frontier, and further illustrate the relation of the agricultural to the mercantile system in Bisipara.

Turmeric is cultivated on steep hillsides by clearing and burning the jungle, and growing the plant in the ash and pockets of soil. It also can be grown in gardens, but the hillside plot is the more usual, possibly because garden-land must be used for subsistence crops. Since I worked among Oriyas, and Oriyas did not grow turmeric, I made no systematic enquiries into its cultivation. But there are certain obvious points about the technique of growing turmeric which account for the fact that it is not more extensively cultivated. The most common technique allows two years for the plant to mature, and throughout this period the field must be protected from the depredations of wild animals. More important, since it involves more labour, is the need to protect the young plant from the heat of the sun, especially from the end of April to early June. In order to do this saplings and brushwood are cut from the jungle around and spread over the entire field to provide shade. This work is considered very laborious, and Oriyas say that they would not grow turmeric because of the labour involved. The need for wood, if turmeric were to be grown on some of the land that now is used for rice, would greatly increase costs, since these fields are relatively distant from the jungle.

If the profits of turmeric, when measured against the labour of cultivation, cannot attract the indigenous Oriyas into growing it, so much the less has it attracted settlers from the plains. So far as I know, turmeric is not commonly grown on the plains of Orissa. This is a further point in assessing the importance of the fact that turmeric rather than rice is the export crop. Rice-growing would probably have attracted settlers from the plains. But to grow turmeric, they would not only have had to venture into a strange country, which had an evil reputation, but also to learn an entirely new agricultural technique.

The local Oriyas know that some Konds make considerable sums by growing turmeric. They can see this from the solidity and prosperity of some Kond houses, from the vast amounts they pay in brideprices, from the possession by some Kond families of jewellery and such trade-goods as bicycles and guns, and from their own dealings as turmeric-traders. Nevertheless they do not grow the crop. The only two plots of turmeric in the village in 1953 were small: one belonged to a DISTILLER shopkeeper and the other to a Kond POTTER. No Oriya cultivated a field on the mountainside. They say the work is too hard, and in any case they do not know the technique. They also say that, anyway, the work is proper to the Konds and not to Oriyas. There is a hint of snobbery and caste-prejudice in their statements, but I have no doubt that they would take to turmeric-growing if they thought the reward commensurate with the labour, and if they could get cash in no other way. The few people who are adventurous in cultivation prefer to grow cabbages and cauliflowers for the market at Phulbani, or, in one case, the more risky and rewarding effort of growing sugar-cane. The postmaster had grown sugar-cane five years ago and was planning another crop for the 1954–5 season.

The fact, then, that turmeric and not rice is the export crop of the Kond hills is responsible for the continued integrity of subsistence cultivation of rice,[1] and, indeed, the continued existence of the village as a community. There have been important changes in the social structure of Bisipara, but they would have been much greater than they were, had the system of cultivation itself been altered by the extension of the economic frontier of India.

But, while in this way the system of cultivation and its attendant rites and observations have been preserved in the new economy, the distribution of the resources of village agriculture has been radically altered. This change arose firstly through the differential ability of individuals and groups to profit in the new system, and secondly from the fact that the land itself became involved in the money economy.

The fact that it is often the stranger who, in the first instance at least, profits from the extension of the traders' frontier is one aspect of a differential ability to profit in the new system. Here the difference lay in managerial skill and experience and in con-

[1] M. Gluckman (1943, p. 49) remarks upon the integrity of the agricultural system, when money can be obtained from other sources.

tacts with the world of commerce. These factors are still important to-day, since they qualify outsiders alone—although not all outsiders—to take part in the higher commercial activities.

A second aspect of the principle that men as profit-makers are not equal is the result of the combined effects of the caste-system and Administrative action. The examples are obvious. The DISTILLER caste-groups alone are qualified to trade in drink. The drink-trade was made extraordinarily profitable by the Government's ban on home-stills. The Government was interested in Excise Revenue, and it is possible that local officials were subjected to a 'DISTILLER lobby', but the profits which accrued to the DISTILLERS over a period of forty years were not primarily the result of their business acumen or entrepreneurial exertions. They were 'windfall' profits. A similar illustration of the fact that differential ability to profit from the new economy was not solely dependent on the capacity of individuals is provided by the WARRIOR caste-group. Their leaders have benefited from the Administration's preference for the traditional rulers. Likewise the Scheduled Castes and the Adibasis enjoy the protection of discriminating legislation in the competition for salaried posts.

Thirdly, spectacular success in the new economy has in a few cases resulted from individual business ability and caste-qualification, not helped out by the actions of the Administration. The man who trades in hides is an example. In so far as his success depended on his being an OUTCASTE, these were windfall profits. The fact that he alone among his caste-group profited is a reflection of his individual luck and skill as a man of business.

In the history of the redistribution of land between different caste-groups in Bisipara, it is striking that profits gained purely by business acumen and hard work have played a much smaller part than have windfall profits, which depended ultimately on Government actions and policies. This is particularly true in the case of the DISTILLERS.

The differential ability of persons to profit in the new economy is not necessarily parallel to their success in the agricultural economy. This has a profound effect on the traditional social structure of the village.

It is obvious that the role of a man in the old economy is not without influence on his role in the new economy and his ability to profit by it. In some cases a position of power and wealth in the agricultural village gave a man a good start in the new economy. The clearest example of this is the continued dominance of the WARRIOR headmen. In other cases substantial success in agriculture enables a man to profit in the mercantile economy. The lenders and sellers of paddy are examples.

On the other hand it is equally clear that a lowly position in the agricultural economy did not—and to some extent does not—debar a man from profiting in commerce. This is a reflection of the duality in the economic system and the political system. Those who were humble in the politico-economic world of village-and-agriculture could achieve success in the new economy, with the protection of the Administration and sometimes with its assistance, either in the shape of direct legislative discrimination, or indirectly by windfall profits.

On the other hand, it is to be noticed that although the more spectacular sources of wealth in the new economy—the drink-trade, merchant-shopkeeping, and trading in hides—are concentrated in the hands of a few persons owing to the factors I have been considering, nevertheless certain other opportunities in the modern economy are relatively widely diffused and not so much limited by differential ability. This is one aspect of the fact that the traders' frontier is made up of heterogeneous elements, involving different types of goods and demanding different kinds and degrees of skill from participants. The work of the lowest rung in the ladder of middle-men who handle turmeric and liquor-flowers is open to almost everyone, and although superior abilities and luck might cause one party of traders to profit more than others, yet the gap between them and their less successful competitors is not of the same order as the gulf between those who could, and those who could not, deal in drink. In volume, turmeric is by far the most important export of the hills, and it probably is the biggest single source of wealth which the modern economy has brought to the village. Yet, since the chance of profit is widely diffused, and not limited by the caste-system, nor by Government action, nor to any great degree by skill and experience, its effect has been to conserve the traditional system of agriculture, as I described above, and to slow down the redistribution of the village lands. In other words, the significance of the traders' frontier as an instrument of social change in Bisipara lay not in the volume of goods which it brought to the community, but in the fact that its wealth did not always accrue to those who controlled the agricultural economy, and who had the power in the traditional political structure of the village. This is true both in the external relations of Bisipara and in its internal structure. Bisipara, the political capital of its Kond domain, became in the new economy a trading metropolis. The wealth provided by the trade in turmeric did not at once upset the subordinate relation of Konds towards Oriyas.[1] Similarly, inside the village, such changes as have come about have not been the result of turmeric, which in volume is the most important trade-good, but of windfall profits in goods, the handling of which was limited by differential abilities.

The mercantile economy has impinged on the system of agriculture, because those who profited as merchants, traders and earners of salaries invested their money in land. This suggests three questions. Why did they do so? What made it possible for them to buy land? What has been the effect of the redistribution of land on the social structure of the village? I am concerned here with the first of these questions.

There is no need to ask why the peasant who makes a windfall profit in trading or work for the Government should invest that profit in land. The notion of land as the one secure, permanent and unchanging source of wealth is firmly fixed in his mind. But the reason why men whose life has been devoted to commerce, and whose wealth has been derived from commerce, should also find land a desirable investment, is not so obvious.

One factor, although not the most important, is the prestige attached to owning land. In Bisipara to be a leading man (*bhodro loko*) is also to be a landowner. This prestige obviously derives from the time when land was the sole source of wealth

[1] M. Gluckman (1941, p. 79) remarks upon a similar situation in Barotseland. 'Nevertheless, this early entry of trade-goods did not at once radically alter the balance of the economy. The dominant position of the Lozi, and especially of the Lozi king, was further validated, since the new commodities, of which they largely had a monopoly, were eagerly desired.'

and consequently the sole source of power. Land, indeed, is still the largest source of wealth in the village.

A more important factor is the proximity of even the larger entrepreneurs (the merchant-shopkeepers) to the land. They and their ancestors were all born in villages. None were town-dwellers. Their system of values is similar to that of their peasant customers. They all are familiar with the techniques of agriculture. In the larger world of commerce they are little men, and although their calling stems in part from an industrial economy, nevertheless they are closer to the village craftsman and even to the village servant than they are to the businessmen of the cities. They are the foreigners whom the traders' frontier has introduced. But there are degrees of being foreign and the traders who came to Bisipara are not so foreign as are, for instance, the Indians in Africa. In social structure and in culture the villages in which the traders settled are basically similar to the villages from which they came.

This is important, since it lies behind the third reason prompting shopkeepers to buy land. They made their homes in Bisipara. It is true that they all retained—and still do—close ties with their villages on the plains. At least three of them own estates in their ancestral villages and their wives come from that area. Nevertheless they have settled in Bisipara. They are not adventurers out for quick profits and holding before themselves the prospect of retirement to their ancestral village. They are residents of Bisipara, and its basic cultural similarity to their ancestral villages makes this residence feasible.

But the most important reasons why those who profited in the new economy invested in land are economic, and apply equally whether the successful man was a newcomer or one of the long-settled Oriyas. Firstly there was very little else in which to invest.[1] I have already described how the profits of the drink-sellers had willy-nilly to be invested in land. There are, of course, other investments, but these either are limited or are much less attractive than land. Some money is invested in jewellery. This has its advantages, but such investment is not productive. Money can also be invested in any of the minor business enterprises described in Part II of the book, but these

[1] J. S. Furnivall (1948, p. 87) says, 'Others also, merchants and shopkeepers, bought land, because they had no other investment for their profits.'

are more risky than land, and carry less prestige. Moreover, the region is on the margin of the commercial economy and the opportunities for investment in local commerce are limited.[1] Money can be put into the Post Office Bank, but this is a novel proceeding and its profits seem remote and intangible and rather small.

Secondly, investment in rice-land was profitable. There was an internal market for the sale of rice. Apart from the Government officials who for a time lived in the village, there were those people who earned cash in the mercantile economy and had to buy rice to feed themselves. A man did not need to limit his holding to what was required to feed himself, his family, and his clients. The bigger the estate, the bigger was the surplus, and the consequent earnings of cash. When discussing turmeric and rice, I argued that the changes in Bisipara are less than they would have been if rice had been the export crop. The obverse of this is that although Bisipara, as a village, has remained a unit of subsistence cultivation, so far as concerns rice, nevertheless within this unit a market economy in rice developed. Without this internal rice-market, the changes in the social structure of Bisipara would not have been as great as they were.

The economic mechanisms and the modifications of the kinship structure, which made it possible for those wishing to buy land to find sellers, have been discussed at length in Part II. Here I am concerned not with the economic mechanisms operating immediately in the village, but more with economic forces and Governmental policies at work in the background.

What evidence there is suggests that by the middle of the nineteenth century at least a large part of the cultivable rice-land around the village was already under the plough. Further increase in population made it more and more difficult to find new land to cultivate and seems soon to have driven potential land-investors into buying land rather than using their resources

[1] I was told that a rich Kond had given the enormous sum of Rs.5000 (£375) to a Ganjam DISTILLER shopkeeper in Bisipara for use in buying and selling gold. The profits were divided, five parts to the Kond and three parts to the shopkeeper. I never heard of another investment on a similar scale, or, indeed, of a similar kind.

to bring new land under cultivation. The limitations of the environment, natural growth of the population and growth by immigration, the presence of capital to invest, the profits of investing in rice-land, and the absence of investment avenues other than in land, are the moving forces behind the redistribution of land.

The processes by which these forces are manifested in the village are twofold. First there was the break-up of the joint-family, which was in effect a change in the system of inheritance whereby the elementary family became isolated from its fellows. Secondly this involved a reduction in the size of some estates to the point at which they disintegrated under pressure of contingent expenditure.

A permissive factor in the process of land-transfer is the full title of the landholder and his right to buy and sell. This, in India, is usually represented as the work of the British, who, indeed, were proud to claim it as their greatest achievement. Hunter,[1] in rolling English prose, says :

> The great public works with which we have dotted the country will last our time and disappear. The silt of the delta will cover our roads and railways, as it has covered over the temples and palaces of preceding dynasties. The fortresses on which science has lavished her ingenuity will noiselessly sink down into jungle-buried, shapeless heaps of brick. The river will swallow up our iron-girded bridges, or leave them high and dry across their deserted beds—massive screw-pile monuments of a Cyclopean age, scarring the bright face of the rice-crop. . . .
>
> It is by what we have implanted in the living people rather than by what we have built upon the dead earth, that our name will survive. The permanent aspect of British Rule in India is the growth of Private Rights.

But land is not sold merely because legislation confers the right to sell, as Hunter himself shows. Land is bought and sold only when land is scarce. Undoubtedly the British, in their anxiety to create a Bengal Squirearchy, anticipated economic processes. But increasing pressure on the land of Bisipara and the presence of eager investors would sooner or later have

[1] W. W. Hunter, 1872, Vol. 2, p. 200. Hunter gives a clear and well-documented account of the growth of proprietary rights in land in Orissa in Chapter IX of this work.

produced at least *de facto* methods of disposing of land, even if it had not legitimized them *de jure*.

There are no accounts of the system of land-tenure in the Oriya villages of the Kondmals before the arrival of the Administration.[1] But since the Oriyas came from Boad, which was one of the Tributary States of Orissa, and since Hunter described their system of land-tenure, it may be assumed that his description applied to the Oriyas of the Kondmals. The sole proprietor of land was the Raja. Land might not be sold, since the cultivators had a right of occupancy, contingent on their status as subjects or servants of the Raja. In the old Hindu Kingdom of Orissa the land was divided into Great Districts, 'comprising a large number of Fiscal Divisions, with many Villages in each Fiscal Division'. This arrangement was in force in the heart of the land. On the borders, which in the west had to be protected against the hillmen and on the eastern seaboard against pirates, the land was made over to a 'feudal nobility', who enjoyed a grant of land in return for the maintenance of military forces. They were called 'Fort-holders'.[2]

In the light of this, it seems probable that the Oriya chiefs in the Kond hills were in a feudal relationship to the Raja of Boad similar to that of the Fort-holders or the Divisional Headmen to the Hindu King of Orissa.[3] In theory they held their land as the servants of the Raja of Boad: and the men of the village held land as the servants first of the Oriya chiefs and ultimately of the Raja. In practice, as I have described, the Oriya chiefs were independent of the Boad Raja, a situation which has obvious parallels in English history. This was caused by poor communications and probably was not the case in the relationship of the Oriya chief to the men of his village. It is very unlikely that the Raja of Boad had any control over the distribution of land in the Kond hills. But it is probable that anyone who wished to acquire land in one of the Oriya hill villages had to apply for it to the Oriya chief. The land

[1] W. Macpherson (1865, p. 62) gives a brief account of the system of land tenure among the Konds and records a method of transferring land.

[2] The title of the head of a Fiscal Division, the equivalent of a Fort-holder, is *Bisoi*, which also is the name of the ruling WARRIOR lineage in Bisipara.

[3] This account of the organization of the Hindu Kingdom of Orissa is taken from W. W. Hunter, 1872, pp. 215–21.

belonged to him as the representative of the community and of the Raja. The cultivator had what the British described as a right of occupancy and not a full title which would enable him to sell the land.

This, however, is conjecture. I cannot state for certain that land was not sold before the British imported into the Kondmals the institution of freehold right, especially as the evidence given by Macpherson for Kond villages conflicts with this. But, taking into account the traditional system of land tenure in the Hindu State of Orissa, and the fact that the economic conditions, which in fact caused land in Bisipara to be sold, only came into existence after the Administration had arrived, I think it unlikely that sale of land was usual before 1855.

The point about the system of land tenure is relevant, because evidence from Africa shows how a similar system of land-holding can keep land (at least in its distribution) out of entanglement with a money economy, even when land is short 'In Zululand in 1937 people were fined for selling and buying land . . . and the paramount . . . in his judgement preached that land and its raw materials are owned by him, for the people, and are not things to be trafficked in, as among Whites.'[1] Throughout southern Africa the reaction to shortage of land is not, so far, the development of proprietary right, akin to freehold, but rather an effort to see that every subject has some land.

In Zululand the traditional system of land-tenure had introduced an element of planning in the face of land-shortage. In Bisipara a system of land-tenure probably similar to that of Zululand in its main features has fallen down before the play of market forces and legislative encouragement of private rights. The two situations are different. The Oriya chief never had the powers of the Zulu kings and chieftains. The technique of agriculture differs in the two places, since in Bisipara it is possible for a man to grow far more than he can consume, and sell the surplus. Land, in other words, is a profitable investment, and it would take a very strong chief to maintain his traditional

[1] M. Gluckman, 1943, p. 50. There is an extended discussion of the effects of the modern economy on African agriculture in this book, pp. 46–64. A similar judgement is recorded by I. Schapera, 1943, p. 152.

rights in land against the pressure of potential investors, when land was limited and profits unlimited.

The difference in the two situations is that the sale of land in Bisipara was not under the jurisdiction of the district headman. There could be no question of his fining the buyer and seller of a piece of land. The Zulu Paramount benefits from the support, or at least the indifference, of the Administration. In the Kondmals the new Administration ignored the traditional system of land-tenure and elevated private rights. Land escheats to the Government and not to the headman. As the holder of the land, the headman is supplanted by the Government.

I repeat that this is conjecture. It is possible that private rights were well developed before the British took over the Kondmals. What is certain is that after the British took control, if a system of land-tenure of the type I have described did exist, it offered no obstacle to the transfer of land that subsequently took place.

In the most general terms, the problem which I have been discussing is the interaction of a 'backward area' with the economy of the modern world. This is a problem manifested in many parts of the world and in many different ways. To conclude this section I shall point out some of the features which differentiate the process going on in Bisipara from that in other places.

The first and most obvious limitation is that the 'backward area' is a peasant economy, and that the modern economy arrived in the form of a traders' frontier. The latter is the result primarily of the environment. Communications are poor. There are no known mineral resources to attract industry. There are, of course, other factors at work to prevent the growth of industry, but this is beyond the scope of my enquiry and I have taken the peasant economy and the traders' frontier as the given point at which to begin the analysis.

The first qualification is that Bisipara is on a settlers' frontier. By race, language, religion, and culture the village is distinct from the majority of villages in the region. The inhabitants are alien. They also are akin to the inhabitants of the region from which came the traders. They own the best land. Politically they dominate the region.

This combination of circumstances made Bisipara into a village of traders. This, in its turn, meant that the Oriyas could obtain money and trade goods without having to alter their system of agriculture. This has been an element of conservation in the subsequent social developments in the village.

Another element of conservation is that a large proportion of the population of the village was able to profit from trade. In this respect the consequences of differential ability were lessened, since the wealth acquired from trade went not solely to the big traders, but also to cultivators.

The second qualification is the caste system. This was partly responsible for the fact that some persons could profit in the new economy more than others. It sharpened the natural difference in human business capacities.

The third qualification is the activity of the Administration. Firstly it combined with caste to bring about windfall profits, and these, more than anything else, diverted the new wealth from those who already were wealthy in the agricultural system. The caste system and the policies of the Administration, together with inborn human capacities, ensured that wealth from trade did not necessarily accrue to those who were rich cultivators. Secondly, the Administration, in its tenderness for private rights, broke down the indigenous system of land-tenure and allowed economic forces to commercialize the land.

There was an increasing pressure of population on the land. At the same time the mercantile economy split the joint-family. The property-holding kinship unit was reduced in size. Some estates came down to a level where they disintegrated under pressure of contingent expenditure. The new economy had brought wealth to those who formerly had no land, and land became a desirable investment, because it was limited and because its produce could be sold to those who gained their living from the mercantile economy. The replacement of the client system by wage-labour set no limit to the size of the unit of management and made it easy for those who invested in land to cultivate the land efficiently.

This, in brief, is the effect on agriculture of the traders' frontier, which, in Bisipara, represents the modern economy of India and the world.

The Village and the State

Just as the economy of the village can be analysed into two systems, the agricultural and the mercantile, so the political life of the villagers is the product of their membership of the village and their status as citizens of India. This is the dichotomy, familiar in colonial countries, between the Administration and the indigenous political system. These four systems are connected. The village polity and agriculture are organically linked with one another. The Administration and the mercantile economy are similarly interdependent systems. The village polity cannot be described without reference to the agricultural system on which it is based : agriculture has been changed by the mercantile economy : some important features of the mercantile economy are the result of Administrative activity : and the presence of the Administration gives effect to changes in the village polity, which are touched off by changes in the village economy.

I am once again concerned only with Bisipara. In discussing its relationship to the Administration, I shall touch upon differential policies of the Government towards Kond and Oriya only when they seem relevant to events and processes inside Bisipara.

The relationship of the village polity and the Government, as represented by the officers in Phulbani, is, in one respect, a simple ordination in an administrative hierarchy. This is an obvious fact, but it needs amplification. It is this relationship which accounts for the attitude of the villagers to the Administration, their efforts to exclude the Administration from their lives, and the way in which groups within the village can manipulate the Administration to gain their own ends. The village and the State are embraced in one society. To describe the social structure of Bisipara at the present day without reference to the Administration would result in distortion. But they are two worlds. They share neither the same values nor the same culture.

The ties which bind Bisipara to any other Oriya village are many and complex. There is hardly a man in Bisipara who cannot trace an effective link with at least one household in every other Oriya village in the Kondmals. These links are of many kinds. In some cases the tie is one of agnatic kinship. More often it is one of affinal or uterine kinship. Kinship ties ramify, and are extended through the usage of village solidarity, and, other things being equal, such extended links are effective when they cross the boundary of caste and even of pollution. Thus, visitors used to descend upon a HERDSMAN household in Bisipara for a snack (if caste were appropriate), or to eat their own food, or to rest and gossip, and they were welcomed because they came from the natal village of the householder's wife. Some of these visitors belonged to untouchable castes. The welcome they received depended on their importance and the closeness of the tie, but at least they would be allowed to sleep in the courtyard. All the Oriya villages of the Kondmals are inextricably bound to one another by ramifying ties of this sort.

But the link between Bisipara and the Administration is the single thread of *imperium*. No-one in Bisipara is mother's brother to the Deputy Commissioner. The social roles of the administrators and the men of the village do not overlap. Even caste is irrelevant.

This division persists inside the Administration, as one would expect, since the Administration is an organization and not a community. Those who are recruited locally as policemen or messengers remain members of their village communities and retain the outlook of a villager. Their attitude to the Government (*Sircar*) is fundamentally the same as that of the ordinary cultivator. Their loyalty remains with the village, and this applies even to the headmen, whose position I will consider later.

There is, in fact, in rural India a parody of the four castes of Hinduism. In this parody there is the Gazetted Officer caste, the Non-Gazetted Officer caste, the *Babu* (clerk) caste, and the rest, comprising the menials in the Administration and the villagers. In the Kondmals they do not inter-dine and they do not intermarry, and it is very hard to get from one class to the next above.[1] There is only one University Graduate from the Kondmals. He is the one local-born Gazetted Officer and is himself something of an outsider, since his grandfather, a Chris-

[1] 'Parody' is defined in the *Oxford Dictionary* as 'a feeble imitation'. I would not like this flight of fancy to be taken literally.

tian, came to the Kondmals in the service of the Administration. Every other Gazetted Officer has come from outside, either from the metropolitan districts of Orissa, or from Bengal or from South India. The same applies to the larger part of the Non-Gazetted Officers. It applies even to the clerks, for there are very few natives of the Kondmals with the required educational qualification.

The social distance between the higher ranks of the Administration and the villagers is further maintained by the rapidity with which officers are transferred. Service in the area, which is totally lacking in the social and recreational facilities to which the educated classes are accustomed, is not popular. The climate is considered bad. The District is thought of as a backwater, or, at best, as a stepping-stone to more important positions.

The villagers look upon the Administration—although not necessarily upon individual officers—as unpredictable, unsympathetic, ignorant, and immeasurably powerful. In reporting this, I am not attacking the Administration, since this is a common attitude to 'the Government' anywhere in the world. To those who understand it, the working of the Administration is far from unpredictable : lack of sympathy and ignorance of the wants of the common man is no more to be found in the Kondmals than in a bureaucracy anywhere ; and the power, though real, is tempered by the relatively small segment of village life in which it is exercised. The attitude of the villager is a reflection not of the attributes of the Administration, but of the fact that these are different systems. Officers may understand the village *ethos*—indeed those who were brought up in villages usually do : but the villager does not look upon himself as a citizen, having common interests with the Administration, but as a subject. Civic sense stops at village boundaries.

The combination of xenophobia and unwillingness to see themselves as anything but subjects is illustrated by a story told to me and designed to illustrate the incorrigible stupidity of the native. A junior official arrived on the bus. He got out at the market-place with two cases and discovered that the Government buildings were half a mile away. He offered two annas to a man and asked him to carry the bags. The man, a Kond, looked at the money and walked on. The newcomer made several more unsuccessful attempts to find porters, when my informant came along on his bicycle. They talked and the newcomer explained his predicament. My informant ordered another passer-by, whom he had never seen before, to carry the luggage. Without demur, the man picked up the cases and carried them to the Courthouse. He was not paid.

This tale—which occurred in a discussion of the welfare activities of the Administration—was given in support of the thesis that villagers must be made to do what is good for them, since their prejudice prevents them from seeing their own interest. This is a mode of thinking found among upper classes everywhere, and, indeed, in opinions expressed by individuals in the Administration, class attitudes were apparent, ranging from the patriarchal and benevolent to ignorant prejudice. The majority held the former attitude. But I listened to one man saying, 'Why do we spend money digging wells for them? They'd just as soon drink out of the ditch (*nala pani*).' This is a cultural variation of the coals-in-the-bath theory.

Class differences are apparent also in dress. Officers wear trousers and a bush-shirt or a jacket. The younger clerks wear similar clothes or shorts. Older clerks and older junior officials might wear European clothes—usually with a solar topee—but the majority of them are clothed in the long *dhoti*, reaching to the ankles, with the long pocketed shirt, tails worn outside. The villagers, including the district headman, wear a shorter *dhoti* (called *gamucha*) to the level of the knees, and on the upper half of their body either a cotton shawl or a waist-length shirt (*ungi*). On their head they wear a turban. Boys and youths wear shorts. The villagers resent their fellows adopting clothes appropriate to upper classes unless they have special qualifications. Some of the schoolmasters wear the long *dhoti* and the pocketed shirt and this calls forth no comment. But other villagers may only wear these without exciting derision when they are going to a festival or visiting relatives. Bitter scorn is poured on a WARRIOR youth from another village, who 'dresses in trousers, shoes, and a jacket, and sits all day in the hotel drinking tea and smoking cigarettes—like a *babu*'.[1]

[1] The point of the cigarette is that the villager's proper smoke is a *bidi*, a roll of leaf with rubbed tobacco inside. The hotel in Phulbani is not, as the English word implies, the resort of officials. It is a tin shack in the bazaar, from which tea is sold.

The existence of these attitudes, which I have said are typical of social class in our society, does not imply political consciousness, in the sense that the villagers think of their relationship with the Administration in terms of class conflict, or look forward to the day when they themselves will take over the reins of government. If the tag existed in Oriya, the villagers would agree that the Government, like the weather, is always with them. Government is something exterior, inevitable, and not always convenient.[1]

There is an historical basis for this attitude, since, until *Pax Britannica* was imposed on the Kondmals, systematic administration of units larger than the village did not exist. There seem to have been confederacies of a kind, and the Oriyas owed some allegiance to the Raja of Boad, but, as I have implied earlier in the essay, the region had the segmentary, rather than the hierarchical type of political organization. Civic rights and duties did in fact terminate at the village boundary.[2]

The primary functions of the Administration are to keep the peace and to collect revenue. These I will consider later. Leaving aside for the moment the unpurposed economic consequences of its policies, I will now discuss certain deliberate activities by which the Administration influences village life. It has established a school in the village. It maintains a bungalow there. It has caused wells to be dug and it has contributed to various irrigation schemes. Until recently a Veterinary Assistant practised in the village. There is a Post Office. A by-road and a bridge into the village are maintained. Until 1947 the Administration regularly exacted compulsory labour (*bheti*) from the villagers. The Forestry Department controls the exploitation of jungles in the vicinity of the village. The Agricultural Department offers certain facilities, including monetary loans. Under the direction of the Civil Surgeon measures of hygiene

[1] It will be interesting to observe the working of the new statutory councils (*panchayats*), which are in part designed to bridge this gap between the village and the Administration. One was functioning in Phulbani during my visit, but I did not have time to make systematic observations of its activities.

[2] It is to be noticed that while the Administration possesses all the attributes which the Boad Raja lacked—power, continuity, systematic governmental machinery, and so forth—it could not take over the one function which he performed: the Raja was the spiritual head of Oriyas in the Kondmals.

and prophylaxy are put into effect. Wells are chlorinated and there is periodical vaccination against smallpox. In Phulbani a free medical service is offered.

The villagers accept most of these services philosophically and are prepared to admit their good points. Education is respected and the usefulness of the school is appreciated. Water from a well, in spite of the opinion quoted above, is preferred to ditch water. The village greatly missed the veterinary service when it was removed, and have petitioned for its restoration. A large number of adults voluntarily offer themselves for vaccination, when the assistant comes to deal with children, but the hospital is regarded with suspicion and usually patronized only *in extremis*. I have recorded above the reaction of the village to a proposal to close the Post Office. There are no strong opinions about the Forestry Department, since Oriyas are not axe-cultivators, and the work of the Department impinges little on their lives. The agricultural loans, offered until recently, were widely taken and in most cases put to good use. Even forced labour, so far as I could gather, was regarded with equanimity—at least in retrospect—when it was clearly for the public weal. I heard several times comment upon the solidity and technical excellence of a bridge over the Salki, built by compulsory labour, when compared with a dam, built by a contractor, which twice had collapsed. For its own public works—a new temple and a smaller dam to replace the one which broke—the village still uses forced labour and calls it by the same name, *bheti*. Compulsory labour on roads, on the other hand, was bitterly resented, since the villager on foot and in his ox-cart had a different idea of what constituted an adequate surface, from the idea of the British officer of the early nineteen-thirties in his tight-sprung motor-car.

But the suspicions of the villagers persist, even against the welfare activities of the Administration, particularly when these are not conspicuously successful. Some years ago an energetic demonstrator persuaded the villagers to grow a type of lentil crop, novel in the region, on land previously devoted to rice. The seed was supplied on credit, and almost the whole of one field-area was planted with this crop. It failed completely. I did not have a chance to discuss with the Agricultural Department the reasons for this failure or to get their version of the experiment. I suggested, in a discussion with two intelligent men, one of whom has the reputation of being the most skilful cultivator in the village, that there might be good scientific reasons for the failure and it might be worth trying again. Their technique might have been wrong. It might have been a bad year. Perhaps they had misused the irrigation system : and so forth. Normally the failure of a familiar crop is accounted for in these terms. But they refused to think along these lines, put the whole blame on the Agricultural Department, and shifted the discussion into the usual channels of the difference between Government things and village things, and the essential danger of having dealings with Government agencies. To illustrate the latter they alleged that the Department was now claiming payment for the seed, although it had written off the debt when the crop was a failure. For the former topic they turned to the argument commonly advanced against agricultural agencies, that if the peasant had the resources of the demonstration farm, he too could grow fine crops.

Each side has a sterotype of the other. The peasant is stupid, indolent, and greedy. The ' we ' and ' they ' attitude between Government and governed is found here, as everywhere else. ' They ' do not know what is good for them. ' They ' have no road-sense. ' They ' want things for nothing and will not help themselves. From the other side, ' they ' do not understand ' our ' problems. ' They ' make unreasonable demands. ' They ' should repair the bridge. ' They ' should mend the dam. ' They ' ought to do something about the rice-blight. What do you suppose ' they ' will do about the locusts ? ' They ' would take months to mend the big bridge, while the Leaf Company will do it in a day and at a quarter of the cost. The sharp distinction which the villagers make between their own communal activities and the projects of the Administration was brought home to me by a discussion which followed the second breach in the big dam, which had been built with Government help some years before. An older and smaller dam, which the villagers themselves built and which had been submerged in the larger lake, was repaired by the villagers. I asked why they should not repair the big dam, which gave a much better supply of water. A lot of reasons were given. The hole was too big. The dam was fundamentally unsound.

They would need concrete—and so forth. But one informant closed the discussion with an air of finality by saying, 'Besides, why should we repair the dam? It's not ours. It belongs to the Government. Let them repair it, if they wish.' This was said in spite of the fact that the dam served no-one but the village. Nor did the disclaimer prevent them from applying for a grant from the Government to restore their own smaller dam as a permanent structure, during the next dry season. They wanted the best of both worlds.

So far as concerns such welfare activities, Bisipara has had the best of both worlds, since the Administration does not do direct violence to the communal life of the village. Such changes as have occurred are the result of unleashing unforeseen economic forces. In its conscious acts of policy the Administration is very tender towards the village community. The welfare activities which I have been discussing in this section for the most part do not tend to break down village ties or to destroy village autonomy.

In most general terms, the reason why this autonomy is preserved in the face of Administrative action in the internal affairs of the village, is, firstly, that no multiplex ties are created between the Administration and the village. The thread is mainly the single downward one of *imperium*. The school or the Veterinary Assistant or the application by individuals for agricultural loans do not set up ties which conflict with village loyalties, or a relationship which is not wholly one of super-ordination and subordination. The school becomes 'our school'. The assistant is 'our Stockman'. The agricultural loan does not even create affection or a sentiment of loyalty towards the wider polity which has provided it. The schoolmasters are all recruited in the Kondmals, and while there is a strong *esprit de corps* among schoolmasters, this fellowship does not include the Department of Education and its higher officials. In the same way the Stockman might be 'one of us', but the Veterinary Service remains 'them'.

The second reason is that almost all Government action of this type is routed through the communal institutions of the village, and not through individuals. A single exception was the agricultural loan. In all other cases, if the village wants something, then it petitions as a village. From the other direction

Government orders come down to the headman, who passes them through the village council. The man who brings small-pox vaccine is a native of the Kondmals, and he comes to the village and sits on the headman's verandah, where the people attend him. He vaccinates the village : the villagers do not go as individuals to be vaccinated in Phulbani.

One reason why the Administration uses village institutions for its welfare activities is that almost all these projects concern public works or public welfare, and not, directly, individual welfare. But there are also historical reasons, which justify my assertion that so far as concerns direct Administrative action, Bisipara gets the best of both worlds. These reasons are, firstly, that the village community was already firmly in existence when the British arrived, and, secondly, that there was no wider political organization, which the presence of the Administration would tend to upset. Diagrammatically the villages are small circles, representing organic and functioning communities. The State is in the centre, linked to each village by a line representing *imperium*. The important point is that in order to establish itself, the State did not first require to draw the small circles.

The same is not true of all parts of the world. The Kondmals were fortunate in so far as their indigenous political organization (speaking here of Oriya villages) was of a type understood by and approved by the conquering power. Sometimes Government has created political authority *de novo* purely out of ignorance.[1] In Burma, partly through excessive familiarity with the Indian village system, and partly through an inability to understand a system of authority not co-incident with territorial boundaries, the Administration interfered with the indigenous political organisation and thereby allowed economic forces to disrupt the existing communities. As a result it was barely able to maintain law and order.[2]

In its primary functions of keeping order and collecting the revenue, the Administration had no higher indigenous political official with whom to deal than the Oriya chiefs, who became *mutha* headmen. The Meriah Wars had demonstrated that the

[1] Cf. E. Colson, 1948, *passim*. M. Fortes and E. E. Evans-Pritchard (editors), 1940, pp. 15, 265. M. Fortes, 1945, pp. 13, 250.

[2] J. S. Furnivall, 1948, pp. 36–8 *et passim*.

Raja of Boad had no effective authority in the Kondmals.[1] There was no hierarchy of chieftains. Consequently the only person whose role transcends the boundary between the Village and State is the *mutha* headman.

The *mutha* headman is the head not only of his own village but also of Kond villages in his *mutha*. But here I am not primarily concerned with the Kond-Oriya relationship, and I shall discuss his role without reference specifically to his Kond subjects. Although the nominal village headman of Bisipara is in fact another person, nevertheless it is the *mutha* headman who is ritually and politically the apex of the village, and it is his role that penetrates the Administration.

If the system of land-tenure was based on the right of the chief to distribute land, then the coming of the Administration, its assumption of the reversionary right in all land, and the elevation of a system of private freehold rights, must inevitably have diminished the authority of the chief. Studies in Africa demonstrate how the chief, in spite of the conflict of values and loyalties to which he is subject, and in spite of the opening of new sources of wealth unconnected with the land, has yet been able to maintain his authority, because the indigenous system of land tenure is as yet relatively intact.[2] There are vestiges of this system in Bisipara. Unsettled land, usually garden and house-site land in and near the village, is reserved by the Government and its distribution is *de facto* in the control of the headman. In the same way appointments as militiaman or watchman, which carry a grant of land, are on the recommendation of the headman, and he uses these powers for the benefit of his henchmen. Furthermore, although the Government has removed his ultimate control over the land, nevertheless he is now their representative in the village, and he and his predecessors have by various subtle means created the impression that the headman is a dangerous enemy or a valuable friend in matters of land. But these are mere vestiges, and it requires a degree of subtlety and intelligence to use such pressures effectively, and they can be used only when chance offers suitable circumstances. These

[1] *Selections from the Records*, 1854, pp. 78, 80, 89 *et al.*

[2] For the point about land, see M. Gluckman, 1943, p. 50.

There is a brief discussion on headmen in the Rampa Agency of Madras, in C. von Fürer-Haimendorf, 1945 (2), pp. 167–78.

powers are a small perquisite for the cunning of the headman and they are in no way comparable to an accepted right to distribute the land.

The *mutha* headman does make constant, and, so it seemed to me, extremely subtle use of the gulf between the village and the Administration, in order to maintain his authority in the village. He does the same among his Kond subjects, as I described in an earlier chapter, but there he appears straightforwardly as the representative of the Administration and is inclined, if he thinks it necessary, to threaten the mailed fist. In village affairs his strength lies not in any claim to the favoured ear of the Administration, but partly in superior knowledge of its ways and partly in a suggestion of its omnipotence and omniscience. On the rare occasions when he does call in outside authority, he presents the case to his fellow-villagers as if he were merely anticipating the inevitable and averting the wrath of the Government from himself and the village.[1] Behaviour of this kind is made possible by being a headman : but it is not structurally inherent in the headmanship. It is a refinement introduced by headmen who have the required abilities.

For there is no doubt that in social structure and in the sentiment both of the headman himself and of the villagers, he belongs with the village. This is true from every point of view. He is part of that complex ramification of ties between men and villages which I described above. His position in the village is validated by ritual observances. Socially he belongs with the villagers he dresses like them, and he shares their activities and recreations. He receives a commission on the tax he collects, but he does not thereby become a salaried official, as the headman became in Burma.[2] I never heard any suggestion that he was a tool of the Administration or that he was more interested in pleasing the Administration than helping the village, although towards the end of my stay I heard many discreditable stories from his enemies in the village.

The headman is able to maintain this position because, although he transmits Administrative orders and carries out Administrative

[1] There was a perfect example of this in 1953. Unfortunately I cannot write it down, since I can think of no way of relating it that does not seem to be libellous of one party or the other.

[2] J. S. Furnivall, 1948, p. 37.

policies, he is not expected to deal with recalcitrants. Prosecutions for non-payment of tax are levied by the Revenue Department. The villagers all know that the headman cannot protect such offenders and cannot conceal their offence. They do not expect it of him. Contraventions of the Excise laws are detected and punished by the police and the Excise officers. It is not suggested to the headman that he should be responsible for preventing illicit distilling in his village. It is unusual for the headman to be summoned to Phulbani to receive orders. A messenger comes to the village and delivers the orders to the headman in his compound or on the veranda, where there are always three or four men standing about, who in this way see that the orders have come from the Government. If there is a major question of local policy to be decided, or a major investigation to be conducted, then the Administration comes to the village, which is represented not by the headman alone, but by the headman-in-council. In short, the way in which the Administrative machine functions does nothing to break the natural solidarity of village and headman.

I have described the integrity, unity, and exclusiveness of the village in its dealings with the Administration, and I have given some reasons for these characteristics. When the Administration came to the area the village was already a community, geographically and socially distinct, autonomous, with its own

---

Plate VIII

(*a*) THE HEADMAN WORKING

The photograph was taken in an unlevelled upland field (see page 280). It adjoins the village and was formerly the site of Government buildings, which now have entirely disappeared.

The headman is winnowing *mugo* (*phaseolus radiatum*).

In dress and in the work he is willing to do, the headman belongs clearly with the village rather than with the Administration. The humblest clerk would not deign to do work of this kind.

(*b*) LABOURERS AT WORK FOR THE HEADMAN

The photograph was taken in the same field on the same day. The headman stands in the centre in the background.

The labourers are threshing *mugo*. One is the plough-servant of the headman and by caste is a Kond HERDSMAN. Another is a HERDSMAN: another a SWEEPER; and the last is the headman's younger son. The HERDSMAN and the SWEEPER were engaged as casual labourers.

(*a*)

(*b*)

PLATE VIII

responsible government, and capable of supplying its own social wants. This was a form of government with which the Administrators were familiar and of which they approved. The words 'Village Community' had, indeed, acquired an emotive force,[1] which is still strong to-day. The village fitted neatly into the scheme of administration, and there were no more embracing political institutions which might come into conflict with the new Administration. In its direct and deliberate policies and activities the Administration makes use of the village as a unit, and *in this field* does not tend to thrust upon the individual duties, allegiances, and interests which might conflict with his role as a responsible member of the village.

The village is a community: the Administration is an organization. Villages are bound to one another in a complex web of kinship and quasi-kinship and friendship. But their tie with the Administration is the single one of *imperium*. This is, of course, an inherent characteristic of an Administration, considered in abstraction: but in fact there are sometimes Administrations the personnel of which are connected by individual ties with subjects of the Administration, and partake of a common culture and a common way of living. But the Administrators of the Kondmals have always come from outside. They have a different way of life from the villager. In education, wealth and outlook they are of a different social class. These factors serve to keep the Administration and the village as mutually exclusive units. There can be no doubt whether the role of any individual lies in the one or the other. He must be either one of 'us' or one of 'them': he cannot be both.

The Village Council, the Government Courts, and Mercantile Wealth

In spite of the great gulf between village and State, and in spite of the strong sense of community felt by villagers, individuals and groups within the village can make use of the State to further their own ends. Under the shadow of the Government courts are fought out conflicts which arise from a changed economy. The State is partly responsible for these conflicts, since its presence allows new economic forces to function and sometimes gives

[1] See the quotation from Sir Charles Metcalfe given on page 3 of this book.

them unintended aid. Equally the State, by its presence and its power, permits modification in the political structure of the village, to accord with the changed economic structure.

In civil cases, the initiative in drawing the attention of the Administration to village affairs lies with individuals, although such action is made possible by the State, which claims the right to hear appeals from any decision of a village tribunal or a caste tribunal. Such appeals do not necessarily subvert the authority of the village council, since the Magistrate will often decide that their decision is correct, or will pronounce that the decision must lie with the village or the caste, and is not within the cognizance of a Government court. I will discuss later the significance of civil suits as a factor in disrupting the village community.

The Administration has abrogated the right of the village council to sit in judgement on criminal cases. These cases, for the problem I am here considering, fall into two categories. The one category, which includes such things as contravention of the Excise laws or failure to pay tax, is new, pertains solely to the Administration, and is alien to the system of village morality. In the other category are such offences as homicide, which would formerly have had to be judged by the village council, and which is recognized by village ethics as wrong, but which now lies solely within the jurisdiction of the Government courts. It would be beyond the competence of the village council to sit in judgement on a case of homicide.

Although, strictly speaking, the arrest of a villager and his trial for tax evasion or Excise offences represents a diminution of the juridical autonomy of the village, the villagers do not see it in this way. They do not think that a reform bringing such cases under the jurisdiction of the village council would give them greater independence and greater autonomy. Excise and tax are things of the Administration. When someone falls foul of these laws, then that is an affair between him and the Administration, but not between him and the village. Indeed, as I stated in discussing the role of the headman, the Administration's willingness to act alone in detecting and prosecuting offenders against its Excise laws has been an important factor in maintaining village integrity.

Abrogation of the right to judge cases of homicide is an important modification in the indigenous judicial system. It has removed the possibility of open feud and of warfare, and has taken over a key function from the political institutions of the village. But once again, the village seems content to concede this right to the Administration. The penalties for doing otherwise are too great. The village can with impunity turn a blind eye to illicit distilling, since this is an affair between the Administration and the distiller. But it cannot treat a murder in the same way, firstly because the Administration demands that it should not, and, secondly, because the presence of an aggrieved party in the relatives of the victim makes it almost certain that information will come before the Administration. Thirdly, a murder sets up a state of tension in the village, which needs to be resolved, and since the village itself cannot achieve this, the case must come before the Government courts.

The presence of an aggrieved party is crucial in this instance, and it brings these cases, in the perspective of my problem, into a line with appeals in civil cases. The initiative in calling in Government lies with a member of the village, either the aggrieved party or the headman, who, by doing so, is simply anticipating the relatives of the victim. There were no murders in Bisipara during my visit, nor did I hear of any in the recent past. But there were two alleged murders in the vicinity, and I will use these to illustrate the important effect of the presence of an aggrieved party. A man was alleged to have been murdered in the jungle. When the body was found the father of the victim made an immediate report to the police. They came to investigate and decided that the man had been killed by a tiger. In the other case an itinerant trader from the plains was reported to have been killed by a tiger near a remote village in the Kondmals. Very little of the body was found and the case was recorded as a tiger-kill. Some months later I heard allegations that in fact the man had been murdered and his goods and money stolen. I must emphasize that these allegations are hearsay and must not be taken as casting doubt on the official records that both these incidents were tiger-kills. The point is this : in the first case an aggrieved person immediately summoned the authorities ; in the second case, if this had been a murder, there was no aggrieved party to call in outside help, and the villagers could have dealt with the death in the way most convenient to them—by ignoring it.[1]

An aggrieved party is precluded by the law of the Administration from seeking redress before a village tribunal in a case involving homicide. But there are also a large number of civil cases which come before the Magistrate, not because the village court is forbidden to hear them, but because it is unable to bring effective sanctions in support of its decision. An obvious example is a case involving persons resident in different villages, the commonest of which are theft and fraud. In these the village council again turns a blind eye, and it is left to the injured party to call in the police.

But the village council is also an ineffective tribunal in some cases which concern two parties from its own village. These are cases which are not felt to involve the public weal, and the most common of them involve title to land. The reason is partly that the one effective sanction at the disposal of the village council is ostracism. If ostracism is to work then there must be a high degree of consent from the village. The mere infringement of the rights of an individual is not enough. The offence must be beyond doubt heinous, and obviously a contravention of the *mores* of the community. Thus ostracism was readily invoked to back the actions of the community in its prosecution of persons who kept maleficent spirits. It was also invoked by the WARRIORS and the clean castes during the latest conflict with the Boad OUTCASTES, against anyone who revealed proceedings in the village council to a Boad OUTCASTE. But it was not invoked in two recent cases involving title to land. In one a BRAHMIN had bought a field from a Ganjam OUTCASTE, giving in payment a gold necklace. But the OUTCASTE continued to cultivate the field. The BRAHMIN went before the Magistrate and sought either for the transfer of the field or the return of his necklace. He did not come to the village council. Discussing this case, an informant said that there would be nothing to gain by going before the village council, because the Ganjam OUTCASTE would take no heed of them in an affair like this. He was a rich man. In any case, the informant added, the BRAHMIN was not very popular at the moment.

[1] The role of an aggrieved party in similar situations in Bastar is illustrated by W. Grigson, 1949, p. 285.

But another case demonstrates that the disdain in which that particular BRAHMIN was held at the time had no influence on the issue. In a precisely similar case the *mutha* headman himself, who, if anyone, could move the council and the village to action, had to go to court to gain the use of and to register the title to fields which he had purchased.

There is, however, another element at work here. It is not simply that the general public is indifferent to disputes over title to land. Titles to land are part of the system of private rights in land and are foreign to the village system. The system of registering transfers of land was initiated by, and is maintained by, the Administration. Effective title cannot be obtained in the village council : it must come from the Government.

The obverse of this is the case of the maleficent spirits. This is an affair which belongs entirely within the village *ethos*, and of which the Administration takes no cognizance. Indeed, it would be likely to treat penalties imposed by the village council for such an offence as against natural justice. Therefore the village exacted an oath that no-one should invoke the Administration. The plaintiff in such a case cannot get justice (as the village conceives justice) out of a Government court : the case must be conducted within the traditional juridical system.

The village council and the Government courts differ in several characteristics, which have an important influence on the readiness of individuals and groups to bring the Administration into village affairs by going before a Magistrate.

The fundamental fact is once again that these are different systems. The law of the Administration is codified and developed and proper representation before this law requires the services of a lawyer. The law which the village council administers is appropriate to a small group, which is characterized by face-to-face relationships. Village law is based upon widely known and accepted norms. There is no room for the specialized lawyer. The Government courts have a much narrower standard of relevance in hearing evidence than has the village court. The former treats the parties as they appear before the court in one particular issue : the village council is prepared to consider the total role of the parties as members of the village community. The village council is informal, and cheap, and does not intimidate: the Government court is expensive and formidable.

There is no doubt that these characteristics of the Government court serve to restrict litigation. A man who is poor and timid will not venture to seek justice there. He will rather abandon the struggle. The wealthy and the worldly can make more effective use of the Government courts. They do not even need to go to court. It is a firm belief in the village that to hire a lawyer is to win a case, and this deters people who cannot afford the lawyer's fee from trying their strength against those who can.

Title to land cannot be validated ultimately in the village council; it must be sought from the Government, and if there is dispute, the decision rests with Government courts. These courts are believed to be weighted in favour of the wealthy. Differential ability to profit in the new economy, the scarcity-value of land, and the internal market for rice, have given land to those who formerly were without land and without political power in the village. Now such power is irrelevant, since the political authority which underwrites the distribution of wealth in the new economy is no longer the village council and the chief, but the Administration. These are the forces which have weakened the juridical authority of the village council.

In the economic sphere the premeditated welfare policies of the Administration have been of relatively slight importance in breaking down the traditional structure of the village, when compared to the unintended benefits, which it conferred on limited categories of persons. In the same way the Excise Inspectors, the officers of the Revenue Department, and even the police in search of a murderer, are relatively secondary agents in demolishing the traditional juridical autonomy of the village. The prime agent is the fact that the traditional authorities control neither the new wealth nor the land.

Caste in the New Economy

The traditional rulers in Bisipara were the members of the WARRIOR caste-group. The changes which have followed the new economy and the coming of the Administration appear in the village as the emancipation of other caste-groups from the power of the WARRIORS.

In this final section I shall illustrate the modification which has taken place in the functioning of the caste-system during the last hundred years.

Caste, in the sense in which it is used in this book, is a system of relationships between certain groups. Membership of one of these groups is allotted by birth and maintained through the individual's life by an elaborate system of ritual avoidance. Some features of a caste system are well known. It is a system of rank, highly ritualized, and of a rigidity which strikes every observer. This has made 'caste' a term signifying hereditary and more or less exclusive social classes in other parts of the world.

In the Kondmals castes are dispersed over several villages, and each village is made up of several caste-groups. Professor Srinivas has characterized the tie which binds the caste as 'horizontal unity', while the village-tie is an example of 'vertical unity'.[1] I had occasion to discuss some aspects of horizontal unity in considering the role of village servants, but my main concern is with the village and consequently with vertical unity. The role of caste-courts under the Administration and the differing degrees to which the various caste-groups of the Kondmals are integrated are problems in themselves, and I do not deal with them except where they impinge on the role of a man as a member of a village community.

Attention has been drawn to the ritual interdependence of caste-groups within the local community.[2] Equally striking is their economic interdependence, which arises from functional specialization. Speaking of a community in the Punjab, Dr. M. W. Smith says:[3]

> The grain farmer is absolutely dependent upon the vegetable farmer for the maintenance of a balanced diet and the service groups are equally dependent on each other. Not only cannot the farmer grow his grain without the carpenter but he cannot store it without

[1] M. N. Srinivas, 1952, pp. 31–2.
[2] M. N. Srinivas, 1951, p. 105.
[3] M. W. Smith, 1952, p. 51.

the carpenter or potter, depending on his type of storage bins, and the carpenter must keep the potter's wheel in repair or he himself has no water jugs.

Organic solidarity arising from the division of labour is something seldom overlooked in studies of the economic functions of caste.

But there is another aspect of the system of caste-groups in a village community. Certainly in Bisipara, and probably in village communities elsewhere, the ranking system of caste-groups was validated not only by ritual and social usage, but also by differential control over the productive resources. Unless this fact is taken into account, it is impossible to understand the forms of conflict to which economic change in Bisipara has given rise.

In the traditional village the main productive resource was the land. This was under the control of the WARRIOR caste-group. Other caste-groups derived a share in the produce of the village land by virtue of a subordinate relationship to the WARRIORS. By serving the WARRIORS, and secondarily by serving one another, they made a living. This system still survives to-day in the tithe payments. This applied to those whom I have called 'village servants'. It applied also to the 'client' castes who worked land belonging to the WARRIORS. It applied even to the BRAHMIN, who, although ritually superior, was nevertheless an economic dependent and a political subject of the ruling group of WARRIORS. The WARRIORS' control over the land was sanctioned finally by their monopoly of physical force, a product partly of their numbers and partly of their traditional calling.

There was a high degree of coincidence between politico-economic rank and the ritual ranking of caste. This is a reflection of the general rule that those who achieve wealth and political power tend to rise in the ritual scheme of ranking. It is what is meant by saying that the ranking system of caste-groups was validated by differential control over the productive resources of the village. But the correlation is not perfect, since at each end of the scale there is a peculiar rigidity in the system of caste. The consequence of this for the untouchables will be discussed later. For the Brahmin it means that his ritual rank is secure from the vagaries of economic fortune. For caste-groups in between these two extremes, their ritual rank tends to follow their economic rank in the village community.[1]

The BRAHMIN seems at first sight to provide an exception to the general rule that ritual rank is underwritten by differential control of wealth. The position of the Boad DISTILLERS seems to contradict the second statement that other caste-groups derived a share in the product of the village land by virtue of a subordinate relationship to the WARRIORS. But the role of the DISTILLERS in the traditional village is not altogether clear. It is unlikely that they served the WARRIORS by a tithe arrangement, as did the BARBER or the WASHERMAN, since WARRIORS do not drink. Even this is not certain. Although they deny it now, it is possible that the WARRIORS once did drink, and it is equally possible that they needed liquor for various rites. On the whole it is probable that the Boad DISTILLERS sold their product for immediate payment and not by an annual tithe. It is also probable that their custom came from the other service caste-groups and from Konds who lived in other villages. But this does not mean that they were thereby less subservient to the WARRIORS than was any other caste-group in the village. They were few in numbers. They had no martial traditions. The custom on which they depended in the village was itself dependent on the WARRIORS. Nor can this custom have been very considerable, since the liquor trade boomed only after the Government banned home-stills. Finally the WARRIORS possessed the ultimate sanction of physical force, untrammelled by the presence of Government.

The WARRIORS to-day are still the dominant group within the village polity, but their superior position has been impaired by economic change. They no longer control the productive resources.

On the whole this is not the result of any conscious desire of the Government to destroy the dominance of the WARRIORS. By appointing the WARRIOR chief as *mutha* headman and by ruling through the traditional village authorities, the Administration

[1] The anomalous position of the BRAHMIN in some communities, where he is obliged to combine the role of ritual master with economic and political subjection, has been remarked upon by other writers. See, for instance, M. N. Srinivas, 1952, p. 43, and M. E. Opler and R. Datt Singh, 1952, p. 180.

at first confirmed and perhaps enhanced the power of the WARRIORS. In most general terms, this development has taken place because the Administration opened up sources of wealth which are not derived from owning land and do not depend on the recipient being in a particular subordinate relationship to the owners of the land. These opportunities were not restricted to the WARRIOR caste-group, so that men of other castes have been able to profit by them and become persons of property and substance, eligible for political power.

At the same time the wealth in the hands of the WARRIOR caste-group was reduced. In the original village the land had been divided between a number of WARRIOR joint-families. The fact that estates were held by joint-families meant that they were large relatively to their size to-day. But the chance of getting wealth by using resources other than the patrimony tended to break down these families into elementary families and in time partition at the death of a father has become all but automatic. This, combined with a growing population and the elevation of private rights in land, with full title to sell, reduced some estates to the point where they could not meet the cost of the normal contingencies of their owner's lifetime without selling land. Land came into the market and those who had profited in the new economy invested in land.

The breakdown of the joint-families and the reduction in the size of estates was one factor which made clientship uneconomic. From the other direction clients were attracted away from their masters by the chance of making a living in the new mercantile economy. This further expedited the transfer of land, because the new owners were able to rely on a pool of labour from which men could be hired on purely economic terms and without reference to the social status of the employer. This, in its turn, further weakened the position of the WARRIORS since they were deprived of lordship over a category of persons who had been towards them in a position of formal dependence.

At the same time the traders' frontier brought to the village a category of persons who had never been part of the social and political structure of the village, and who were not, initially at least, constrained since childhood into regarding the WARRIOR caste-group as naturally dominant in village politics.

In this way economic change has attacked the superiority of

the WARRIORS from all sides. By a reduction in the size of the property-holding kinship unit, the WARRIORS were compelled to sell land. At the same time land had ceased to be the sole source of wealth, and the new sources were not monopolized by the WARRIORS. Further, a share in the product of the village land was no longer dependent on having a particular subservient relationship to the WARRIORS. The population had been increased by newcomers who had not the tradition of respecting the WARRIOR caste-group as the political rulers of the village. Finally, many of the new economic opportunities not only were not the monopoly of the WARRIORS, but sometimes, as with distilling or handling hides, were exploited by means which the WARRIORS could not employ.

All this, it must be remembered, was taking place at a time when the WARRIORS had been deprived of the overt use of force.

If the ranking system is validated by differential wealth, then it will be upset by changes in the distribution of wealth. The changed economy demands social mobility. But the rigid system of caste-groups in the village either has canalized these forces into its own system, or, by seeking entirely to inhibit them, is tending to destroy itself.

Although it is the rigidity of a caste system that has attracted most comment, observers have also noticed that under certain conditions mobility in the system of ritual ranking is possible.[1] Rajas could by decree elevate castes to a higher rank.[2] Kingly families are known to claim a high origin, when in fact they are descended from low castes.[3] The laws of Manu recognize mobility of this sort.[4]

> As the son of a Sudra may attain the rank of a Brahman, and as the son of a Brahman may sink to a level with Sudras, even so must it be with him who springs from a Kshatriya, even so with him who was born of a Vaisya.

But the second and third cases given here, in which individuals pass from one caste to another, are unknown in Bisipara, except

[1] E. Senart, 1930, p. 75.
[2] L. S. S. O'Malley, 1941, p. 364. J. H. Hutton, 1946, p. 82.
[3] M. N. Srinivas, 1952, p. 219.
[4] Quoted by L. S. S. O'Malley, 1941, p. 364.

when a person marries into a lower caste and is expelled from his own group.

It is a peculiarity of the caste-system in the social structure of a village, as distinct from its formulation in Manu or its manipulation by kingly families, that mobility in the system of ritual ranking attaches not to individuals but to groups. Unless this peculiarity of caste is given full weight, it is impossible to see why the conflicts resulting from the new economy have continued to be fought out in the idiom of caste and between caste-groups, and why the situation has not produced class-groupings along the lines of economic differentiation and across the borders of different castes.

In seeking to improve his position in the ritual system of rank in his own community, the rich man cannot throw off his poorer caste-fellows : he must carry them along with him. There are clear reasons for this. The new economy has done nothing to break down caste endogamy. Therefore a man must find a wife from among his own group. He depends on the rest of his caste for help in the rites of marriage and death and at numerous other crises in the course of his life. With such ties as this, the most that the wealthy within a caste-group can do to lighten their upward passage by jettisoning poorer caste-fellows is to form a sub-caste. This sub-caste must consist of at least two unrelated families in the first instance, otherwise marriage will be impossible. Since the members of a caste-group often derive from one ancestor, social conditions are not always favourable for sub-caste development, even when economic conditions are appropriate. Fission might be made difficult by existing ties of kinship, which would conflict with the new sub-caste ties : the claim to a new status might even mean physical movement out of the caste street. It is probably such factors as these that have prevented sub-castes emerging among the Boad OUTCASTES, and have caused the rich and poor among them to be associated in efforts to improve status. The same ties, and the same knowledge that mobility adheres to groups and not individuals, instils a sense of solidarity in the caste-group, and causes the poor to support their own 'middle-classes' in the struggle against higher castes.

But the factors preventing individual mobility in the ranking system do not lie solely within the aspirant caste-group and in its solidarity. They lie also in the solidarity of higher caste-groups, for these close their ranks against rich men of lower caste.

Within the village community and its system of ranked caste-groups, social mobility arising from the new economy belongs to the caste-group and not to the individual. The forces of change are thus canalized into the idiom of caste, and, given certain conditions, the structure of caste-groups is unimpaired, although the ranking of units within this structure may be modified in accordance with their changed economic rank.

The Boad DISTILLERS provide an example of this. As their wealth increased, so, by increasing Sanskritization,[1] they elevated their ritual rank. The process goes on with struggle and conflict, but it does not do violence to the institutions of caste, nor did it, in this case, destroy the local structure of caste-groups. Ritual rank continued to be validated by differential control over productive resources.

But in other cases the localized system of caste-groups proved unable to accommodate the new economic reality. This was the result either of the magnitude of the economic change, or of certain irreducible features in a caste-system.

One of these features is localization. This precluded individual mobility. The rich man remains tied to his fellows by kinship and excluded from higher groups by their knowledge of his origin. If a man is determined to improve his position apart from the rest of his fellows, then his only course is to separate himself from the local community, either literally by going away, or structurally by abandoning Hinduism.

Even to abandon Hinduism is not, from the individual's point of view, an entirely satisfactory solution. In spite of the dogma of Christianity and the efforts of the missionaries, the rank of a Christian in the local community continues to depend on the caste from which he was converted. This persists among the Christians themselves, even to the third and fourth generation. A BRAHMIN family which was converted to Christianity four generations ago refuses to associate with Christians who were converted from untouchables, except in the formal assemblies in the Church building. They do not dine together, nor do they

[1] This is the name which Srinivas (1952, pp. 212–14, *et al.*) gives to the process which I have described in Chapter IX.

intermarry. The same internal stratification causes converts to attempt to conceal their origin. A young Boad OUTCASTE in Bisipara, who became a Baptist, has dropped his typically OUTCASTE lineage name and taken a Brahmin name.[1]

But localization has another aspect. The new economy has come in the guise of a traders' frontier. The wealth it brings comes to Bisipara. The men do not go away to work. They do not join Trade Unions : they are not caught up in modern political machinery : they have no experience of industrial townships where caste loyalties come into the shadow of class affiliations. They are not subjected to the disturbing influence of travel. Caste is not attacked by spatial mobility. The battle is only in the field of social mobility : and even this is fought on the home ground of the caste-system. This is the reason why the conflict is carried on in the idiom of caste, not only when the local structure of caste-groups can cope successfully with economic change, as in the case of the Boad DISTILLERS, but also in the cases of the Ganjam DISTILLERS and the Boad OUTCASTES, when the local structure of caste-groups reacted to economic change by extruding these groups and thrusting them into the larger polity, where the Administration rules.

The second feature is untouchability. In this, its most rigid institution, the localized structure of caste-groups has failed entirely to adapt itself to changed economic conditions. The structure has not reacted by internal adaptation. It has not accommodated the aspirant group in a suitable place in its hierarchy. It will finish by extruding the untouchables.

The Boad OUTCASTES were originally fully integrated in the organic structure of caste-groups which made up Bisipara. In ritual their function was music-making. In the politico-economic organization they were the instrument by which WARRIORS exploited the land and freed themselves for the tasks of government and warfare.

Their position on a traders' frontier has given the Boad OUTCASTES opportunities which untouchables elsewhere do not enjoy. It facilitated their emancipation from clientship to wage-labour. The settlers' frontier has given them a chance to make

[1] J. H. Hutton (1946, p. 106) discusses caste-attitudes in Islam and in Christianity.

effective use of discriminating legislation.[1] They have become free, and, relatively, they have become wealthy.

Wealth alone will not explain the present conflicts between the Boad OUTCASTES and the rest of the village. The Kond POTTERS, with about the same numbers and only slightly less average wealth, work amicably within the traditional structure of caste-groups. The Kond POTTERS are within the group of clean castes and their mobility is not restricted by the concept of pollution.[2] It is untouchability that drives the Boad OUTCASTES into conflict with the rest of the village. Without this they might have risen in the manner of the Boad DISTILLERS.

The Boad OUTCASTES are driven to use the Administration. The local caste-structure of the village cannot grant them the position they feel is rightly theirs. It is not a forum before which their claims will be heard.

Although they do not hesitate to invoke the Administration, nevertheless they are neither happy nor sanguine in doing so. They do not feel loyalty towards the Administration. Their mentality remains that of the villager. They have all the fears and antipathies and suspicions which characterize the attitude of any villager towards the Government. Indeed, since they contravene the Excise laws frequently and are a by-word for rascality in local Police circles, their relations with the Government are, if anything, less happy than those of the rest of the village. Nor are they particularly skilled in putting their case before the Government, for they have to present it in terms which will make the Administration take notice. They could not allow a blow which an old man gave to a youth to be discussed in the village council in the shadow of the caste system, because there the blow was a heinous offence, to condone which would be to attack the fundamental concept of untouchability. The issue would be decided before it was discussed.

[1] All the Boad OUTCASTE schoolmasters teach in Kond schools. They have an advantage over their Kond competitors in that they are born into Oriya-speaking households. Their position in a predominantly Hindu area would be more difficult.

[2] There are, of course, other reasons. Wealth among the Boad OUTCASTES is concentrated in fewer hands, and consequently there are more ambitious men among them than among the Kond POTTERS. Another factor is Gandhi's campaign against untouchability.

Nor could the Boad OUTCASTES make out a case for their man on the grounds of the respect which youth owes to age. But the blow itself is too trivial an issue for a Government court, which could take no cognizance of the fact that the blow was inflicted by an untouchable on a person of high caste. Instead the Boad OUTCASTES had to present their case as an incipient riot. They could not claim that they would be denied justice before the village court. Nor could they present the real issue, which was untouchability. The case in the Magistrate's court would have to be judged on the evidence for or against riotous action by the villagers against the Boad OUTCASTES, since this was the issue which the Boad OUTCASTES themselves raised.

The combined pressures of economic progress and of their untouchable status are driving the Boad OUTCASTES to become citizens of the Administration rather than members of the village, in spite of the fact that culturally they are with the village and in spite of the inherent difficulties of making use of Government courts to achieve ends within the caste-structure of the village. This, indeed, is an impossible goal. They would like to rise within the village polity, within the local structure of caste. In the end they will be put outside the local structure. It cannot now accommodate them.

For different reasons the Ganjam DISTILLERS are in a fundamentally similar position. There is not the same bitter conflict that occurs between Boad OUTCASTES and the village, nor are they affected by barriers of untouchability. Nevertheless, their economic role and their economic status makes membership of the local structure of caste-groups irrelevant and unimportant. The point, again, is localization. The structure of caste-groups within Bisipara was underwritten by differential control of productive resources, which amounted to control of the village land. But the economy in which the Ganjam DISTILLERS operate is wider than this. It covers a field in which caste is irrelevant and in which the juridical authority rests with the Government. They have no need to seek accommodation within the local structure of caste-groups.

These are the ways in which the coming of a traders' frontier is modifying the structure of caste-groups in Bisipara.

Caste itself is relatively unimpaired. Everyone, including the Ganjam DISTILLERS and the Boad OUTCASTES, 'believes in' caste. They observe the rules of endogamy and inter-dining. Caste usages affect every aspect of their lives. The solidarity of caste-groups has not been lessened.

But the local structure is undergoing a fundamental change. It is losing its politico-economic function. This function rested on the fact that productive resources were allotted according to caste, and control of these resources was organized by a localized structure of caste-groups. In one case the structure has adjusted itself successfully to the new economy. But in other cases it has failed. The new economy is widespread : caste-group organization is appropriate to a localized economy. The new economy demands social mobility : but untouchability is at once a cornerstone of caste and an insuperable obstacle to mobility. Localization and untouchability are the rocks against which beats the tide of the new economy.

The men of Bisipara to-day derive their right to a share in the resources of production not by membership of a caste, but as citizens of India. In the village the hierarchy of caste-groups is no longer a complete reflection of economic realities, nor an adequate means of ordering political relations. Under pressure of economic change the political functions of caste are beginning to be taken over, as one might expect, by the ultimate political authority, the Government of India.

APPENDIX A

THE CONSUMING POPULATION

BOTH paddy and rice are measured in the village not by weight but by volume. A 'measure' (in Oriya *tambi*) is roughly the equivalent of a two-pint pot: twenty of these measures are put together to form a 'unit' (in Oriya *khondi*).

The people of the village consider that the average adult man consumes one quarter of a measure [1] of rice at each of the two daily hot meals. It is on this basis that casual labourers are fed. It is recognized that old people or sedentary workers, such as schoolmasters, might eat less than this, and that gluttons can eat more. By this reckoning a grown man needs, to provide his two daily meals, one-half measure of rice per day, fifteen measures per month, and one hundred and eighty measures or nine units per year. Since the volume of paddy is almost twice that of a similar amount of rice, a man's yearly requirements of paddy can be considered to be eighteen units.

It must be emphasized that this is not an absolute and exhaustive account of a man's needs. Not only does he require paddy for other purposes (for parching, for gifts, for entertaining, for purchases at the shop, and so forth), but also he needs other forms of food, such as dal or vegetables, oils, salt, and so forth. But in making comparisons between the different households of the village, these other foods can be ignored and paddy is a sufficient criterion. This question is taken up again in Appendix B.

In assessing the needs of a household I have considered all persons of fifteen years and over as full consumers, those from ten to fourteen as half-consumers, those from two to nine as quarter-consumers and I have ignored those under two years old, since the amount of rice they eat is negligible. In this way the needs of each household were ascertained according to its composition, and although such a figure could not be used as a measure of nutrition, it is sufficient for comparison of the size

[1] For this the English word 'glass' was commonly used in the village.

of households as consuming units in relation to each other and in relation to their incomes.

It seemed sensible, when comparing the income from the village land of caste-groups, etc., according to their proportions of the population, to measure population not by heads but by making allowance for the different status of consumers. Thus a family of two adults and two twelve-year-old children are, for this purpose, three consumers. Population is reckoned according to this method throughout, unless otherwise stated.

A man's yearly requirement of paddy for food is 18 units. The average price of a unit throughout the year is Rs.3/5. Accordingly I reckoned that for paddy a man needs each year Rs.60. The same price (Rs.3/5) was used to convert the figures of the annual value of estates from units of paddy into rupees and annas.

Two measures of paddy, if well husked and cleaned, will produce a little under one measure of rice.

APPENDIX B

THE SIZE OF ESTATES

AT an early stage of the research it seemed necessary to find out the size of estates owned by individuals. At first I hoped to be able to use the survey of the Revenue Department. This proved impracticable. The original survey was not accurate and the registers have not been kept up to date. The settlement was made between 1920 and 1924, the purpose being to register only lands in the possession of Oriyas, in order to prevent further alienation of land by Konds. It was sketchily performed and very little supervised. As a settlement it suffers from almost every defect that can affect such a record.[1] No new settlement has been made since that date and land brought under cultivation and improvements in existing holdings have gone largely unrecorded. I have translated that part of the Record of Rights which refers to Bisipara and I found that it contained several families which have since died out, and that the greater part of the plots are in the names of a generation which now is dead. Adjustments necessary for the collection of tax are made in the mind of the *mutha* headman. It seemed pointless to go further in this direction.

The following factors were relevant to making a new plan:

(1) Rice is the main crop.

(2) Rice is grown mostly in permanent fields, which range in size from one-hundredth of an acre to half an acre. Fields are rarely bigger than this.

(3) Estates are not made up of contiguous fields.

(4) The greater part of fields owned by the villagers are adjacent to the village.

(5) Enquiries into income and the size of estates are not met with enthusiasm.

Rice is the main crop. Rich landholders differ from poor in their stock of rice, and not in growing other crops. Secondary crops are important in the diet, for life cannot be sustained on

[1] Z. C. Misra (unpublished manuscript).

rice alone. But from other points of view, crops other than rice are not important. More hours are spent on growing rice. More land and the best land is planted with rice. In bulk, rice forms the greater part of the diet. Rice is used for gifts and payment, and in ritual. The word for ' food ' is the same as the word for ' cooked rice '. I have therefore assumed that both rich and poor landowners grow secondary crops according to their needs, and do not increase their output much beyond what they eat. Rich landowners can be distinguished from poor by measuring their income of rice and ignoring secondary crops.

Rice is grown in permanent fields which with rare exceptions give a crop every year. These fields are called *khetu*, a word for which there is no simple equivalent in English. *Khetu*, levelled and banked to hold water, are used only for rice. Fields of another type are *anto*, unlevelled, which grow both rice and secondary crops. Rice grown in *anto* is quick-maturing and has a low yield. This rice forms a small part of the total crop, and it was ignored in measuring income.

The yield of *khetu* depends on their size, on the number of months for which they can be irrigated (on which depends the variety of paddy sown—the more water, the slower the maturation and the heavier the yield), on the amount of manure put on the field, and on the thoroughness of cultivation. These characteristics, both of the land and the cultivator, can be ascertained, so that in an ordinary year the yield of any permanent field can be forecasted.

The fact that fields are small and are scattered around the village makes identification of the owner and assessment of the yield laborious, but not impossible.

Such enquiries arouse suspicion and people are unwilling to talk of their income except in the most general terms. The work goes more easily if the investigator is known and considered harmless, and if the assistants are appropriate to the group with which they work. Such men must have personal experience of cultivation and yet be literate : and they must be able to take time off from their own land, for the survey can be made only in the cultivating season. But the more literate a man, the less he knows about cultivation and, as a general rule, the less he commands the confidence of the village. Confidence is essential, since the survey cannot be done without the co-operation of at least some of the cultivators.

The most accurate survey would be done by measuring the area of every field, and, just before the harvest, taking a sample cut from each, from which to work out the total yield. With limited resources this is not possible. There are too many fields. They are irregular in shape. I could rely only on statements from the owner and from others about the size of the normal harvest in any field.

The following three methods gave the information needed.

First a sketch-map made of the different field-areas (*berna*) around the village, by which the fields are grouped. Each field-area has a name. The smaller ones were grouped under larger ones to provide convenient units of survey. Then each field-area in turn was mapped in a sketch to show every field. When these maps had been checked for major omissions—there was no time to check field by field—they were taken out in the first five hours of daylight, when people were working, and each field was identified as to its owner and its yield, a balance being struck between the estimate of the surveyor and the statement of the cultivator, if he was present. The results were then put together to show for each landowner and cultivator the number of fields in, and the income of paddy from, each field-area.

Secondly each person was asked

(1) to enumerate his fields, both *khetu* and *anto*, both in Bisipara and in other villages;
(2) to state the crop grown and the expected yield;
(3) to say from whom and when he had bought the fields and the price paid; and
(4) to say what fields belonging to others he had taken in pledge or share-cropped.

The results were then collated for comparison with the results got from maps, taking into account only rice grown in *khetu*.

To some extent these two surveys show up each other's mistakes. Fields which a man has omitted to mention appear on the map, and *vice versa*. But the method is not foolproof. There is no check on the fields which a man owns in other villages, since lands there have not been mapped. Nor is there any protection against the contingency of the same field being overlooked by the map-maker and omitted by the owner.

Thirdly, a cultivators' diary was kept. At the beginning of the cultivating season five men were selected. Their fields were listed and described by name and situation. Then, day by day, the following items of information were collected for each field :

(1) The name (when possible) and status of the person working (i.e. relative of the owner, casual labourer, plough-servant or share-cropper) ;
(2) the hours worked ;
(3) payment, if any ; and
(4) what work was done.

This survey showed, among other things, the relative importance of *khetu* and *anto* in terms of the hours spent working in them.

The method is open at least to these errors : the map may be incomplete or wrongly drawn ; the fields may be inaccurately identified ; or the estimated yield of rice may be incorrect.

There are two methods of making a correct map. One is by drawing to scale ; the other is by aerial photograph. In principle both these are possible and would produce accurate results. But the aerial photographs were not available. Mapping to scale would have taken a single person a very long time, since the fields are small, irregularly shaped, and numerous.

In making a sketch-map the easiest mistakes are to omit or to duplicate fields, especially at the boundaries of the different field-areas, when these are not marked by a path. The risk is lessened by employing one person to map all the fields between obvious natural bounds, so that he may begin each day where he left off the day before, and need not find the place where another person's map ends. On the other hand, when possible, a different person was used to identify the owners of the fields, since this provided automatically a check on the accuracy of the map. In principle there is no reason why the same person should not check his own map : in practice I found people more ready to look for mistakes in another's work than in their own, and, when possible, I exploited petty enmities for this purpose. Finally, it is possible to miss out a whole field-area. This happened when the first sketch-map was made. Efforts to check the map by a bird's-eye view from the mountain-side were obstructed by trees. The mistake appeared when comparing the results of the mapping with the results of the questioning, in which the missing field-area several times appeared.

The second survey, done by questioning, provides the best check on the accuracy of the map. It is not a perfect check. Minor errors remain undetected. But major errors of omission or duplication show up.

Two things made the identification of the owners of fields more difficult. Firstly, time was limited and it was not possible to identify the owner of every field by waiting until someone was encountered working in that field. However, many people know the history and present owner of a large number of fields, and almost everyone knows at least the owners of those fields which adjoin any one of his own. This knowledge was used. It is a potential source of inaccuracy. But the work can in this way be completed in a reasonable time.

The second difficulty is that the owner is not always the cultivator. The latter may be a share-cropper or he may have taken the field in pledge. There is not so much difficulty about identifying the owners of fields which are share-cropped. But if a field has been pledged for many years, the owner tends to be forgotten by everyone except himself and the pledge-taker, whose interest it is to conceal the true situation. If he does wish to conceal his actual right in the field, the pledge-taker will say, when questioned, that it belongs to him. Questioning the owner corrects this, but the discrepancies were so numerous that it was not possible to investigate all of them. Identification of share-cropped fields produced few discrepancies. However, in measuring income from land it is of no concern whether the income comes from a field owned or a field taken in pledge. We know who gets the paddy, and that is enough.

The major weakness of the method is that knowledge of the yield depends on an estimate and not on measurement. However, with the exception of two out of the ten field-areas, the same person made the estimate of the yield. If he has a tendency to over-estimate or to minimize, at least the error is the same for all fields. Systematic over- or under-estimation of the total yield would be serious if our purpose were to compare rice cultivation in different parts of India. But since the comparison to be made is between the incomes of individuals and groups within the village, an error which is common to all is not significant.

The final figure used for comparing the incomes of individuals was reached in this way. The number of fields which a man possessed according to the maps in any field-area was compared with his statement about that field-area. In most cases the number of fields agreed. There were some discrepancies. Occasionally fields which the map showed to be in X field-area were stated to be in Y field-area. Sometimes two adjoining fields were stated as one field. Inquiry in this way accounted for most of the discrepancies, but there remained a few which proved to be concealment of fields in the statements, or omission or wrong identification of fields on the map.

When the number of fields a man owned in each field-area had been fixed, his statement of their yield was compared with the map-maker's estimate. In all but a few cases the owner tended to reduce the yield. Old women, in particular, seem to have cut it down by half. In a few cases, when the yield was stated to be more than shown on the maps, it was noticed that one of the map-makers systematically underestimated large fields.

When the estimates of income had been adjusted in this way, each figure was raised to the nearest multiple of five units of paddy, in order to make calculations easier. This number was used in all subsequent calculations.

GLOSSARY

English to Oriya

BARBER	Bhandari
BASKETMAKER	Dombo
casual labourer	mulya
cooked rice	bhato
DISTILLER	Sundi
field-area	berna
FISHERMAN	Keuto
flaked rice	chura
HERDSMAN	Gauro
Kond HERDSMAN	Kondho Gauro
Kond POTTER	Kondho Kumbharo
Kondmals temple	Sibhomundiro
measure	tambi
Meeting-house	Mandap
militiaman	paiko
OUTCASTE	Pano
paddy	dhano
parched paddy	lia
parched rice	muri
pledged (of land)	bondha
plough-servant	holya
rice	chaulo
ritual friend	maitro
share-cropper	bhagwali
street	sahi
SWEEPER	Ghasi
TEMPLEMAN	Mali
tithe	jejemani
unit	khondi
Village headman	gram polis
Village temple	Akoraghoro
WARRIOR	Sudo
WASHERMAN	Dhoba
watchman	chaukidar
WEAVER	Kuli
WRITER	Mahanti

ORIYA TO ENGLISH

anto . . . . . an unlevelled upland field
bheti . . . . . forced labour
dosa . . . . . a funeral rite
khetu. . . . . a field used for paddy, levelled and banked. If stream-irrigated it is called *pani khetu* : if rain-irrigated it is called *dipha khetu.*
meriah [1] . . . . . the victim of a Kond rite of human sacrifice
sudho . . . . . a funeral rite

[1] Informants thought this word was derived from English, like ' Christian'.

REFERENCES

Census of India, 1951.

Selections from the Records of the Government of India. No. V. History of the rise and progress of the operation for the suppression of Human Sacrifice and Female Infanticide in the Hill Tracts of Orissa. 1854. Calcutta. Bengal Military Orphan Press.

Campbell, J., 1861. *Narrative of operations in the Hill Tracts of Orissa for the suppression of Human Sacrifice and Infanticide.* London. Hurst & Blackett.

1864. *Personal Narrative of Thirteen Years Service among the Wild Tribes of Khondistan for the suppression of Human Sacrifices.* London. Hurst & Blackett.

Colson, E., 1948. 'Modern political organization of the Plateau Tonga', in *African Studies*, June–September 1948.

Darling, M., 1925. *The Punjab Peasant in Prosperity and Debt.* London. Oxford University Press.

Fortes, M., 1945. *The dynamics of clanship among the Tallensi.* London. Oxford University Press.

Fortes, M., and Evans-Pritchard, E. E. (Editors), 1940. *African Political Systems.* London. Oxford University Press.

Fürer-Haimendorf, C. von, 1945. (1) *Tribal Hyderabad.* Hyderabad. The Revenue Department.

1945. (2) *The Reddis of the Bison Hills.* London. Macmillan.

Furnivall, J. S., 1948. *Colonial policy and practice.* Cambridge. Cambridge University Press.

Gluckman, M., 1941. *Economy of the Central Barotse Plain.* Rhodes-Livingstone Papers, No. 7. Rhodes-Livingstone Institute, Northern Rhodesia.

1943. *Essays on Lozi Land and Royal Property.* Rhodes-Livingstone Papers, No. 10. Rhodes-Livingstone Institute, Northern Rhodesia.

Grigson, W. V., 1949. *The Maria Gonds of Bastar.* London. Oxford University Press.

Hancock, W. K., 1940. *Survey of British Commonwealth Affairs.* Volume II. *Problems of Economic Policy, 1918–1939. Part I.* London. Oxford University Press.

1942. *Part 2. Op. cit.*

Hunter, W. W., 1872. *Orissa.* London. Smith, Elder & Co.

Hutton, J. H., 1946. *Caste in India.* Cambridge. Cambridge University Press.

Macpherson, W. (Editor), 1865. *Memorials of Service in India from the correspondence of the late Major Samuel Charteris Macpherson, C.B.* London. John Murray.

Misra, Z. C. *The Khonds and the Khondmals.* Unpublished MS.

O'Malley, L. S. S., 1908. *Bengal District Gazetteers : Angul.* Calcutta. Bengal Secretariat.

(Editor) 1941. *Modern India and the West.* London. Oxford University Press.

Opler, M. E. and Datt Singh, R., 1950. 'The division of labor in an Indian village', in *A Reader in General Anthropology*, edited by C. S. Coon, London. Cape.

1952. 'Two villages in Eastern Uttar Pradesh (U.P.), India: an analysis of similarities and differences', in *American Anthropologist*, Vol. 54, No. 2, Part 1. April–June, 1952.

Schapera, I., 1943. *Native land tenure in the Bechuanaland Protectorate.* The Lovedale Press.

Senart, E., 1930. *Caste in India* (translation by E. Denison Ross). London. Methuen & Co.

Smith, M. W., 1952. 'The Misal: a structural village-group of India and Pakistan', in *American Anthropologist*, Vol. 54, No. 1. January–March, 1952.

Srinivas, M. N., 1951. 'The social structure of a Mysore village' in *The Economic Weekly of Bombay*, 30th October 1951.

1952. *Religion and Society among the Coorgs of South India.* Oxford. Clarendon Press.

INDEX

Date Due

JAN 24 '61			
MAY 9 '63			
MAY 16 '63			
10/24/63			
MAR 26 '64			
APR 9 '64			
NOV 26 '69			
APR 9 1981			
APR 1 1982			
DEC 9 1982			
MAY 1 9 1989			